Maybe You Know
My Kid

Maybe You Know My Kid

A Parent's Guide to Identifying, Understanding and Helping
Your Child With Attention-deficit Hyperactivity Disorder

By Mary Cahill Fowler

A BIRCH LANE PRESS BOOK
Published by Carol Publishing Group

First Carol Publishing Group Edition 1992

Copyright © 1990 by Mary Cahill Fowler

A Birch Lane Press Book
Published by Carol Publishing Group

Editorial Offices   Sales & Distribution Offices
600 Madison Avenue   120 Enterprise Avenue
New York, NY 10022   Secaucus, NJ 07094

In Canada: Canadian Manda Group
P.O. Box 920, Station U,
Toronto, Ontario, M8Z5P9

Birch Lane Press is a registered trademark of
Carol Communications, Inc.

Manufactured in the United States of America
ISBN 1-55972-097-2

10 9 8 7 6 5 4 3 2

Carol Publishing Group books are available at special discounts
for bulk purchases, for sales promotions, fund raising, or
educational purposes. Special editions can also be created to
specifications. For details contact: Special Sales Department,
Carol Publishing Group, 120 Enterprise Ave., Secaucus, NJ 07094

For my husband, David and my sons, David and Jonathan—the
spirit behind the words,
and to
my mother and Mark

Contents

Acknowledgments

Throughout the course of writing this book, I received a great deal of both moral and technical support from many people. I wish to thank my friends Margaret Mary Bambury, Sylvia Boyd, Kathy Burke, Jan and Gene Flood, Anne Gridley, Constance Owen, Allison Schlosser, Barbara Szostak, and Barbara and Ben Van Vliet. I am also very grateful to Claudia Bepko, Inger Gotterup and Pat Rosiak. Without their gentle prodding and enthusiastic encouragement this book might have remained a concept. A special thanks to Doug Fleming and Sarah Rossbach Fleming for a place to write when I needed quiet, and to Sarah, a fellow author, who with knowledge and intuition always managed to be in the right place at the right time. My appreciation to Terri Steineckert, her children Heidi, Troy, Tyler, Brandon and Shane, and Russ and Sandy Thomas for the kindness and hospitality they gave me during my travels.

I owe a debt of gratitude to the mothers, fathers, children with ADHD and their brothers and sisters who took me into their confidences. Your stories are an important part of this book and I wish to thank you for sharing so openly and honestly.

Chris Aboreille of the Education Law Center in Philadelphia, and Lisa Meehan of the Statewide Parent Advocacy Network in New Jersey and Pat Sokolow of the Monmouth County L.D.A. provided helpful behind the scene resources and I thank them for the information about special education law and parent advocacy. I also thank Sandra Thomas, President of CHADD for the many resources and referrals she provided.

My appreciation to Gabor Barabas, M.D., Kathy Collins, M.S.W., Randy Mendelson, Ph.D., Richard Reutter, M.D., Fran Rice, and Judy Welch, M.A. M.F.C.C. for their contributions to the text. A very special thanks to Jean Bramble, R.N., Dr. William McMahon and Sam Goldstein, Ph.D., for the time and care you gave me and for your clinical insight and your contributions to the text.

I feel fortunate to have had the opportunity to meet and speak with Dr. Russell Barkley, Dr. C. Keith Conners, Dr. Melvin Levine, Dr. Bennett Shaywitz, Dr. Sally Shaywitz, and Dr. Paul Wender—experts internationally recognized for their outstanding contributions to this field. I thank you for giving me so much of your time and expertise and for so graciously contributing to this book.

I am especially grateful to Richard Zakreski, Ph.D., for his moral support, technical assistance and painstaking review of the manuscript. Thanks for your care and patience.

I also wish to thank David Minter for his encouragement, Joan Raines, my agent, for her guidance and handholding, and my editor Hillel Black whose careful attention and wise suggestions shaped this manuscript and its author.

Finally, I thank my family for all your support, your encouragement, your love, and the inspiration.

Maybe You Know
My Kid

CHAPTER ONE

Attention-deficit Hyperactivity Disorder: An Overview

Maybe you know my kid. He's the one who acts before he thinks. It's usually upon some rash impulse that scares the living daylights out of me, like seeing how fast he can ride a big wheel down a long, steep, curvy hill. He's the one who says the first thing that comes to his mind. It's usually with a loud voice in a quiet crowd, and it makes me wish I could evaporate into thin air.

And he cannot remember a simple request. So I long for a trained parrot that can tell him ten times in five minutes 365 days a year to go upstairs, brush your teeth, get dressed and make your bed. He's the kid who scrapes his knee and screams so loud and long that I worry the neighbors think I am beating him. Then, just when I'm about to call the doctor, he eyes a monarch butterfly and chases it through the trees until it disappears, just like his hysterics of seconds before. He's the kid in school with ants in his pants who could do the work if he really tried. Or so we have been told over and over.

Maybe you know my kid really well. Maybe he reminds you of your own child or someone else's. But maybe you didn't know that children like this aren't really pain in the neck kids with lousy mothers. They are the children with Attention-deficit Hyperactivity Disorder, commonly called ADHD. This syndrome is characterized by inattentive and/or distractible, impulsive, and overly active behaviors. It is estimated that three to six percent of all children have ADHD in varying degrees of intensity.

ADHD is not a new phenomenon. A very similar pattern of behavior was first noticed by physicians in the late 19th century.

Their patients, who suffered from either brain injury or illnesses that affected the central nervous system, appeared overactive, impulsive and distractible. However, similar patterns of behavior eventually became noticed in children without any brain injury. Over the years, numerous investigators delved into the reasons behind the cause of such behavior in children who otherwise appeared perfectly normal.

As a result of these investigations, the name of this symptom complex changed numerous times to reflect advances in the scientific community's understanding of the disorder. During the 1960s, the syndrome became known as Minimal Brain Dysfunction or MBD. Around 1970, excessive motor activity was the most visible symptom, so the children formally said to have MBD came to be called Hyperactive or Hyperkinetic. Since the hyperactivity slowed considerably around the time of puberty, many practitioners believed the child's problems ended then.

By 1980, inattention appeared as the primary problem of most children. But not all children who exhibited attention difficulties behaved in a hyperactive, "always on the go" fashion. So in the third edition of the *Diagnostic and Statistical Manual of the American Psychiatric Association,* researchers broke the disorder into three subgroups; ADD type one with Hyperactivity (ADD-H), ADD type two without Hyperactivity (ADDnoH), and ADD-RT (residual type) meaning symptoms carried into adolescence and adulthood. People frequently describe the ADDnoH children as the "spacey" or "absent-minded professor" types. Often their inability to focus and sustain attention does not become problematic until they go to school where demands for attention and concentration are made. The notion that one need not be hyperactive and that symptoms could exist beyond puberty proved a breakthrough in the understanding and treatment of this disorder.

After the publication of DSM-III, the notion that a person could be inattentive and not hyperactive and vice versa was advanced. Consequently, when DSM-III-R was published in 1988, the name changed again to Attention-deficit Hyperactivity Disorder. DSM-III-R assigned ADHD the medical code number 314.01. A separate category, 314.00, called Undifferentiated Attention Disorder, was created for children who exhibited significant attention difficulties but no hyperactivity or impulsivity. Throughout this book, I refer to children with or without hyperactivity by the ADHD label.

The fourth edition of the DSM is currently under consideration. Whether or not the name or the criteria for this disorder will change remains to be seen. Dr. Paul Wender, Professor of Psychiatry and Director of Psychiatric Research at the University of Utah Medical School, says, "It would be better if we did not use the terms Attention Deficit Disorder and Hyperactivity because each term, i.e., 'hyperactivity' and 'attention problems,' suggests itself to be a critical necessary symptom of the disorder."

No one knows for certain what actually causes ADHD. But we do know that it doesn't come from diet, allergy, or bad parents. In the opinion of Dr. Wender, "By and large ADHD seems to be a genetic disorder. It is hereditary, but it does not breed true. Different combinations of symptoms occur in individual instances." Thus, he explained, even within families, differences in the characteristics of the disorder exist. For example, one family member might be hyperactive, inattentive, impulsive and have associated dyslexia, while another sibling might be inattentive, impulsive and poorly coordinated or not have the disorder at all.

According to Dr. Bennett Shaywitz, Professor of Pediatrics and Neurology at Yale University Medical School, in a very small percentage of children, a disorder that looks much like ADHD occurs as a result of brain injury due to head trauma. In other cases, Dr. Shaywitz finds that Attention Disorder and Learning Disabilities arise as a result of hypoxic (lack of oxygen) brain injury. However, Dr. Shaywitz strongly emphasizes that such cases are quite rare and that most children are believed to have ADHD because of "inherited disturbances in certain chemicals in the brain's neurotransmitter systems." Neurotransmitters are chemicals which regulate brain cell function and thereby facilitate the manner in which the brain regulates behavior. Exactly how that chemical disturbance occurs is unknown. Dr. Paul Wender explained the current best-guess theory points to a decrease in activity in certain brain systems caused by decreased activity in neurotransmitter systems which use the neurotransmitters dopamine and perhaps, norepinephrin.

But what causes ADHD, or even what name it has, doesn't change what is known about this condition. We know the disorder is most commonly found in children. But, in one third to two thirds of these cases, symptoms carry into adulthood. Children with ADHD come in all shapes and sizes. Some have very severe degrees and have all of the symptoms. Many areas of their lives are affected. Others have symptoms so minor that the condition almost goes unnoticed. Some have associated disorders as well.

Most clinicians and researchers agree that certain symptoms constitute the disorder. However, an individual need not have all the symptoms to have the disorder. In the opinion of Dr. Paul Wender, "ADHD patients have a mixture of inattentiveness, sometimes but not always motor hyperactivity, impulsivity, variability of mood, short fuse, hot temper, disorganization, stress intolerance; children are disobedient."

We know that at different ages, different features of the disorder are more problematic. Impulsive behavior is a danger for a toddler, but attention is not a skill required or expected at this stage of development. The symptoms can create problems in all areas of a person's environment or in just one area. For instance, the child with ADHD who has moderate attention difficulties may have trouble in school, but not at home where there are less tasks that require concentration.

We know that in half the cases, children evidence signs of the disorder prior to age four. But we also know that these signs often go unrecognized until the child goes to school. Boys are more commonly diagnosed. But we now know girls also have it. Researchers only recently have begun to study ADHD as it affects girls. Whether there are actually more boys than girls with ADHD is yet to be known.

These children come from all socio-economic backgrounds. But ADHD seems to be more prevalent in lower stratas. This phenomenon might in part be due to the fact that children with ADHD are often underachievers. Underachievement is not a function of their capability. ADHD children span the range of average, above average and superior intelligence.

Despite all that is known about ADHD, many children go undiagnosed. Instead they are misunderstood. Some are even blamed for behaviors which are the very features of this disorder. ADHD children act in a way that comes naturally to them. Thus, they are at the mercy of their disorder and its symptoms. Parents may suspect that all is not as it should be. But without knowledge and understanding of ADHD they are puzzled and worried by what they see.

As the fellow parent of a "difficult" child, you probably know that I hurt too, and have felt alone and scared, frustrated and angry, helpless and hopeless. Maybe you also suffered from the looks you were flashed by people who didn't know your kid couldn't help it. Maybe you didn't know this either. Maybe you cried and hollered when you sent your child to school hopeful that he would succeed and he returned home angry. Maybe you were scared when you realized the system understood him less than you did. And maybe you saw what little self-esteem your child had go down the tubes.

There is no cure for ADHD. But our children and families do not have to be stressed to a breaking point. Some of the qualities that compromise ADHD can be assets for the child and adult who learn how to channel them. A positive outcome is best accomplished through diagnosis and proper management of the symptoms of this disorder.

The recommended approach is multi-faceted. It begins with education of the parent, the child and the child's teachers about ADHD; parent training in behavior management techniques; modification of the child's educational program, and possibly medication. Where indicated, family psychotherapy and/or individual psychotherapy to address self-esteem and peer-relationship problems are also suggested.

I am one of the lucky mothers. I now understand why my son behaves the way he does. I know what to expect from him and how to manage his ADHD symptoms. I know when and where to go for help. I know now that the disturbing behaviors which appeared at various stages of his development were neither of his own doing nor my fault. If you are the parent of an ADHD child, I want you to know this too.

This book is intended to serve as your guide. The following chapters present a picture of what Attention-deficit Hyperactivity Disorder is and what to do about it. The chapters are organized in a developmental fashion. Each one describes the patterns and characteristics of ADHD at a particular stage of the child's development, and where possible, outlines the recommended treatment for the disorder.

Chapters are divided into two sections. At the beginning of the first section, signs and symptoms of the disorder are discussed and illustrated using anecdotes from my own family's experience.

The second presents the manifestations of the disorder predominant to the particular developmental stage. Since every ADHD child does not manifest the exact same signs and symptoms of ADHD, the second section of each chapter discusses the experiences of other mothers, fathers, siblings and ADHD children. In order to observe the ADHD child's right to privacy, these others have been given pseudonyms.

That this disorder presents itself differently from child to child is a point to be emphasized. As you read, try to identify with the patterns of the disorder and how they may pertain to your situation. Try not to compare your situation to each child's actual circumstances, for as we know, many factors contribute to the individual's development whether or not he has a disorder. No two children are the same.

Section two also provides a clinical point of view based on interviews I had with practitioners who are nationally and internationally recognized for their work with this disorder, and with professionals in private practice. The effects ADHD has on those who interact with the child is discussed throughout. Where pertinent, a summary list at the end of each chapter provides specific information contained within.

I offer this book with the hope that it will broaden the general knowledge of Attention-deficit Hyperactivity Disorder. Its information is well documented and its treatment recommendations proven. You may recognize yourself, your own child, or someone else's within these pages. If so, you are on the road to getting help. But I caution against self-diagnosis and self-treatment. Just as you would seek the expertise of an eye doctor for a problem with your vision, find a practioner who is reputed to be knowledgeable about Attention-deficit Hyperactivity Disorder.

CHAPTER TWO

The Infant

I have always believed that when it came to the birth process, mother and child worked together. But David, my first born, is and always has been his own person. His birth came on his terms in the form of a swift hard kick that ruptured the amniotic sac and left me in a puddle of water alone and wondering at 1:00 AM if this was the long awaited moment. The doctor's examination just hours before revealed that I was nowhere ready for birth. Yet at 2:00 AM, without having so much as one single contraction, I was admitted to labor and delivery. My egg had decided to hatch.

Nineteen hours later, my son was born on his due date, September 25, 1979, the United Nations year of the child—a good omen for a superstitious mother like his. David was 7 lbs. 7 oz, 19½˝, and he was beautiful. Except for the fetal monitor tangled in his long black hair, his voyage into the world of the newborn didn't leave a mark on his body. His face was perfectly rounded, and though he was slightly blue at birth, his color improved within minutes.

As I lay on the delivery table watching the nurses wrap him in the garments of the outer world, I was struck with a sense of astonishment. Here was this little tiny body, having just emerged into our world after what turned out to be a very long day, alert, moving his limbs, full of life, while I, his mother, could barely move a muscle. I've always tried to make sense of what seems contradictory and so I rationalized that this was as it should be. After all, I had done the work.

Six hours later, when the nurses brought the babies to the room for feeding, I had my first taste of motherhood. No more dress rehearsal. Though physically I felt like a dishrag, my sense of excitement became so great that it didn't take more than a second before I was fully awake, holding my baby who was sound asleep. He looked and smelled as all babies do, so innocent and pure, though to me he was not like any other baby. I felt such a sense of pride and joy and bewilderment that within so short a period of time I could go from taking care of my own needs to suddenly having the responsibility of someone else's. For a brief second, I allowed that I felt unsure about the kind of job I would do. Then I quickly dismissed this thought and went back to feeling elated.

From the very beginning, David seemed to have a profound effect on everyone. Visitors to the hospital would go to the nursery first and then report. "Oh Mary," my sister said, "he's a beautiful baby and what an active soul!"

My sister-in-law exclaimed, "He's really strong. The little guy bucked himself to the top of the bassinet. He lifted his head and looked straight at me! I can't believe how he looks all over the place. The other babies just seem to sleep."

Well, being a proud mother, what could I think? That he performed feats of strength could only mean that he was naturally a super athlete. Because he was highly stimulated by his environment only meant that he was exceptionally bright. Both my husband and I felt this child was a gift we would have to manage very carefully.

So with this attitude, it is not surprising that I grew furious at the events of his second day on Planet Earth. At 4:00 PM, the nursery staff buzzed my room to inform me that David had raised such a ruckus, the staff still could not comfort him after two hours of trying. "So Mrs. Fowler would you please come get your baby?" What was wrong with those baby nurses that it took them two hours to realize that this newborn needed his mother.

I brought David to my room, gave him my undivided attention, fed him, changed him and off to sleep he went. Simple. Until day three. Then I had trouble quieting David. He screamed so uncontrollably I thought certainly something must be terribly wrong with him. Rocking only made him squirm so hard that I feared that I might drop him. I put him in the bassinet and held a water bottle to his lips, and gradually he went to sleep. I couldn't understand why my roommate could hold her baby all day long and I would have to put mine down after ten minutes. The answer became clear. Her baby was a girl and girls cuddle; mine was a boy and boys do not.

By the end of day three, I realized I was off to a bad start with parenting. I became very high strung. To make matters worse, I had some minor complications that restricted my activity, and David developed jaundice, which is quite common in newborns, but nonetheless upsetting. Then he added a new twist to his reper-toire. Choking! Everytime I tried to feed him, be it breast or bot-tle, he would gag. Even my roommate, who was the picture of serenity, suggested I call the nurse.

Congestion. That was all. "Nothing for you to worry about," said the nurse as she stuck a long rubber tube down his throat and sucked through the other end. After removing the worst of the mucous, she gave me the baby, and for the first time in two and a half days, he slept once again peacefully in my arms. Congestion. No wonder this little fellow had been so disagreeable. I became calm.

That was a big mistake. The pressure I felt in the hospital could not compare to the stress in store when I had the full responsibility for the baby at home. David Sr. expected that I knew what I was doing. I expected that he knew what he was doing. God only knows what the infant expected. Whatever he figured on, I did not meet his needs. The baby cried every twenty minutes from 8:00 at night to 6:00 in the morning. His high pitched voice pierced my ears and ran through my body jangling ever nerve ending. No sooner would I fall asleep than "screech" and up I'd get. First I tried to feed, then change, then rock, then let him cry himself to sleep. After three weeks, I was beating my pillows, screaming into them, feeling furious that I had ever con-ceived this kid, ashamed that I could feel this way about my son.

I tried to tell my husband that I felt strung out, but was too afraid to admit I felt scared. He acted as though David's behavior was normal, that all babies keep their mother's awake round the clock. Since he had a son by a previous marriage, I figured he knew what he was talking about.

David Sr. had no awareness of my need for emotional support because I had not shared the doubts I had about my mothering abilities with him. Yet I desperately wanted reassurance that I wasn't just one of those women reputed to be "not cut out for motherhood," so I turned to friends and family for guidance and backing.

Some, like my one sister-in-law, were sympathetic and assured me that eventually baby David would establish a routine. My mother seemed very empathetic, but above all she was a mother and thus needed to share the wisdom of the ages, which is "That's what babies are like." Since she had five, she could recall numerous incidents to verify her point. And she happily reminded me that at least my husband helped with the baby when he wasn't away on his weekly business trips.

That certainly was true during the daylight hours. But David Sr. and I agreed he needed sleep to be alert for his very demanding job. So during the night, our son fell entirely into my care. After all, I could grab a nap with the baby during the day. That is, if the baby napped, which he didn't. Deep inside I felt abandoned.

Fortunately, we lived near many relatives who pitched in. My first good night's sleep came when I developed a kidney infection and my sister-in-law Terry spent the night at our house since I was too ill to care for the baby and David Sr. was away on an overnight business trip. The next morning, I felt reborn and forever grateful for that night. Terry was exhausted but seemed to have developed a new respect for me. This was no easy kid.

Yet I couldn't help feeling that somehow David was special, different than other children. He just seemed so alert, so active, so advanced. When I reported that he rolled over at two weeks, another sister-in-law, the mother of three, told me in no uncertain terms, "It's not possible, Mary. Babies can't do that." When I insisted that I put him face down and found him face up, she quoted from Dr. Spock and allowed that this was no doubt a freak incident that wouldn't happen again. I began to question myself. I knew I saw what I saw, but it was not clear how David had performed this feat. I surmised that through crying and screaming, David rolled over by accident.

I called the pediatrician, not so much to say that the baby had rolled over, but to ask if maybe he had colic and could that explain why he screamed so much. He said it was possible but improbable since he would scream round the clock if he were colicky. He then suggested that maybe David was one of those hungry babies "who need solid food in addition to breast milk." At four weeks, he had solids. And he loved them. Though I had made the commitment to breast feeding, I did not in the least mind the compromise. At this point, I would have killed for a good night's sleep.

The solid food seemed to do the trick, and once again I thought we were bound for smooth sailing. David woke only periodically, and though he still did not sleep much during the day, I at least had more energy to deal with the constant attention he demanded. Despite his having a wealth of toys, little seemed to keep him interested very long. He hated the playpen and the crib. By two months, he perched himself on his hands and knees and rolled across the floor from one place to another. Both my husband and I were thrilled at his every move. Friends and relatives marveled at his stamina and persistence. My sister Margaret affectionately nicknamed him "wiggle worm."

It has always been my nature to make light of situations when I'm scared. So at two and a half months, when David came down with bronchitis and was placed on a bronchodilator medicine, I assured my husband that this was a usual childhood illness. But within a couple of hours, David had a reaction to the medicine. He behaved like Superboy until he lost all control. Then his body began to flail wildly about. Neither of us could restrain him. The pediatrician told us to keep him safe and ride it out. A few hours later, he crashed into a sound sleep. I spent the night on the floor next to his crib, terrified. From then on, it didn't take much for me to call the doctor who within the first ten months of life saw David twenty-six times. Some of those visits were for normal check-ups. Most were for upper-respiratory and ear infections.

Did he ever have ear infections! But he never cried or screamed in pain. Instead he would "dolphinize," a term I coined to describe his high-pitched wail. This sound reached such a pitch that friends who telephoned would hang up because it drove them crazy. David's dolphinizing was like a rising barometer. The noise was there all the time but it would gradually escalate when he was in distress. As the cry turned shriller, he became more difficult to manage. When I tried to hold and quiet him, the sound would grow louder. Distracting him worked only momentarily. After hours of hearing him cry, my ears would start to hurt. The more I tried to soothe my son, the more disturbed he became and the more frustrated I felt until eventually I was totally distraught, screaming at him to shut up. When I reached the point where I wanted to jump out a window, I realized that something was wrong and called the pediatrician.

"Why don't you bring him in Mrs. Fowler," he would say. Then, after he examined him, "Mrs. Fowler, his ears are infected. Look at this." I peered in the scope and saw a blister the size of a pea. No wonder the poor child screamed. "What are we going to do with this kid, Mrs. Fowler?"

I simply didn't know what I was going to do with this boy. Only a few things seemed to work. Humor was one of the coping tools I used. For the first six months of David's life, I would joke with the pediatrician and tell him I was in the market for a band of roving gypsies who might want to add a beautiful blue-eyed boy to their clan. Once I suggested that I didn't really need a pediatrician, that perhaps an exorcist could drive out the evil demons who deemed that he behave horrendously instead of cry like normal babies when he was ill. Though the doctor understood my attitude and laughed along with me, others found me disrespectful. I could not imagine why. After all, not much in our house smacked of calico and apple pie.

By the time David turned six months, our house became a crazy place. I remember one night when a business associate of my husband's came by unexpectedly. We still functioned under the misconception that infants do not really interfere with the routine, and so we invited this traveling salesman for some good company and a home-cooked meal. The child seemed to have radar. Though he was usually dead to the world from 6:00–10:00 PM, on this particular night he awoke at 8:00, dolphinizing. Realizing that I would be preoccupied, my husband offered to barbecue the chicken.

Hank, our guest, watched in amazement as little David crawled up my leg, down my arm, over my head, across the back of the chair, and up his leg. Hank was a bit astonished at the energy level of this little baby but found a ready explanation, "He's just like his Dad isn't he." We all laughed, though it wasn't a belly laugh. It was more like the laugh you make when you're not sure what behavior is appropriate.

The chicken came in from the grill black. No one had to worry about the risk of infection from this bird. We sat down to dinner with little screaming David lying on his stomach across my knees, my elbow pinning him while I tried to sway him into sleep. I decided not to mention the spider dangling from a long strand directly over Hank's rice. Fortunately, the insect retreated from the grating sound made by our guest's knife as he sawed through his chicken. Our companion thanked us profusely for a very nice evening but declined in no uncertain terms our offer to stay the night. Hank was the first in a long line of guests who didn't overstay their welcome.

Gradually, my husband and I became separated from our friends with grown kids and our friends with no kids who preferred the more civilized pleasures. Our home was quite simply chaotic and not at all soothing to the nerves. Only on rare occasions did we function as a team. Since my husband was away on business trips at least three full days each week, I saw the evenings when he was home as an opportunity to break away from what was fast becoming a prison. When I returned to find the baby had given his Dad a hard time, instead of offering sympathy, I would seize the opportunity to complain.

David Sr. would acknowledge that managing the baby could be difficult, but certainly no reason for me to lose my temper. That statement sent me into orbit which only proved his point. I knew I had to do something to get myself on an even keel.

I soon developed a group of friends, all of whom were young mothers, figuring that maybe if I had a social life during the daytime I would feel more satisfied and might even speak in sentences again. Most afternoons, we would gather at my house since David was the only baby who would not nap if the daily routine changed in any way. Unlike my relatives with grown children and friends who thought I was ridiculous to remove all perishables from harm's way, the other mothers liked the security my home offered. It was not just child proof. It was a veritable fortress.

But even these seasoned mothers found David's antics to be phenomenal for a six month old. When they observed as I changed him, one asked if I had developed a unique technique for diapering boys who are prone to hose down whatever leans over them. As you know, most babies are placed on their backs and the old diaper is removed. But David had to be placed on his stomach while my elbow pinned his chest to the table. Otherwise, I was apt to catch him in mid-air as more than once he catapulted off the table. Had it not been for the modern science wonder of stickum diaper tabs, I would have been unable to change him. While the other women thought my solution to be clever, some relatives thought maybe I bent over backwards for this kid. "You should make him stay still," I heard them say more than once. It seemed to me that they thought I took some perverse pleasure in complicating matters, that I liked the sensationalism and encouraged David's behaviors.

After spending a lot of hours together, the gals soon began to tell me how exhausted they became just watching me keep up with my fearless little dare-devil. At seven months, he stood and climbed, and soon the floor no longer sufficed as his playpen. He found the view from on top of the tables and the backs of chairs to be far more inviting. The stairs gave him absolute delight. When we gathered at the kitchen table, he discovered he could join the party by climbing the rungs of the ladder-back chairs.

This stunt proved relatively harmless until the time I didn't know where he had gone. Seeing my baby sprawled on the floor with a chair on top of him while he screamed at the top of his lungs scared me to death. I thought for sure he had been crushed. The more I tried to comfort him, the louder he hollered. I was quickly losing patience, and finally out of sheer frustration, plopped him in the playpen where he soon found a suitable distraction and stopped crying. My friends stood by horror-stricken. I felt like a total failure believing that a mother's gentle touch was the best curative. With David, my touch only made him scream louder.

On days such as these, when my husband came home from a hard day's work or a week on the road, I would recite a litany of antics David had pulled off while he had been away. Proud Papa loved having a rough and tumble boy and never thought he was abnormal. Instead, he thought my response to our son was overstated. He said I lacked patience. That attitude stung! My emotions became totally confused. I realized I had trouble coping with my son. Still I loved him. I simply did not know what I was supposed to do to please him.

With David the rewards were few. As long as I would watch from afar, or provide a myriad of stimuli to keep him constantly occupied, peace reigned. But the minute I tried to have a peaceful moment with my baby, there was no rest. I eventually learned that holding David meant bouncing him on my knee or throwing

him in the air. Though he still breast fed, he never concentrated
on suckling. His eyes flitted all over the room while his hands
tangled my hair or tore at the hoop in my ear. The least distraction and he interrupted his feeding entirely. I couldn't understand
why this baby was unreachable. Again I concluded that boys will
be boys and mine seemed so alert he must be destined for great
things.

Or at least another trip to the pediatrician. After eight months,
a pattern began to emerge in David's behavior. While he was
always very active and curious, his behavior sometimes crossed
the line from being overly stimulated to frenetic. When this happened, I recalled the kitten we had named O.B. O'Brien. One
day, when O.B. was barely ten weeks old, we left him outside
while we went off to shop. On returning, we found O.B. wildly
racing in circles around the yard. At first my husband and I
laughed, but as O.B. persisted, we somehow saw that he was in a
pathetic way. I picked him up and discovered his eyes were swollen shut and his fur was coated with a mass of bee stingers. It
seemed that poor O.B. got tangled up with a hive and had been
driven crazy. Though he eventually calmed down, O.B. remained
somewhat neurotic after that.

Whenever David reached that frenetic state where nothing I
could do would calm him, I began to feel that maybe I, too,
behaved like O.B. O'Brien and would do something rash if I had
to spend one more second with this baby. This reaction supported
my suspicion that I lacked the nurturing abilities for being a good
mother. Though I loved my child, I felt ashamed that I could not
cope with this little boy who was my own flesh and blood.

I covered these painful feelings with a veneer of bravado and
entered what I call the black humor stage of motherhood. Some
people thought it was funny that I nicknamed the baby Rasputin.
Others found me irreverent. Naturally I spent most of my time
with the gang that liked to laugh, which included my sister-in-law
and her fifteen-month-old. Every day we met at the beach. This
was no simple feat. First, we had to carry the boys across the hot
sand and find some unsuspecting stranger or friend to watch them
for a few minutes while we ran back to the car to get the diaper
bag, the toy bag, the wooden corral which easily weighed ten
pounds, the blanket, the towels, the umbrella, and the cooler.
Then we set up all this paraphernalia for a relaxing day of sun
and surf.

My nephew Johnny was an industrious toddler who entertained himself for hours. When he fussed, he was generally hungry or ready to nap under the shade of the umbrella. Not David! He hated that corral and alternated between throwing the toys outside, "dolphinizing" and taking the toys from Johnny. I jumped up and down like a yo-yo, and after an hour, had about all I could take. Yet getting there turned out to be such a major production, I could not bear to leave early. Rasputin was simply going to do things my way.

David proved so disruptive, he became the center of attention by default. The gals who sat with us would remark about his escapades and his activity, but always they ended by saying, "He's such a good looking boy!" "Look at those blue eyes." "He's really beautiful."

My reply, "He needs to be." Some were nice enough to tell me to ignore him and enjoy myself. People not sitting with us just glared at me with that look, "Why doesn't she do something about that kid!" If only they knew.

After two weeks of his pick-me-up/put-me-down routine, David realized he could wedge his big toe into the parts of the corral that formed a "V" shape and pull himself up. I dubbed him Spiderman and watched with the others in awe as he climbed to the top and then out. "There goes the neighborhood," was my comment. There went any chance of sitting peacefully.

David quickly discovered the ocean. Since he seemed to hate the feel of the sand on his knees, he improvised by walking on his hands and feet, and like a little crab, headed straight for the sea. I expected that the pounding surf and cold water smacking him in the face would dissuade him, but this lemming kept to his march. So I learned to tie a long rope around his middle. At ten and a half months, he walked. It didn't take long for me to realize that once again we would do things his way.

That August, David had yet another ear infection. The ear specialist told me that a surgical procedure called a myringotomy was indicated. Panic set in. Though I knew older children had this minor procedure, this was my child the surgeon would operate on, my little fellow he would put under anesthesia. When I told my husband the news, he reacted with as much panic as I.

However, unlike me, on the day of the operation, David's father appeared totally composed. He even calmed me when the nurse told me hospital policy did not allow parents to accompany their child to surgery. The nurse suggested we put his favorite stuffed animal in the bed with him. But my baby had no favorite toy, no special animal he would fall to sleep with night after night, no blanket he would cuddle for comfort. Dad handed the nurse his pacifier. He understood how helpless I felt when, on the way to the operating room, young David saw me sitting in the hall, and jumping to his feet, he almost fell off the gurney. "Boy, he's an active fellow. I've never had one do this before," the nurse commented. His fragile and frightened look tore me apart. This was the first time I realized just how much my son and I depended on each other. While he slept off the sedation, I held him close. I felt like a mother who knew how to care for her baby.

Once again, I saw David as being special. Since his first birthday fast approached, I no longer expected him to be a cuddly teddy bear. Junior Frolic, a nickname given by his Dad, seemed more than appropriate. Weaning him from the breast was not traumatic. I knew it was time, and besides, I was pregnant again. I was ready to part with the infancy stage. The day before his twelve month checkup, David ran full speed through the hall, stopping abruptly when he crashed into the bathtub. He now sported his first shiner. He too became ready to enter the world of the toddler.

I am given to sentimentalism and thought I would mark his first birthday and each subsequent birthday by writing him a letter. In that letter, I intended to write about all the milestones he had achieved during the year. I began, "Dear Junior Frolic, your Dad gave you this name because you were so active, so full of life." But as I went on I found it increasingly difficult to report just what exactly had occurred during the year. Much that I had to say was uncomplimentary. Much that I had to say seemed unmotherly. And so we gave him the usual toys: a little big wheel, a set of building blocks, and puzzles.

David was not the only family member to receive puzzles that first year. Both his Dad and I were frequently confused by his behavior. On the surface, most of the things he did seemed ordinary. At times all babies fuss and cry, refuse certain foods, have difficulty establishing routines. But these behaviors are not ordinary when they are consistently exhibited to the extreme. Though David could be charming, engaging and interesting, "difficult" is a more accurate overall description of him then.

At this stage, there was no way for anyone to know that David had Attention-deficit Hyperactivity Disorder. ADHD has no physical marking. One cannot look at a child and say, oh I recognize that mark. That kid has ADHD. In fact, even a difficult and demanding infant cannot be assumed to have ADHD. Most ADHD children were not necessarily difficult infants. For most parents, obtaining this diagnosis proves to be a christening of trial and error.

The reason ADHD is virtually impossible to diagnose at the infancy stage is due to the nature of the condition. ADHD is not a disease. There is no test one can administer to determine pathology. It is a medical syndrome. As such, one has to decide if a given constellation of symptoms characteristic of a specific disorder is present in an individual before a diagnosis is made. An individual with a medical syndrome does not have to exhibit all the symptoms associated with that syndrome in order to suffer from it.

The Diagnostic and Statistical Manual of the American Psychiatric Association, revised third edition, specifies this diagnostic criteria. To have ADHD, a child, prior to the age of seven, must exhibit any eight out of fourteen symptoms listed below. In order to be a symptom, the behavior must be inappropriate to the child's age, and the disturbance must be present for longer than six months. The symptoms as listed in DSM-III-R are as follows:

1. Often fidgets with hands or feet or squirms in seat (in adolescents, may be limited to subjective feelings of restlessness).
2. Has difficulty remaining seated when required to do so.
3. Is easily distracted by extraneous stimuli.
4. Has difficulty awaiting turn in games or group situations.
5. Often blurts out answers to questions before they have been completed.
6. Has difficulty following through on instructions from others (not due to oppositional behavior or failure of comprehension), e.g., fails to finish chores.

7. Has difficulty sustaining attention in tasks or play activities.
8. Often shifts from one uncompleted activity to another.
9. Has difficulty playing quietly.
10. Often talks excessively.
11. Often interrupts or intrudes on others, e.g., butts into other children's games.
12. Often does not seem to listen to what is being said to him or her.
13. Often loses things necessary for tasks or activities at school or at home (e.g., toys, pencils, books, assignments).
14. Often engages in physically dangerous activities without considering possible consequences (not for the purpose of thrill-seeking), e.g., runs into street without looking.

The severity of the condition depends on how many of these behaviors the child exhibits. The criteria for severity of Attention-deficit Hyperactivity Disorder as it appears on page 53 of DSM-III-R are as follows:

Mild: Few, if any, symptoms in excess of those required to make the diagnosis and only minimal or no impairment in school and social functioning.

Moderate: Symptoms of functional impairment intermediate between mild and severe.

Severe: Many symptoms in excess of those required to make the diagnosis and significant pervasive impairment in functioning at home and school and with peers.

The qualities of inattention and impulsivity are appropriate in babies. Their nervous system is not mature enough for them to concentrate for periods of time or to control their impulses. Thus, a diagnostician cannot look at these qualities in infants as behaviors indicative of ADHD. Though some children are diagnosed as toddlers, the average age at which a child is determined to have ADHD is around eight years, or the third grade. Then the demands for attention and self-control are greater, and one can easily observe the child who is not able to meet age-appropriate expectations. Teachers, in particular, may notice when a child does not meet the norms of behavior, and so they frequently initiate child evaluations.

Unlike the core symptoms of impulsivity and inattention, that of excessive motor activity is visible early in life. However, as a symptom, hyperactivity alone cannot be diagnostic of ADHD. First of all, it is only one of the possible core symptoms that can comprise the disorder. Secondly, a child can have all the other symptoms of the disorder and still have a normal activity level, i.e., not be hyperactive at all. Some ADHD children are even underactive and may appear lazy or lethargic. As explained by Dr. Paul Wender, the noted ADHD researcher, "Hyperactivity is a red flag. It is analogous to a fever or temperature in medicine. A fever tells you somebody is ill, but it does not indicate which illness the patient has."

Certainly, David was more active than the typical baby. When I described this behavior to the pediatrician, I got the distinct impression that, while being sympathetic, he thought I was the nervous and overreactive type. I accepted that kind of response back then. I do not today. Then, having only limited information, I guessed that I was a big part of the problem.

So did most of the fifteen mothers I spoke with who had children eventually diagnosed with ADHD. Most of these mothers typically described their babies as colicky, given to frequent and persistent crying, not easily soothed. Some of these babies, but not all, had a "high energy" level as well. Many of these infants were poor sleepers and fussy eaters. You would think that difficult, demanding, overactive infants could be earmarked as children who will eventually be diagnosed with ADHD. Yet, research indicates that these traits in infants do not predict the disorder. However, such traits do identify the infants as "at risk."

Dr. Richard Reutter is a neurodevelopmental pediatrician and co-director of the Child Evaluation Unit at Monmouth Medical Center in New Jersey. He believes ADHD infants are difficult because they have a hard time regulating state. They are the babies who, for instance, cannot calm themselves after a frenzied crying. Rather than responding to a parental attempts to settle them, Dr. Reutter notes, these infants tend to continue crying until they literally wear themselves down.

Throughout the course of a day, infants pass through many different states. As described by Dr. Reutter, they may go from quiet and alert to quiet and sleepy, or from awake and irritable to full crying. He says the ideal state for a baby is quiet and alert because that is the time it is able to respond to stimuli in the environment and to learn from it. Dr. Reutter thinks those "at risk," ADHD babies for example, have a hard time getting to the quiet and alert state and are not able to maintain it. Thus, these infants are deprived of the good interactions with the environment which are facilitated by this state.

Like myself, the mothers of difficult infants I interviewed thought they were bad mothers. Some because they could not seem to please the baby no matter what they tried. Others because they found it difficult to cope with the constant effort the baby required. We assumed we must be doing something wrong. Most of us felt ashamed of and responsible for the negative responses provoked by the baby's difficult and demanding behavior. We assumed "good mothers" would never respond to an innocent baby with anger and frustration. Though we may have suspected that the baby could not be held accountable for his or her behavior, we felt uncertain about our role in causing the baby's distress.

Lynn White felt particularly guilty. The pregnancy which produced her daughter Susie was unplanned. The only way she could explain such an active and aggressive little nine-month-old girl was to surmise that her baby acted up because she somehow sensed her mother's reluctance to have another child. As it so happened, Susie had to be sent in mid-year from second grade back to first before her symptoms were identified as ADHD. Yet, Lynn White characterized Susie's overall behavior as problematic in her first months.

In addition to the guilt many mothers place upon themselves, Dr. Reutter has noticed, quite often others reinforce the mother's guilt feelings. The classic example is the irritable breast-fed baby. He finds that mothers of such babies often get advice from either the baby's grandparents or aunts or uncles that she is not feeding the baby enough, or the baby needs food, or her milk is no good. As a result, many of these mothers switch from nursing to bottle feeding, and may switch from one formula to another in an attempt to satisfy the baby. Dr. Reutter explained that the baby, of course, cannot be satisfied because this is not a problem of food, but rather one of regulating state.

Dr. Reutter has observed that parents of difficult and demanding infants often feel cheated in addition to their pangs of guilt. Their expectations of what the interaction should be with their babies and what actually occurs are quite different, and they tend to feel angry and frustrated and embarrassed. Dr. Reutter notes that relatives and other people are often too quick to make punitive remarks to the parents of difficult, demanding babies, such as "you are spoiling the child" or "you don't punish the child enough and that's why he acts that way." Such comments fuel the parent's negative feelings. ADHD children are at risk for physical and emotional abuse.

Dr. Reutter believes that parents of difficult, demanding infants need some anticipatory guidance to recognize that these sorts of angry feelings are natural when a baby cries a lot and nothing the parent does to soothe it works. He advises parents to acknowledge such feelings when they occur and to deal with them, for example, by calling somebody and talking about what they are experiencing. This step generally diffuses the frustration so parents better can handle the situation.

In terms of helping parents cope with difficult and demanding infants, Dr. Reutter emphasizes the importance of parents recognizing that the problems are not the results of something they are or are not doing. He urges parents to expect babies who do not regulate state easily to have trouble with transitions and changes in routine. Besides every day transitions, Dr. Reutter says that parents also need to recognize "virtually anything that comes along, such as illnesses or routine immunizations, will challenge this type of baby more than others." Such situations warrant the physician alerting the parents in an anticipatory way about what should be expected in different situations and various stages. Such anticipatory guidance also proves extremely helpful for parents of difficult infants who are born to families where there is a history of the ADHD disorder.

Once parents understand the whys and wherefores of their baby's behavior, Dr. Reutter says they can then work on various techniques that might help the baby settle state better. These include smoothing transitions, establishing steady routines, and not overstimulating the baby. Dr. Reutter advises parents of difficult infants to establish routines by doing the same things at the same time, in a set manner each day, and to be consistent about these routines, because infants who have difficulty regulating state need that kind of order.

Parents also need to avoid overstimulating the difficult baby. Along this line, Dr. Reutter explains that these babies will often become overly stimulated by a simple routine playing activity, and parents will often continue interactions when the baby has gone beyond the point of being responsive to such activities. Thus, parents need to learn to recognize the cues given by the baby. Sometimes these babies will cry irritably, Dr. Reutter notes, or avert their gaze and withdraw from the situation to avoid the excess stimulation. If the stimulus is physical, the baby may arch or pull away. When the parents interact with the baby, Dr. Reutter suggests they do so during the baby's quiet, alert state. But as he pointed out, in difficult babies, this state may exist for only a few minutes out of each hour.

Other techniques exist which parents may use to soothe the agitated baby. However, Dr. Reutter says that such techniques depend on the individual baby. Some babies respond to swaddling. Others respond to the stimulation that comes from being walked or rocked. And still others will only fall asleep easily when they are riding in the car. As I myself found, there were nights when Claudia Kreiger resorted to drives in the car to settle her baby. Dr. Reutter told me that today there is a device you can attach to the crib that provides the sensation of a car traveling at 55 MPH.

Parents of difficult infants also need to take care of themselves. Dr. Reutter advises getting some type of a respite. If one parent does most of the caretaking, then the other parent assume a greater share, he suggests. In cases where both parents are stressed, hopefully they can leave the baby with a relative or a friend for short periods of time while they get a break away from home.

Not all difficult infants will continue to have problems as they grow older. However, parents of hard-to-manage infants still need support during these months whether or not the baby's difficulties are self-limiting. Anyone who experiences parenting difficulty, regardless of the cause, should take initiative and ask a health care professional for help. But I offer a word of caution. Not every doctor can give what is needed. As many of us know quite well, often we were told our baby's behavior was normal. Dr. Reutter says this behavior is not a normal phenomenon of infancy and that such responses do little to help the parents who really need guidance and instruction. Support will come from a doctor who, as Dr. Reutter outlines, treats your concerns seriously, offers information about your baby's possible behavioral patterns, and has specific recommendations to help ease the distress.

Dr. Reutter says that parents who have difficult, demanding infants should arrange a special appointment to speak with their pediatrician outside of the doctor's regular working hours. He explains that many pediatricians have high volume practices, and tend to dismiss these types of concerns when they are raised during "well baby" checkups, because they do not have the time to deal with the problems. Once a parent makes a special effort and if the doctor is unresponsive, Dr. Reutter suggests seeking out someone or someplace that deals with infants who have special problems.

A good starting point to find support for the difficult infant is the local hospital. If that hospital does not have a child evaluation unit or any specific programs to deal with infants who have difficulties, it might have a referral system where names of physicians in the area dealing with this kind of situation can be provided. If the local hospital cannot be of help, Dr. Reutter recommends contacting either the county or state chapter of the American Academy of Pediatrics for the necessary information to obtain these types of services.

Everyone needs to realize that "bad parents" and even "good parents" do not cause Attention-deficit Hyperactivity Disorder. Dr. Paul Wender, Director of Psychiatric Research at the University of Utah Medical School, says the studies he conducted on adopted children "show fairly convincingly that there is genetic transmission." He reports that current research is focused on finding the chromosome(s) which carry the disorder, and perhaps within the next ten to twenty years investigators will be able to identify the specific gene or genes involved with ADHD.

The child's environment does not cause the disorder either.

However, the ADHD child does not exist in a vacuum and we cannot overlook the interplay between this child and environmental conditions. Research indicates that the ADHD child's environment often exacerbates his or her symptomatology. For instance, practically every mother I interviewed told me that her ADHD child did well in school under the guidance of a sympathetic and understanding teacher. Conversely, with a stern and rigid teacher, the same child did not fare as well.

Conditions at home also effect the ADHD child. Dr. Wender explains that parents do not cause ADHD, but they may aggravate the child's symptoms. "ADHD kids need a parent who is consistent, sympathetic, even-tempered and unflappable." Instead, he notes that the parents of an ADHD child often have any number of problems themselves, such as depression or even ADHD. When present, these problems often restrict the parent's ability to cope in a calm, consistent manner. Though I am not the ADHD parent in our family, certainly my emotional reactions to my son's behavior helped make his problems worse. Yet I think we parents of ADHD children need to place our responses to the child's behavior in context, particularly when we are operating without a diagnosis and knowledge of the disorder.

ADHD is not user-friendly. As Dr. Paul Wender explains, because the child has ADHD he may be overreactive to ordinary family troubles. Just as the child overreacts to ordinary family troubles, those troubles become intensified by this ADHD child's behavior which dominates all daily interactions. The stresses created by the disorder leave little time or energy to deal with ordinary problems and pressures, let alone complications such as marital discord. Usually, every individual's needs go unfulfilled. Families gradually become enmeshed in a dysfunctional pattern which begins so subtly that individual members grow accustomed to negotiating in a disordered environment to such an extent, the abnormal takes on the guise of normal. A vicious cycle is created because the ADHD child feeds on family troubles and family troubles feed on the ADHD child's behavior.

We can't blame the child for his disorder. Nor can we blame the parents for the difficulty they have coping with the situational demands. Until researchers solve the genetic puzzle, we need to know how to cope with the effects of this disorder. One way is to maintain a sense of humor. And so I offer you Dr. Paul Wender's aside made in jest about the lesson he has learned from genetic studies to date.

"You should breed with exquisite care, then marry whomever you choose." Since this notion is probably too revolutionary for most people, early diagnosis of one's prospective spouse and treatment might be a suitable alternative. The sooner the child is diagnosed and the family is in treatment, the better the opportunity for families to break that vicious cycle and be restored to normalcy.

Summary

- Attention-deficit Hyperactivity Disorder is a medical syndrome.
- This syndrome is identified in children who exhibit any eight of fourteen age-inappropriate symptoms for over six months and before the age of seven years.
- Average age of diagnosis is eight years.
- ADHD cannot be diagnosed on basis of hyperactivity alone.
- Usually ADHD is not diagnosed in infants, but difficult, demanding infants can be identified as "at risk."
- Difficult infants have a hard time regulating state.
- The quiet and alert state is ideal for baby because baby responds to environment and learns. "At risk" infants are seldom in this state.
- Mothers of difficult infants feel like bad mothers. They also feel guilty, ashamed, embarrassed, angry, frustrated and resentful.
- Parental guilt feelings may be reinforced by input from relatives and friends.
- Difficult infants do not meet parental expectations of how an infant should behave.
- Parents of difficult infants need anticipatory guidance to cope with the negative feelings that arise, and the baby's poorly regulated behavior.
- Parents of difficult infants need to learn to smooth transitions, establish routines and avoid overstimulating the baby.
- Parents need to recognize cues babies give about how they are responding to environment and to interact with babies in

the quiet and alert state.
- Parents of difficult infants need time away from baby.
- Supportive doctors will offer guidelines and instructions to help parents manage a difficult baby.
- Parents should make a special appointment with pediatrician to discuss baby's difficult behavior.
- Parents can contact a local hospital or the American Academy of Pediatrics to locate services they need.
- ADHD is a non-user-friendly condition.
- Interplay between the child and all environments can make symptoms worse.
- ADHD children overreact to ordinary family troubles.
- Every family member is affected by the disorder.
- No one is to blame for the disorder.
- Early diagnosis and treatment make the disorder easier to cope with and manage.

CHAPTER THREE

The Toddler Years: Ages 1–3

From the time David's life passed the six month mark, I guessed he appeared frustrated because his embryonic body placed restraints on his attempts to explore. So I welcomed the toddler stage of development with the foolish belief that David would be more content once he came into his own realm. "Toddlers are supposed to be active," I told myself. "They are supposed to get into things. Toddlers are supposed to be somewhat independent, not like a baby monkey on its mother's back."

But I did not know what the ADHD toddler was supposed to be like. Within a few short months, I found the monkey on my back was now loose in the house. I no longer had full control of him. David had mobility. He had strength. He had the ability to run circles around me. Which he did. Being four months pregnant did not make coping with this one-year-old boy any easier. To keep a semblance of order in our house, I realized David, unlike other toddlers I knew, needed undivided attention unless he was asleep.

And to think, once his Dad and I foolishly pretended not to notice the great deal of time and energy required by this one small child. I gave up trying to restrict his activity level. Instead I became a mother/vacuum cleaner who followed him around, swept up after him, and swallowed all traces of disorder. Friends who marveled at this display of spit and polish asked in awe, "How do you keep the house so neat with a one-year-old around?"

Little did they know it turned into a full-time job. When David woke from his nap, he not only threw the toys from his crib, he also tossed out the sheet and blankets. When he wasn't in the process of rearranging the house, he became engaged in inventing

28

new uses for household objects. By thirteen months of age, he knew the stairs were for climbing, but found they could be turned into a slide. A bannister became a Jungle Jim to be scaled from outside the staircase. It was not unusual to find him dangling in mid-air.

No matter what the activity, David gave it new meaning and purpose. Pots and pans turned into frisbees. Windows made wind chimes. When you bang on them with a truck, they make a shrill melodic sound. The drapes became rope swings, electric cords lassoes. The dog, he chased. David refused to acknowledge the word "No." Unless, of course, it spilled from his lips.

When I called friends and relatives to say, "You won't believe what he did today!" they laughed and said. "He's a piece of work." No one branded him as exceptionally wild. Not even as they watched him progress to the point where he always walked one step ahead of me. Based on their responses. I assumed I over-reacted to his behavior until my mother asked, "How are you ever going to manage little David and a new baby?" I knew I could barely manage my first child, and I had absolutely no answer for my mother's question. Since I was a few months pregnant, within a short time I, indeed, would be faced with finding a solution.

Meanwhile, David's energy level physically drained me. Yet I knew I could keep him from harm until he grew older and developed better judgment skills. But his contrary response to my efforts to please him left me disheartened. We never got into sync and I never knew what to expect.

On Halloween, I thought for certain he would be thrilled to give our candy to the neighborhood ghosts and goblins. But when a seven-year-old witch appeared on our porch, David screamed bloody murder until I closed the door. I figured this sinister creature proved a little too chilling for his bones. But even with the princesses and fairy godmothers he threw a fit. When nothing I did calmed him, I surrendered the notion that mother's instinct was a guide I could rely on through his darkest nights.

By the time David's dad came home, my nerves were shot. "You should have stopped answering the door," he said. To my way of thinking, this answer was no solution but rather a stopgap measure. Years later, when once again a witch swept our home into an uproar, I remembered we lived under a very strange spell.

Perhaps then if my husband and I knew our son's extreme reactions to be symptomatic of an underlying problem, we might have had a chance to address the problem more effectively. But we did not. Instead, we took each symptom as an isolated behavior and tried to explain it as best we could. When illness could not be considered a factor, we blamed ourselves or each other.

Over the course of my second pregnancy, our preoccupation with David's finicky eating patterns grew in direct proportion to my girth. When I told David's dad I felt frustrated because our son would eat nothing except cereal and milk, he responded as though I said David would only breathe on alternate Tuesdays. "He needs green vegetables. He's probably sick all the time because of what he doesn't eat. Maybe if you had better eating habits . . ." Bang!

I knew my eating habits didn't cause David to be such a fussy eater. I even knew my cooking could not be considered at fault. Maybe, I thought, the problem existed because it was I who fed him. But that possibility didn't make me feel good. So I decided I simply did not know what kids like to eat. My friends with small children told me what they prepared. But when I placed these tidbits in front of David, in one fell swoop he brushed them to the floor which made Pogo the dog/vulture very happy.

Shortly before the new baby was born, David Sr. moved his office into our house. For the most part, I felt happy too. Dad had more time to spend with our son. There were times though when I felt inadequate and jealous, especially when I watched them play together. While my instincts about how to nurture this child seemed lousy, Dad's roughhousing with our son pleased young David. While I complained about how frustrating David could be, Dad found him to be "a real kick!" But where we had hoped for a boy our first time around and had one, this time I hoped for a nice, quiet, cuddly little girl.

It was so hard for me to see that I meant anything at all to my son. Whenever I tried to share my affection, David ran in the opposite direction. At times I felt guilty for believing this little guy set the tone of our relationship. At times I just felt very sad.

In order for a pleasant interaction to occur, we needed a calm place and a routine activity. Every morning I made sure we sat side by side on the floor of his room and did puzzles together before nap time. At age one-and-one-half, this child could piece puzzles geared for a five-year-old with very little help. Nurturing David came in quiet moments such as these.

The rest of the day, however, was spent in an effort to keep David out of trouble. This task proved much harder with each month that passed. Whenever I talked on the phone or visited with a friend, David waged an all out assault on the house. Seasoned mothers told me "Don't worry. David's just one of those kids who is into everything. You'd rather have him inquisitive instead of dull." True. But what concerned me was David's seeming lack of fear.

After his new brother Jonathan was born that May, David lost all caution. His stunts became dangerous. I lived in constant fear that one day David would move just a little too fast, do something just a little too impulsive, and not be able to stop the course of action. I worried that one day I might bring my son home in a box.

My fears about David's ability to harm himself were not unfounded. One July morning, while I changed the new baby, twenty-two-month-old David quietly left the room. Seconds later, I found him standing on a second story window sill. Both his hands pushed the thin screen which was fastened to its frame by only a hook and eye. Until I could find a way to distract him, I froze in the doorway, afraid that my sudden movement might propel David into a forward thrust and free fall to the pavement below.

That day I decided to buy iron bars for the windows, but soon learned that even bars were not child proof. The pediatrician emphatically suggested I do whatever it took to keep David safe. "Even if that means you have to tie a rope around his waist and fasten its other end to your wrist."

I already learned to put a harness on him when we walked. David had no respect for traffic. He would run across the street without pausing a second. No matter how many times I tried to teach him to stop, to look, that the street was a dangerous place, he just never listened. But tying us together with a rope? This lifeline was an umbilical cord the likes of which I never expected. I worried he might inadvertently strangle himself. So I followed my mother's advice and watched him like a hawk instead.

Such hypervigilance came with a price. Any semblance of a warm, nurturing relationship severed. Now I was tense, irritable around my older child. My mother asked, "Why are you so uptight? Is anything wrong?"

"No, Mom. I'm just tired," I sighed.

Her inquisition was relentless. "Are you sure? Are you and big David having trouble? Is it the new baby?" I did not want to admit how petrified David's impulsive actions made me. However, I could definitely state my anxiety was not caused by Jonathan.

Unlike his older brother, Jonathan was a good baby, easy to manage, a happy soul. As he progressed through the early years, he took his time and studied a move before he made it. He left his environment intact. He loved to be held. Around him, I felt like a good mother. I could not understand how two boys born of the same parents could be so entirely different. Only years later did I learn that Jonathan had not inherited the ADHD disorder as his brother had, and therein lies the difference between my two sons. Where Jonathan proved the essence of joy, David remained an enigma until my husband and I learned the nature of our older son's problem.

Meanwhile, the stress created by a child who constantly seemed to be testing his limits and ours took its toll on our marriage. Now my husband and I argued, blamed each other and pointed the finger at who did what to cause young David to do whatever. Even when we agreed David behaved in thus and such a way, we argued about the reasons why.

My husband's explanations vascillated between "there's something wrong with him," to "we must be doing something wrong." Afraid the "something wrong" might be me. I immediately assumed a defensive stance and dismissed these comments by saying "quit making such a big deal out of everything. That's just how kids are."

But I didn't know too many kids as testy as David. My mother said, "He doesn't respect you. He's allowed to get away with too much."

"He really loves to bust your chops," my sister observed.

Since the babysitter, Mrs. Hutchinson, never found him to be a bother, I thought the observations of my mother and sister were correct. My sister-in-law, the mother of four, suggested that I "make him sit in a chair when he's naughty. That's what I do with my kids." So I tried. The only way to make David stay seated meant I had to sit on top of him.

Days with David became more and more like a game of Russian Roulette. I could not predict either what he would do or how he would react next. He flung himself into the "terrible two's" with a vengeance. He met with constant disapproval and increasing anger from me. "Don't do this. Don't do that. I said stop that. That's bad." Instead of soothing lullabies, he heard this daily barrage of commands. He followed very few orders.

Jonathan, on the other hand, received only positive and loving attention. As David became more his own person, his behavior became increasingly sullen and aggressive. Everyone, including me, thought he had an extreme case of sibling rivalry. In actuality, David also suffered serious blows to his self-image. Now I realize he had to watch someone else get the nurturing he could not take for himself.

Maybe that's why David stopped calling me "Mommy." Who knows? When I first heard him address me as Mary, I thought my two-year-old was just going through the stage when some toddlers hear their parents refer to each other on a first name basis and do the same. Relatives found his behavior cute and to some degree we all encouraged him. I figured in a short time he would again call me Mom. That did not become the case for a year and a half.

During this time, our family dynamics approximated a three-ring circus. David misbehaved. I reacted generally by yelling since reasoning never worked. Dad criticized my reaction. Then we argued. When David created another naughty diversion, we repeated the entire scene until my husband and I, the adults, eventually withdrew in angry silences. Unknowingly, I gravitated to Jonathan and my husband to young David. Neither of us could see that our reactive interactions split our family down the middle.

Nonetheless, we all felt the tension. I complained about it frequently. One afternoon at a coffee klatch, my friend Pat suggested I call the "Totline," a phone service mothers called for answers from a psychologist to questions regarding their child's behavior. In the child development books I read, David appeared only vaguely in evidence on the pages. Thus, when I turned to them for information, I found instead of answers, more questions. This service, I hoped, would provide me with a plausible explanation.

When I mustered the courage and called the "Totline," my throat tightened as soon as I spoke. In a strange way, I felt as though I betrayed young David. A sense of relief followed after the psychologist assured me most of David's behaviors were normal for his age. "You just have to be consistent with your responses," she advised. When I asked her now to handle his refusal to eat nutritious foods, she suggested I "make a game with the food. You know. Show him how broccoli is like a little green tree." Well, I only knew about airplanes. I couldn't wait for that evening to serve broccoli. But David did not like little green trees either.

I should have predicted such a simplistic solution would not fool David. All along, people told us how bright they found this child. Some even said, "He's too bright for his own good." I wondered if he was too bright to follow the norms.

After all, this child demonstrated he could understand and conceptualize complex events. When he was eighteen months old, his Dad and I watched the televised landing of the first orbiting space shuttle. Young David, who sat at my feet seemingly preoccupied with a flashlight apparently tuned in more then we realized. After the Columbia rolled to a stop, he turned to us and said, "I wish I could go up there some day." Neither one of us could believe what we heard.

Mysteries began to make sense to me. I reasoned David to be hard to handle because his intellectual abilities far exceeded his physiological development. We only had to wait for his mind and body to get into sync. Then, I figured, he would surely behave appropriately. Meanwhile, it seemed sensible to nurture David by responding to his intellect. But in doing so, I perceived David to be older than his years. Once again, in an attempt to explain the nature of this child I took a wrong turn. I expected David to be smart enough to have greater self-control.

He was not. There were so many days I wished he, like the Columbia, could go up there too. Frequently I told him, "David you are driving me nuts." I made similar comments to friends and relatives as well. It did not occur to me to question how such feedback affected this two-and-a-half-year-old boy.

But I did realize David's attention-demanding behavior was not the only aspect of life "driving me nuts." During this period, major life stresses bore down on our family. First, we had to adapt to a new baby. Then, my husband's father died suddenly. My father became terminally ill. When David Sr. came home from the office and announced we had been transferred hours from home, I exploded.

Patience has never been my strong suit, but now I had even less. When I brought both boys to the pediatrician for checkups, he asked, "How's it going Mrs. Fowler?" We had a long history of kibbitzing about the trials and tribulations of being David's mother. Generally, the doctor joked with me and shook his fist while he smiled and said, "He needs a good punch in the nose."

This particular winter's day, I was in an ill-humor. Instead of making light of David's antics, I held back tears and angrily told the doctor in no uncertain terms, "This kid is driving me nuts. There has to be something wrong with him." The pediatrician quickly retorted, "Maybe there's something wrong with the mother."

That remark did everyone a great disservice because I thought to myself, "Maybe he's right." After all, I took my children to him because I respected his medical judgment. I thought David's lack of control probably was my fault. This thought prevented me from seeing any clinical reason for David's difficult nature.

And this thought also made me really angry, but instead of reacting to the doctor's remark, I took my anger out on David. I decided to declare war on his behavior. Whatever it took, this kid was going to slow down, be careful, and do whatever he was asked, or else. Fortunately, before I chained him to a radiator, the business of moving distracted me. For the time being, David had a reprieve.

Clearly, David did not behave like a typical toddler. But I did not know that. Nor did most parents of ADHD children. Granted many of our kids stood out in a crowd. Still we assumed they were just going through a stage. Perhaps this idea was not too farfetched. After all, there had to be a reason that this time in a child's life is called the "terrible two's." Most of us shared the point of view of Brian Doyle, a father who said to me, "I thought he would grow out of it."

The "it" to which Brian referred is the classic out of control behavior exhibited by many children with ADHD. These kids do not grow out of "it" at an early age. If anything, the symptoms of

ADHD intensify as demands from the environment increase.

Psychologist Dr. C. Keith Conners, author of the *Conners Parent Symptom Questionnaire,* a widely used diagnostic guide, believes the pattern of ADHD can be recognized as early as one or two years of age provided you can identify the clues. But at this age, most parents and even many practitioners do not spot the behavior so characteristic of ADHD. Dr. Conners describes these children as restless, impulsive, incapable of sticking to a task, and constantly on the go. Traditionally, the likelihood of early diagnosis remains minimal, even for children who are moderately hyperactive and thereby call attention to themselves.

According to Clinical Psychologist Russell Barkley, Professor of Psychiatry and Neurology, and Director of Psychology at the University of Massachusetts Medical School, mothers often fail to recognize the young ADHD child's behavior as problematic and out of ordinary bounds for a number of reasons. First, new mothers or mothers of only children often lack knowledge and do not see what behavior is abnormal. Second, some ADHD children have mild problems and consequently do not evidence much difficulty in the years before elementary school because they mainly play. As these children grow older, Dr. Barkley notes, more is demanded by parents who assign chores and teachers who assign school work. This work taxes the underlying disorder of the children and their difficulties become noticeable. Third, some of these children are exceptionally bright and do not have to study or pay attention until they are in the higher grades, so they compensate for their ADHD deficits in early school years on the basis of their brilliance.

Beyond this basic inattentive, impulsive, restless framework of behavior, what parents generally see in ADHD toddlers are variations of the theme. Most ADHD toddlers have unstable moods. They explode in emotional outbursts over a seemingly minute problem or for no apparent reason. They are persistent and not readily soothed. They frustrate easily and exhibit very little self-control. They also may be highly curious which might explain why so many ADHD toddlers get lost in shopping malls or why family treasures often are found lying in bits and pieces around their feet. Some learn to walk and talk early. Others have speech delays. Disturbances in the parent-child attachment are frequently noted.

These early signs and symptoms are usually misunderstood. By the time some ADHD children reach the preschool age, they are tarred with much rejection and their world has become a very damning place.

The ADHD toddler often appears to behave in a wilful and deliberately non-compliant way. Child Psychologist Dr. Sam Goldstein reports that parents usually attribute the child's behavior to a conscious choice on his or her part. In actuality, the child has no control.

To further complicate matters, on some occasions an ADHD child can control his or her behavior. Such inconsistency confuses those who do not know that the child has ADHD, or even those who may know. The inconsistent behavior also perpetuates the myth that these are the children who *won't,* when in fact they are the children who *can't.* The attitude that the child *could* if he or she chose to places guilt and blame on the child.

Children who wreak havoc upon themselves and their families do not need rejection. They need the attention of a professional who can determine whether or not there is an underlying problem creating distress. For the child with ADHD, early diagnosis in and of itself becomes prophylactic.

There are a couple of guidelines parents, troubled by their toddler's behavior, can follow. If you suspect a problem exists, regardless of the child's age, acknowledge it and seek a solution. Do not let friends or relatives talk you into believing you have conjured up this notion. That happened to Claudia Kreiger and her husband, both trained child development professionals. They were told, "You're just two professional people looking for something. Leave him alone and he'll be fine." Fortunately, they only waited until their son Jay turned two to learn he had a communication handicap and ADHD.

For those of us lay people who are unknowledgeable about either childhood behavioral problems or the health care system, finding the appropriate support services takes on the magnitude of a quest. The major answers most of us must find are: (1) Does my child really have a problem? (2) What is my child's problem? (3) What type of help do I need? (4) Where do I find that help? (5) How do I know I've found the right help? and (6) How will I afford the help? Since ADHD is both a physical and a mental health problem, there are a number of roads one can travel in search of answers.

Once you suspect your child has a problem, even if you are uncertain that your assessment is correct, try to find a name for the problem. You will probably begin with your child's doctor, and may want to follow the suggestion made in the previous chapter and make a special appointment to discuss the problem. Ask whether the child's behavior is significant of any specific childhood problem. Do not ask if the behavior is normal. If the child's behavior was normal, it would not bother you to the point that you sought help. Once you inquire, if you are told, "It is too early to tell," "I don't know," or "Your expectations are too high," travel along and seek the advice of another professional who is well versed in childhood behavioral problems. In this regard, I am reminded of the sage advice given by one of the fathers I interviewed. "Listen to the mother," Ben Green said. "She is with the child every day and sees the problems." The message to mothers is TRUST YOUR INSTINCTS.

The exact nature or cause of the child's problem and the help he or she will need are closely related. Often the person who determines the nature of the child's problem also manages the treatment of the problem. Parents must find a competent clinician expert in their child's particular problem, which in this case is ADHD. Like myself, many parents, when first presented with a need for professional services, do not have the vaguest idea of where to begin to find these services.

According to Kathy Collins, a social worker who is the Director of Consultation and Education for CPC Mental Health Services in New Jersey, parents should not blame themselves if they get confused and frustrated as they try to find their way through the complicated maze of health care services. When a parent is concerned about a child's behavior, Kathy Collins suggests a mental health center as a good place to begin the answer seeking journey. Though the size and services offered may vary, she says that most communities have mental health centers, and most of these centers are equipped to diagnose learning and behavioral problems. People can locate mental health centers through listings in the phone book or through referrals by their child's doctor. In addition to community agencies, many universities also have mental health clinics that will assess behavioral and learning problems.

Another alternative Kathy Collins suggests as a first place

parents might call is the local hospital, particularly if the hospital is large and/or a teaching facility. She explained that such hospitals often have child evaluation services equipped to diagnose and make recommendations for a wide range of childhood disorders.

Kathy Collins pointed out that parents of school-age children might also look to their school district for either a child evaluation or guidance about where the evaluation process could be started to determine if the child has a problem. Under Public Law 94-142, schools must provide special education to children between the ages of three and twenty-one who are deemed eligible for such services. As reported by Fran Rice, a child advocate, in order to determine who is eligible for special education, by federal regulation each school district must provide free of charge a child study team evaluation of any child age three or older who is suspected to have a learning disability. The composition of child study teams varies according to individual state laws; however, by federal regulation the team must consist of a person knowledgeable in the area of the suspected disability, and other appropriate evaluators that would compose a multi-disciplinary team.

Though ADHD is not called a learning disability per se, many children with ADHD have significant difficulty with learning. Furthermore, specific learning disabilities sometimes accompany this disorder. Bear in mind that a child could have ADHD-like symptoms because of another learning disability. For example, shortly after he entered first grade, my younger son became very frustrated and distractible. He also tore his room apart every day. A child study team evaluation revealed that Jonathan was dyslexic. Betty Garver's son Seth did have ADHD. But he also had a communication handicap which is why ADHD symptoms appeared so severe. Thus utilizing the services of a child study team is well within the realm of possible approaches to having your child evaluated.

However, parents need to realize that ADHD is a neurologically-based disorder which carries a medical diagnosis. Therefore this diagnosis should be made by a pediatrician, child psychiatrist, pediatric neurologist, clinical child psychologist or clinical social worker. Child study team personnel may be able to identify the problem, and to address a child's individual educational needs, but the overall treatment of the disorder rests in other hands.

Exactly which of these professionals to use depends on the individual's training, expertise and area of interest. Most pediatricians are trained in childhood behavioral problems and often prove to be the first doctor parents contact. However, many pediatricians have very demanding practices and do not have the time to coordinate and manage the other areas of treatment which ADHD requires. Parents must determine if their child's pediatrician has the time or inclination to devote to the child's treatment.

Pediatricians often refer ADHD cases to pediatric neurologists or child psychiatrists, both of which are competently-trained physicians who can treat the ADHD disorder medically. Neurologists tend to be more involved with the organic basis of the disorder, while child psychiatrists deal with the emotional aspects of the disorder. Child psychiatrists, unlike neurologists, are also trained to do clinical work with the children and their families. Similarly, child psychologists are trained to treat the disorder clinically. However, they use non-medical interventions often in conjunction with medication prescribed by a physician. Unlike the other specialties, child psychologists have the advantage of being trained to administer psychological tests.

Any of the aforementioned practitioners may chose to specialize in the treatment of neurodevelopmental problems and so they seek additional training to do so. Social workers are also competent professionals. However, they often do not receive formal training in the treatment of neurodevelopmental problems. Parents are wise to inquire about the training and experience when choosing a practioner.

Referrals for a therapist who may be well suited for your needs can come from a variety of sources. Some of these sources will have formal referral procedures. Others may do a word-of-mouth type of recommendation. According to Kathy Collins, every state and most counties have mental health associations, and these agencies generally have a referral system of mental health professionals including information about their specialties. In addition, the same sources you would go to for assessment, i.e., community mental health centers, university mental health clinics, hospital child study evaluation units, school child study teams and family physicians, can also prove beneficial for therapist referrals.

Support organizations such as the numerous ADHD parent

support groups also prove to be a source of invaluable up to date information. In addition to the partial list of such groups provided in the appendix, parents can also locate these groups through the self-help clearing houses now established in many states. They are also listed in the appendix. The ADHD parent support groups generally try to inform local school districts about their activities. You might also check with a member of your child study team to obtain the phone number of the contact person for the ADHD support group, though not all child study teams will have such information.

If you are looking for a therapist highly trained in the treatment of ADHD, many of the ADHD parent support groups offer referrals. Dr. Paul Wender, Professor of Psychiatry at the University of Utah Medical Center, applauds the services provided by these organizations and adds, "Support groups do what medical societies are unwilling to do. They will tell you that Dr. Jones is available and Dr. Smith is not, that Dr. Jones listens to you carefully and Dr. Smith does not."

I think parents need to be wary of practitioners who address a child's behavior only in theoretical terms. Deep-seated psychological problems do not cause ADHD. Even if they did, the symptoms require treatment. We parents need practical advice. Whatever practioner you use, be sure you receive good, solid information based on their training and common sense. TRUST YOUR INSTINCTS.

When you seek the services of a therapist, social worker Kathy Collins suggests these guidelines. First, when you call to make an appointment explain your problem and determine if this practitioner can help. Second, when you go to your first appointment, do not commit yourself to being the therapist's client. Ms. Collins explains that the first appointment is part of an assessment process and should be a mutual interview. Both parties, the therapist and the parent, must decide if the therapist can help. Then the parents need to decide if the situation feels right for them. Third, if you know, for instance, that your child has ADHD, be sure to determine the amount of training the therapist has with the disorder. If you do not know what your child's problem is, Kathy Collins advises parents to describe the child's behavior along with steps the parents have already taken, and ask for a diagnosis and assessment in those terms.

As everyone knows, mental health care can often be somewhat expensive. Ms. Collins says that every community mental health center receives state monies and most of them also receive local and federal funds to provide affordable services for everyone. Each agency has some type of mechanism to provide these low cost services. Some offer discounts; others have sliding scale fees. Most agencies take medical insurance. Many private practitioners will also take insurance payments. Some private therapists will even discount their services or treat a small percentage of patients without financial resources for no charge. In addition, university mental health clinics and hospitals might also offer low cost services. Kathy Collins advises that people with need inquire about the mechanisms in place at the various agencies to provide low cost services and not to think they are asking for something unusual.

Along the line of insurance benefits, you should be advised that many companies are severely limiting the amount of coverage they will allow for mental health problems. I personally believe such shortsightedness is a step back into the Dark Ages. Much documentation exists to demonstrate that untreated mental health problems lead to physical ailments and reduced productivity. ADHD is a combination physical and mental health problem. I think our ADHD children should have the same rights to treatment and affordable services as other children with chronic disorders. You may want to contact your legislators and ask them to press for insurance companies to improve coverage for mental health problems.

In addition to diagnostic services, most parents of ADHD children need some form of training. One way to acquire this is through parent training groups which are generally facilitated by mental health professionals. Most of these groups are not specifically for parents of ADHD children. The techniques they use, however, can be helpful in managing ADHD children. Kathy Collins says that in many instances these programs can be tailored to these special situations when parents tell the group leader about their child's special problem. Two mothers I spoke with, Colleen Patterson and Donna Rothman, turned to Parents Anonymous when they experienced behavioral difficulties with their ADHD children. This organization is nationwide, and though set up primarily for parents who are in danger of abusing their children, some Parents Anonymous groups do offer parent training.

Other places which might offer parent training courses include child guidance clinics, mental health centers, local child protection services, municipalities, community colleges and schools of adult education.

Dr. Richard Zakreski is a clinical psychologist in private practice who works primarily with children, adolescents and families, and has a special interest in ADHD and learning disabilities. I spoke with Dr. Zakreski about the general principles parents need to follow when rearing an ADHD child. The following information is in essence an overview of behavior management principles for these children. Literally, hundreds of books exist on this subject alone. The information below is meant to be informative. In no way should it replace a clinical approach to parent training.

Dr. Zakreski explains that both ADHD children and non-ADHD children need their parents to provide a structure to guide their behavior. This structure should impose rules and limits and parameters so that the child has a clear template to follow in order to determine what behavior is or is not appropriate and acceptable in given situations.

Non-ADHD children are quick to regulate their behavior to follow the rules inherent in the structure. ADHD children, on the other hand, often have difficulty recognizing rules, especially if these are implicitly communicated rather than explicitly stated. They tend to misbehave and frequently break rules because of their impulsive, distractible and disorganized nature. Yet ADHD children behave better when they have a clear template to guide their behavior. Thus, they need a well articulated structure that is consistent and predictable, which means that the child clearly understands what behavior is expected and the consequences for meeting or not meeting behavioral expectations.

These children also need a considerable amount of feedback about the behavioral choices they are making and to be held accountable for that behavior. When managed accordingly, ADHD children, like their non-ADHD counterparts, can regulate their own behavior to external limits. Such control proves very important, because children who are in control of their behavior are more successful in their interactions with others.

When parents create a structure embodied in a set of rules for their children to live by, they need to understand that children do not follow rules simply because the rules exist. A verbal under-standing of the rule does not mean the child will automatically internalize the rule so that it guides his or her behavior flexibly and adaptively across different situations on different days. Just talking about the rule rarely makes the child embrace the rule, particularly when he or she is younger or is an ADHD child. Rules work because they are applied consistently and enforced over time in ways that are meaningful to the child.

Behavior viewed this way is a willful, deliberate choice made by an individual to act in a certain way. How a parent responds to the ADHD child or the non-ADHD child after he or she has made a behavioral decision is what makes the structure work. Even though ADHD is an involuntary, non-deliberate condition, when creating a system to manage the ADHD child's behavior effectively, therapists use the premise that the child is making choices about that behavior. And so, behavior management sys-tems are designed to influence those choices by how parents (or teachers) respond to them.

Influencing behavioral choices is basically a three step process. First, you articulate a certain situation and the kind of behavior you expect from the child in that situation. For example, at dinner time, you might tell the child you expect him to eat all the food on his plate in a reasonable amount of time.

Second, you give the child an opportunity to make a behavioral decision, in this case to eat or not eat all the food in the specified amount of time.

Third, you hold the child accountable for his or her choice by applying a consequence for the behavior. For instance, if he or she makes the decision to eat and does so in the specified time, dessert is given along with praise.

The use of consequences to shape the ADHD child's behavior and influence his or her choices is extremely important. By definition, the word consequence means that which follows. Usu-ally people think of consequences as being negative. But in actu-ality, consequences can be either positive or negative. When kids do something well, a positive consequence delivered by a significant other, e.g., parent or teacher, helps them to recognize that they made a good decision. Praise and recognition increase the likelihood that the good decision will be repeated, because the child knows that a good decision means a good consequence will follow. Conversely, when the child misbehaves, he or she suffers a negative consequence. Then the child understands that a bad decision led to a bad outcome.

Positive consequences come in many forms. They range from an oral acknowledgement, such as "good going" and/or a kiss on the cheek, to material rewards, such as food or toys, to the receipt of certain privileges, such as television time. With any positive consequence, oral praise should also be given. Negative consequences similarly range from disapproval or an oral reprimand such as "I do not like it when you . . ." to a withdrawal of privileges and punishment where indicated. Although a parent may be quite frustrated or angry about the child's misbehavior, it is important that punishment be communicated to the child in a matter of fact, emotionally controlled manner. However, parents of ADHD children need to realize, as Dr. Conners says, "they are human beings under extraordinary stress." Thus, if mistakes are made when delivering punishment, rather than wallow in guilt, parents need to try better next time.

One form of punishment used effectively with all children is time-out. Time-out means that the child is sent to a predetermined location and literally timed out of rewarding activities. For example, if the child smacks a sibling, time-out becomes a reasonable consequence for that behavioral decision, because he or she has violated the social contract of shared living within the household, i.e., no hitting. In time-out, the child no longer has the privilege to choose location or activity, or how he or she will spend his or her time.

The actual location of the time-out spot is chosen by the parent. Once sent to time-out, in general, the child is expected to stay there for five quiet minutes, with emphasis on quiet. For younger children, two minutes is a more appropriate time. Similarly, fifteen minutes may be more appropriate for a twelve-year-old. After time-out, the child should be rewarded with an approval type of statement for a positive change in his or her behavior.

Consequences can also be either logical or natural. Whenever possible, consequences should be logically or naturally related to the original behavioral decision made by the child. Logical and natural consequences can be either positive or negative. A natural consequence means the behavior and the consequence are naturally related. For example, the child who does not eat dinner will be hungry and not satisfied. The baseball glove left in the rain and not put away will be ruined. Logical consequences have a logical connection between the behavior and the consequence and are imposed by people. For example, if you do not put your toys away, you will not be allowed to play with them for X amount of time. If you stretch out your bedtime, you will have to go to bed earlier. If you come home late, you will have an earlier curfew or be grounded.

Behavior management approaches to the treatment are most effective when used systematically. Thus, parents need to establish a behavioral program for home use so that the child is made responsible or accountable for his or her behavior. Such programs become more effective when both parents work together. To date, behavior charts prove the most widely used and effective approach to systematically managing behavior. The benefit of charts is that they provide daily feedback in a consistent fashion which not only aids in shaping the child's behavior, but even more importantly, helps the child develop an inner sense of self-control. We want the child to view his behavior as a series of choices he or she makes and to be responsible for those choices. Because good choices are paid with positive outcomes, the child learns to make appropriate decisions.

These programs should be instituted when children are young and kept in use into the teenage years with modifications made to suit age and need. These programs prove harder to implement with the ADHD teenagers, especially if this is the first time they've encountered this experience. They will predictably balk. The programs should be instituted, however, despite any resistance.

Dr. Russell Barkley, Professor of Psychiatry and Neurology and Director of Psychology at University of Massachusetts Medical School, feels that behavior charts are "nothing glitzy—just good hard work at learning to manage a disabled individual." The hard work stems from the fact that the charts require daily implementation on a long term basis, parental organization and regimentation. After awhile, as Hope Clark explains, "I just want to take things as they come and live like a normal family, so I stop using the chart. Of course, Tommy's behavior deteriorates within a few short days."

Many varieties of behavior charts exist as do many books

which explain the use of behavior management techniques. Various examples of charts are included in the appendix. However, behavior charts need to be tailored to each individual child's needs. Certain guidelines exist to set up a behavior management program as embodied in charting. Since managing the ADHD child can often be complicated at first, professional guidance is generally advisable.

Dr. Zakreski suggests the following as guidelines for the use of behavior management charts. The parents with input from the child first need to select the behaviors to be managed on the chart. The child also must understand exactly what is expected from him or her in terms of these behaviors. To begin with, just a few behaviors should be selected particularly with young children, since they do not have the developmental capacity to work with more. With older children, it is generally advisable to start with just a couple of behaviors and then add additional ones as the child meets with success. However, no more than five behaviors should be charted at any one time so as not to overwhelm the child (or parent).

As the child meets with success in shaping the behavior, then additional ones can be added one at a time. The behaviors should be articulated in a positive way so that the child knows what you expect rather than what you don't expect. For example, rather than "no hitting" the behavior would read "treats other family members in a polite, courteous way."

The behaviors selected for the chart should be daily ones. Examples of such behaviors include going to bed on time, doing homework, and getting ready for school on time. In using everyday behaviors, the child is afforded the maximum opportunity to develop control over them. Once you and your child have developed some expertise with this type of system, you can depart from using daily occurring behaviors and use those which occur less frequently or more irregularly. Whether or not you use a chart for these irregular ones, they should still be responded to with natural and logical consequences.

Once you establish the behaviors, you have to give the child the choice to behave appropriately. Then you must pay attention to the child's behavioral decisions throughout the day, and give the appropriate feedback. When the child makes good behavioral choices, he or she should be rewarded with approval messages and some form of tangible marker such as tokens, stickers or points. At the end of the day, if the child has few or no markers, then he or she did not comply or meet minimal expectations for behavior.

The child is held accountable for the overall performance at the end of each day, because you want to hold him or her accountable for his or her performance over a series of behaviors. Otherwise, the child might do well on four out of five behaviors and be penalized because of the one area where he or she was unsuccessful. The parents use the child's total score to determine the positive or negative consequences earned for his or her behavior over the course of the day. The positive and negative consequences will come in the form of the granting or withdrawal of certain privileges agreed upon when the chart is instituted. Such privileges could include going to bed a half hour later, having time to play Nintendo or watch television, having a friend over or going out for pizza or ice cream. When the system is used in conjunction with natural and logical consequences throughout the course of the day, the behavior is dually consequated.

As you can readily see, such behavioral management systems are, indeed, good hard work. Dr. Zakreski cautions parents to be consistent and stick to the program once they decide to use it, because the child should be given the impression that the behavior is important and that Mom and Dad mean what they say. Dr. Zakreski points out that when you make a rule and then give in, the child learns not to respect your word and gets the message that he or she can turn your "no" into a "yes." For instance, if you withhold food as a consequence after the child makes the behavioral decision not to eat and then whines and cries and wears you down, and two hours later you back down and give him or her food, the child's gotten control and you have increased the likelihood that you will be challenged in the future. Firmness and consistency are the operative words in behavior management.

The point of behavior management is for parents to get better at making the child's behavior his or her own problem than the child is at making the behavior the parent's problem. Even if you are tired or involved in other things, when the child makes a bad behavioral decision, you have to enforce the consequence. If behavior management does not work, then the parents have been unsuccessful at making the child responsible for his or her behavior by experiencing the consequences for it.

Another common pitfall of behavior management is complacency. Dr. Zakreski knows many parents who develop a good program, implement it, and produce positive changes. Then they get really happy and are lulled into a sense that the child is doing great now, so they stop the program. Within a short period of time, the child's good behavior slides and the family is back to square one.

"In order to control their behavior successfully, ADHD children do not need different parenting. But they do need extra parenting," Dr. Zakreski says. Thus, the skills used with ADHD children are the same ones used with non-ADHD children. However, with ADHD kids, these skills must be used in a more articulate, more consistent, more deliberate way because ADHD children need that extra management and organization and feedback from parents.

Summary

- ADHD symptoms intensify as environmental demands increase.
- In general, ADHD toddlers exhibit impulsive, distractible, restless, always on-the-go patterns.
- The symptoms of hyperactivity and impulsivity compromise the toddler's safety.
- Other symptoms present in toddler may include:
  1. unstable mood,
  2. problems with sleeping or eating,
  3. extreme curiosity,
  4. intense response to stimuli.
- ADHD children cannot control their behavior on a consistent basis without parental assistance.
- When parents suspect the child has a behavioral problem, they must find the appropriate health care professional to diagnose and treat the problem.
- For an assessment of behavioral problems, parents can inquire at mental health centers, hospital child evaluation units, university mental health clinics, school child study teams, private practitioners.

- Most ADHD children experience learning problems and may have other learning disabilities.
- ADHD is a medical diagnosis which should be made by a pediatrician, pediatric neurologist, child psychiatrist, clinical child psychologist, or clinical social worker.
- Therapist referrals can come from many sources, among which are mental health centers, mental health associations, family physicians, self-help groups and professional associations.
- Parents should interview potential therapists.
- Many agencies offer affordable mental health services.
- Parent training to learn how to manage the ADHD child's behavior effectively is available through special groups and private therapists.
- Parents of ADHD children can make the symptoms of the disorder less unpleasant by using behavioral management techniques. These include providing a solid structure, with clear rules and pre-set consequences attached to the observance or non-observance of those rules. Parents must be consistent and manage the ADHD child's behavior systematically which is best accomplished through the use of behavior charts. A trained professional may be necessary to guide parents in the use of such techniques.

CHAPTER FOUR

The Preschool Years: Ages 3–5

Once I grew accustomed to the reality of our impending move, I told myself this geographic change would mean a new beginning. Without the lure of friends and relatives to share outside the home activities, I planned to devote my full attention toward shaping David into a quiet and ordered little boy.

But David now approached the time when a child's horizons expand to the world beyond, the preschool era of children aged three to five. Neighborhood children and nursery school beckoned. Soon I would have even less control of him. No longer would we conduct most of our business in the privacy of our own home. Like most parents, I hoped my son would shed the difficult skin he wore and ease into the world beyond his front door.

My husband and I left the children with their aunt the day we actually moved into our new home. When the two boys arrived the following day, their rooms were ready, child-proof locks secured all cabinets, laced curtains on some of the windows. However, before I unpacked his toys, David took ill. As always, I attributed this fever to an ear infection, but the new pediatrician called it "a virus, probably brought on by the stress of the move."

His diagnosis surprised me. Though I knew David overreacted to silly little changes, I expected him to handle the relocation with ease. After all, unlike Jonathan and myself, David, as with his Dad, seemed to thrive on adventure. A few days later he perked up when we attended a welcome coffee given for me by a new neighbor.

Stacy Birdwell invited all the neighborhood ladies to meet me. One of them also brought along her three-year-old son so David would have a playmate. Over the din of our voices we all heard the commotion from the other room where David tried to convince Ryan to "relinquish" a toy. The little fellow stood his ground until my son's persistence forced him to retreat into the folds of his mother's skirt. When our hostess attempted to appease David with another toy, he threw it to the floor. Totally mortified, I slunk further down into my chair.

This image was not the one I wished to portray in our new neighborhood. I wanted our family to be like the sitcom "Leave It to Beaver" where everyone interacted in a courteous fashion, where Ward and June Cleaver asserted their control and Wally and the Beaver aimed to please them, where all problems were worked out quietly and calmly behind closed doors, always within a half hour. But from that fateful spring morning, Ryan's Mom always made an excuse whenever I suggested we get the boys together.

David Sr. attributed our son's aggressive behavior at the coffee to frustration. "David probably felt ignored," he said. Over time, however, I noticed he even played roughly with our dog Pogo despite the fact he had grown old enough to know better. David never behaved nastily. He just ran at that dog with so much exuberance, the poor beast turned her tail and took off in the other direction whenever she saw him. Our neighbor to the immediate left commented many times about the good nature of our pet.

So much of David's behavior these days proved inappropriate and could not be ignored. Every activity became an ordeal, even simple walks through the neighborhood. Logic would dictate that after a few bad experiences a sensible person would know when to quit and make changes. And I did really cut back the number of our outings. I stopped taking David to shopping malls and grocery stores, but I hungered for adult company and so persevered with our daily afternoon jaunts through the streets where we lived. People always stopped me to admire the kids. After a while, I met some of them on a regular basis.

If we happened to speak for more than a few minutes, David impatiently tried to pull me away. Failing this first attempt, he then rode his Big Wheel full throttle, and on his more impish days, headed it directly toward my legs. If this action did not achieve the desired effect, he played bumper cars with Jonathan's stroller. Jonathan accepted these jolts in good nature.

But most everyone else remarked about David's demands for my attention. His actions embarrassed me, and I grew increasingly resentful that he interrupted my conversations. Before long I found myself in the habit of making sarcastic comments about him. When someone stopped to say, "He's so adorable," I invited them to stick around. Those who stayed usually saw my point.

Through no conscious effort on my part, such comments reduced the shock value of David's actions and placed them in the Peck's Bad Boy category. They prepared people to expect the worst. If the worst did not happen, all the better. My remarks also shielded me from my feelings of incompetence and allowed the observer to know though I acknowledged David's bad behavior, it nonetheless remained out of my control.

While my negative comments minimized the effects of David's behaviors on others, they went far to keep the wedge between us. Instead of being my son's best fan, I appeared his worst critic. So many times I felt ashamed of my reactions to this child. I now depended more and more on my positive interactions with Jonathan to feel like a good mother. David, to the contrary, became increasingly resentful of his younger brother.

When the time for nursery school arrived, David Sr. and I, despite our ambivalent feelings, decided to enroll David. He thought David too young. I worried that the teachers might not understand such a loud and unruly child. But I also had concerns about his social development. With Ryan out of the picture, Jonathan remained his only playmate. David bossed his younger brother so much that Jon and I both needed a few hours peace.

The school's director listened to my concerns about David's readiness for nursery school. She told me not to worry, "most children need to adjust." The curriculum centered around play and social interaction. Since David never balked about going, after a time I figured nursery school agreed with him.

One winter day, his teacher, Mrs. Able, stopped my car to hand me an owl he crafted from kidney beans. "David worked so hard on this owl, Mrs. Fowler. I just wanted you to know what an effort he made," she said. Well, I beamed with pride. His mosaic depicted a flawless owl. How sweet of her, I thought, to commend David's obviously talented work in person.

When the first parent-teacher conference arrived a month later, I could not wait to hear more about my son's ability. After I sat down and Mrs. Able said, "Oh, David's coming along nicely," I scratched my head. That comment did not sound at all like the glowing report I expected to hear.

"Hasn't he been doing well?" I asked.

She hesitated to tell me the kidney bean owl represented one of the rare days when David stayed on task. She felt pleased for him and figured if she made a big fuss over his accomplishment, he might repeat it. But most days, David became frustrated about his work and lost his temper quite demonstratively.

"He's not a problem," she assured me. "I just say David, attitude, attitude, attitude! and he catches himself."

What a great response I thought, but when voiced by my lips, Mrs. Able's words brought an even angrier attitude.

Though these days David's attitude also presented an annoyance on the home front, other improvements in his behavior compensated for the nuisance. No longer did I worry about his physical well-being. David, now three years old, seemed less fragile, his actions less rash. Sure he ran across the field during a high school football game while a play was in progress, but he saw his Dad on the other side and the shortest distance between two points is a straight line. And he did stop cold in his tracks when the referee blew the whistle to prematurely stop the play.

He now called me Mom again. True, I had to force the word from his lips, but he gave me this courtesy. He even showed signs of affection. When I landed in the hospital with some mysterious gastro-intestinal illness, I came home to find a teddy bear David propped on my pillow. I praised him and bragged to everyone about this loving gesture he made. Though we still do not get bedtime kisses, every night both his Dad and I each receive a stuffed animal which our son selects with the greatest care.

I'm not certain why my son's behavior improved. Perhaps the change could be attributed to the fact that he had grown older. Or maybe since I had a respite while he went to nursery school, I felt less tense and did not overreact to everything he did. Who knows? But I thought David even handled the jealous feelings toward his brother in a better fashion. Once as I prepared to leave for an overnight trip, David said, "Jonathan goes too."

Shocked at this gesture of good will I skeptically asked, "You want me to take Jonathan?"

"Yes," he replied, "take Jonathan to Granny's and leave him there." Now that young David verbalized his feelings, I figured with speech for a tool, he no longer needed to act on every whim. And so I anticipated an improvement in life around our house, at least where David was concerned.

Even though young David's behavior seemed less problematic, tensions within the marriage flared. Not all our problems arose as a result of trying to manage our son. We each brought problems to the marriage in the first place. Our difficulties with David just tipped the scales and our marriage slipped out of balance. My husband and I found ourselves entangled in a negative interactional mess wherein he blamed me, and I, of course, blamed him for the troubles in our home. Before we could address the issues, life handed us a few major stresses within a period of two months. Our marital situation deteriorated from bad to worse.

David made a career move, and a year to the day, we once again relocated. Since this change brought us back home, neither of us thought a move would be stressful. We had not learned that new jobs, and even brand new houses, upset the status quo. This time I flew into orbit because of the additional stress resulting from the death of my father the day after we moved.

No one during this journey had been stamped "handle with care." Only our belongings arrived intact. But these things broke soon after being unpacked. First, a family room lamp smashed when three-and-a-half-year-old David clipped it with his feet while somersaulting off the couch. Next, a tea cup met its destruction, though not by accident: when David Sr. made a critical remark, I hurled it at the kitchen wall. For months, until I wallpapered the room, tea stains bore witness to my loss of self control.

Young David's reactions, however, proved impossible to cover up. He unleashed his temper with a fury that rocked the nursery school walls. In one morning, he hit a child, pushed another off the slide, and threw sand at yet a third. The teacher, totally exasperated, sat him in the corner for over an hour, and even after I arrived, she refused to allow him to leave that spot until she vented her frustration on me.

He looked so frightened. I could not believe David behaved in such an antagonistic manner without provocation. Since this teacher clearly played favorites, and my little boy did not make her list, I rationalized that she might be partially to blame for his behavior by doing nothing to ease his transition to this new school. I bit my tongue so as not to scream at her, "Why don't you give him a break? Can't you see how this move affected him?"

When I recounted this incident to David Sr., he agreed with my assessment of the nursery school teacher's role. But, as always, he carried his comments a step further and insisted this new teacher did not recognize David's need of special attention. I suspected young David might have some underlying problem that made his life intense, but the possibility that my son could have a hurt which I could not fix felt awful and so I tried to ignore my suspicions. Thus my husband's indications that David needed special attention did more than just make it difficult for me to suppress my fears. His comments stirred my sense of helplessness to a boil. I simply had no conception of what more I could do for my boy.

A few weeks after the school episode, David's outbursts at home intensified with such magnitude that his rages scared me. I confiscated his croquet set along with all sticks and blunt objects. When David got mad, he let them fly at whatever or whomever happened in his path. How I punished him made little difference. His temper could not be controlled.

With the tea from my earlier rampage still a blot on the kitchen wall, I felt responsible as though somehow he patterned his actions after what others now referred to as "my high strung behavior." Young David certainly never rattled his father who more and more said to me, "You're the one having the problem." There seemed no other explanation but the obvious, his mother. My self-esteem hit an all time low. I slipped into a depression.

Life in our home became shrouded in unpleasantness. Young David blamed everybody and everything for his behavior. When he ran in the house and crashed into a table, he smashed that "bad table" to bits. When I said, "David, you did the running," he got angrier. If he fell off his bike, instead of crying like other children, David repeatedly threw it to the ground or into the garage door. Even when playing nicely, David managed to break all his toys. His room always looked like a tornado just passed through. None of the neighborhood children invited him to play except one very mild mannered young boy. Often Jonathan received the full thrust of his brother's fury. But unless he had been physically hurt, Jon just sort of took David's actions in stride, and I felt somewhat gratified that at least my younger son was mellow.

David's dad coped with the turmoil by denying its existence and burying himself in his work. I buried my head under the covers minutes after the boys went to bed. During the daylight hours, I felt tired all the time. A friend suggested I get out more with the boys and take them to the beach. "Well," I thought, "that couldn't hurt." But after a week, my stomach went into severe spasms.

David refused to obey the club rules. Such audacity always resulted in a reprimand from the owner who then flashed me a dirty look. Time and again I redirected young David's attention, but he did not learn to stop even when I forcefully removed him from off limit places. He pushed and pulled until he became free and immediately returned to the scene of the crime. Eventually he wore me down and I either gave in to his whims or left the beach in a huff. The other mothers gave us a very wide berth.

That summer ended when Jonathan landed in the hospital from the effects of a mysterious virus. The week before, my mother commented about how awful and pale he looked, but Jonathan never fussed, so I assumed his health was fine. Years later, our child psychologist explained this incident to be a prime illustration of his favorite cliché, "the squeaky wheel gets the oil." David became the center of all that happened in our house by demanding so much of our time and energy that everyone else's needs went unattended.

Relatives warned both David Sr. and me that our younger son did not receive enough attention. Still everyone laughed when I referred to our boys as Charlie McCarthy the dummy and his ventriloquist Edgar Bergen. David consistently interrupted his younger brother and finished Jon's every sentence. Though I agreed with friends and relatives, David clearly usurped center stage. I quickly dismissed their comments. "But the attention Jonathan gets is always positive," I explained. "David gets nothing but negative press," his father concurred. I could not understand why these people did not see how little we, as parents, had left to give.

Anyone who walked through our door could not avoid the

tension. My husband and I reacted through shouting matches or angry silences. By the fall, the hostility proved impossible to submerge. We individually sought private therapy which eventually led to marriage counseling.

The therapist needed time to sort out the mess of our marriage. Yet he almost immediately realized that our son's behavior, though not the cause of all our problems, acted as a catalyst wherein our negative patterns surfaced. However, why all our family outings ended in disaster and why chaos constantly surrounded us remained a mystery.

After the events of David's fourth birthday party, neither his Dad nor I could continue to make excuses for our son's outrageous behavior. That day after all the little guests arrived, David flipped into a frenzy. His mood grew so dark he zapped all the joy from the event. The birthday party ultimately degenerated into an ugly scene when at the petting zoo David smacked a horse in the mouth, an action which totally stunned his Dad and me.

All along, my husband and I figured our son's aggressive behavior to be a reaction to some provocation. Clearly he hit the horse for no apparent reason, and though initially we felt like strangling him, after the shock subsided, we realized David had no control. Where I once viewed him as the master of his deeds, now I saw he needed help. Though his Dad felt a few reservations, we set out to find the source of what troubled our son.

That journey turned into a pathetic comedy of errors. We spent eighteen months going from one professional to another before we obtained an accurate diagnosis. Our search began at the pediatrician's office. In my initial conversation, I told the doctor everything about David's behavior which puzzled me. After recounting the horse hitting incident, I chronicled his behavior from infancy to date. I ended this recollection with an observation. "Doctor, he will not allow my husband and me to have a conversation at the dinner table. His behavior is not normal, is it?"

The doctor replied, "No, Mrs. Fowler, that behavior is not normal."

The pediatrician sent us to an allergist who saw David in November 1983, and found him to be hyperactive. The allergist told me no one really understood the cause of hyperactivity. Since David reacted positively to house dust, he received shots every week.

The allergist also placed David, a finicky eater to begin with, on an elimination diet to see if foods exacerbated his problems. We then used the Feingold diet which promised to alleviate hyperactivity by restricting certain foods with additives, preservatives, salicylates and sugar. The promises of the Feingold diet proved worthless. I figured I must be doing something wrong. Though none had tried this diet personally, every mother I knew said she heard that it worked miracles with other mothers' kids. A year later, we learned diet and allergy do not cause ADHD and no miracles cure it.

Two months later, we landed in a child psychiatrist's office. After taking a family history and observing David interact with us, the child psychiatrist said, "David is hyperactive." He then told us our son would outgrow his hyperactivity around puberty and we could use medication if we needed to "slow him down" until then.

The real issue of treatment he believed centered around David's angry and ill-mannered behavior. When we asked why our son acted so horrendously, the child psychiatrist said, "because he has an extreme case of sibling rivalry. You introduced another sibling at the crucial individuation/separation stage of development." At ninety dollars an hour in 1984, I figured he knew his material.

This doctor ended the session with the suggestion we read about separation/individuation. He gave us Margaret Mahler's book, *The Psychological Birth of the Human Infant,* a clinical text offering an in-depth discussion of this critical stage and other stages as well. The psychiatrist told David Sr. to give our son at least two hours a day of individual attention so young David could work through this stage again. When we pointed out that Dad traveled every week, the doctor said, "Hire a neighborhood teenage boy as a substitute father." Though our marriage teetered on shaky ground, neither of us believed David Sr. could be that easily replaced. In May, we ceased using this doctor's counsel when he recommended we gag David to stop him from releasing his ear piercing shrieks when riding in the car. Nothing improved in our house under his care.

With the school year drawing to a close, my husband and I faced the decision of whether or not to enroll our soon to be five-year-old son in kindergarten. Having no confidence left in our parenting abilities, we attended a seminar on "Kindergarten Readiness" for direction. As usual, the norms did not fit David. The speaker was a licensed and certified school psychologist. He suggested he evaluate David privately.

The psychologist met with us and evaluated our son for an hour and a half. Though David could sustain performance a full year ahead of his age, the psychologist recommended we not place him in Kindergarten. In his three-page report to us, the psychologist wrote, "David is very active and has a poor attention span. He is easily distracted and will not stay with tasks for very long. He is a very intense young child and given to open displays of anger and yelling. David does not like new or different situations and can not readapt even after some exposure to them." He had described a child who displayed all the behaviors that are the very hallmarks of Attention-deficit Hyperactivity Disorder.

Instead of telling us the source of David's problems, his report contained his recommendations. "I would prefer David to be in a very structured and controlled setting at home. If things are always organized and predicted, and quiet and arranged so as not to stimulate David, he can calm down readily and have some control. His activity is not beyond him."

How ridiculous. David's activity proved beyond him, beyond me, beyond the entire family. For some reason, a knowledge and understanding of Attention-deficit Hyperactivity Disorder proved beyond this child development specialist, just as it had eluded the other professionals from whom we sought counsel and guidance.

The signs and symptoms of ADHD become highly visible at the preschool stage. Except in the very mild cases, ADHD children between the ages of three and five generally experience problems in at least one major setting, at home, in school, with peers. Children, like David, with moderate to severe degrees of the disorder exhibit difficulties in all three areas.

Typical reports from nursery school teachers indicate the child's inability to follow directions and stay on task. ADHD children tend to be away from their desks more than do their classmates. Frequently teachers will describe the child as "immature."

ADHD children evidence nursery school problems in different degrees of severity. While only one teacher made only one serious complaint about David, Jan Lawes received such unfavorable reports about her son Doug's behavior, she became a mother volunteer, her rationale being, "I thought if I did everything they could possible want, they would tolerate my kid a little better." Unlike Doug Lawes, Steven White was not at all disruptive in preschool. Steven does not have the hyperactive or impulsive symptoms of ADHD. Still his mother Lynn heard frequent complaints from Steven's preschool teacher because he daydreamed so much and seldom paid attention. One day, in response to the teacher's comments, Lynn said, "Well, you know some kids march to the beat of a different drummer." The teacher replied, "And some have no drummer at all."

Difficulties with social interactions arise as a dominant problem for many ADHD children between the ages of three and five. Many behave in a verbally and/or physically aggressive fashion with their peers. ADHD boys do not corner the market on aggressive peer interactions either. According to her mother, five-year-old Maggie Anderson did not fit the "sugar and spice, everything nice" mold characteristic of young ladies. When Maggie went to a friend's house, if something did not go her way, she literally knocked her female playmate to the floor. After each incident, Maggie's mother apologized and explained that her daughter had a problem with self-control which she and Maggie's dad were trying to correct. Nonetheless, Maggie would still be banished from the other child's home for a period of months.

The overall social behavior of most ADHD children is aptly described as immature and insensitive. Dr. Russell Barkley, Professor of Psychiatry and Neurology and Director of Psychology at the University of Massachusetts Medical Center, says, "ADHD children lack self-awareness. They are mentally and developmentally immature and so they behave like younger children. Younger children do not pay much attention to how their behavior affects other people or themselves."

In addition to classifying them as immature mentally and developmentally, Dr. C. Keith Conners, Professor of Medical Psychology and Director of the ADHD clinic at Duke University Medical School, describes ADHD children as "socially insensitive." For example, Dr. Conners noted the frequency with which ADHD children will blurt out very embarrassing comments in company. Such gaffes are made, he explains, because ADHD children are insensitive to the demands of the situation, and of how their interactions might affect others. ADHD children tend to apply rules in a hard and fast way, rather than as guides to actions. Since they tend to be insensitive to internal states in themselves, they often prove insensitive to how others may be feeling. ADHD children tend to misread the feedback they receive from others about their social behavior. Says Dr. Conners, "Often these kids are amazed they have had an effect on somebody."

If you consider the ADHD child's immature and insensitive nature and factor in the impulsivity that accompanies this disorder, you can easily see why social problems become a constant thorn in his or her side. ADHD children generally react before they make an appropriate assessment of a situation and determine what behavior is appropriate. They also tend to be disorganized and so behave in a chaotic manner. Dr. Conners explains that the prerequisites for good socialization are being able to wait your turn, to share with others and to follow the rules of the game. Since ADHD children often cannot delay impulses, impulsivity prevents them from learning these basic rules of fairness. Dr. Conners also cites two other factors which contribute to social problems for ADHD children. Because of their hyperactivity, these children are usually not in one place long enough to play a game or to learn the rules. ADHD children frequently have associated visual motor problems, so they are not very good in many sports either.

According to Dr. Conners, "ADHD children are different from the antisocial kid who wants to hurt other children. ADHD children just cannot control themselves." The inability to restrain behavior and to respond appropriately to the demands of a social situation often causes ADHD children to experience negative consequences in every arena of social interaction, be that the playground, the neighborhood, the school bus or the classroom. These children are rejected by playmates, isolated from groups. They receive many unkind comments and are usually the last kids picked for teams—if they are picked at all. Most parents know too well the sad fact that their sons and daughters often find themselves excluded from birthday parties. Dr. Conners makes the point that ADHD children *want* to be liked and *want* to be involved, but their ADHD characteristics often prevent them.

To encourage prosocial behavior, ADHD children often require intervention to remediate their social skill deficits. One form of intervention is parental manipulation of the child's social interactions in the home environment. Dr. Richard Zakreski, a clinical psychologist in private practice, believes that parents need to become highly involved to help their ADHD child build social relationships. He suggests parents create a type of therapy group at home in which they facilitate their child's social development by structuring the child's social time, and by providing feedback about the child's peer interactions, so that the ADHD child comes to understand and appreciate appropriate social behavior.

Dr. Zakreski reminds parents that building relationships takes time and effort. Therefore, parents need to be persistent and involved. Bear in mind, most ADHD children can make friends, but they have difficulty keeping friends. The younger the ADHD child is when the parent helps him or her to build social bridges, the better the chance for success. To this extent, Dr. Zakreski describes the following approach as a possible way for a parent to help and encourage the ADHD child's social relationships.

The parent must first target a child for the ADHD child to play with. The hope is this target child will be someone who will want to interact with the ADHD child in the future. Preferably the parent will take advantage of any natural alliances and make the target child someone with whom the ADHD child has already experienced some positive connection. For instance, if the ADHD child came home from school one day and said, "Johnny was nice to me," Johnny could become a good candidate to be the target child. Once a playmate is targeted, the parents then must make the effort to get the ADHD child and the target child together at their home. To do so, the parent may have to extend the invitation. Dr. Zakreski advises the parents against leaving the initial invitation up to the ADHD child because he or she may never get around to it or be reluctant to make it for fear of rejection.

When beginning this social bridge-building process, the goal is to have positive interactions between the two children. Consequently, the next step in the process is for the parents to structure the interaction by limiting the amount of time the children spend together, and by selecting an activity that lends itself to parental involvement and supervision. For instance, the parent might arrange for the children to bake cookies, or watch a video, or go bowling. Activities such as these allow the parent to control the interactions, to intercede if problems arise, and to give the children feedback about their prosocial behavior.

This bridge-building process is repeated as often as needed to encourage a friendship and a routine type of interaction between the ADHD child and the target child. As these children gradually begin to interact positively and successfully with one another, the parent can then extend the amount of time the children spend together and withdraw some of the parental supervision. Once the ADHD child has established a friendship with this target child, the parent should then repeat the process with a second one. Dr. Zakreski suggests that parents keep the ADHD child's interactions to a one-on-one situation to avoid the possibility of the odd-man-out type of interaction. Parents will want to withdraw their involvement to the degree that the ADHD child demonstrates the ability to take responsibility for his or her own activities. Parental involvement or lack of it is dictated by the ADHD child's social skills and not chronological age.

In order to develop prosocial behavior, some ADHD children may need professional intervention. Social skills training is one available therapy for the ADHD child. However, Dr. Russell Barkley, author of *Hyperactive Children: A Handbook for Diagnosis and Treatment,* categorizes this treatment as promising but still experimental. In the clinic where Dr. Barkley practices, children must be nine years old to engage in this therapy because he has found that "below this age they do not seem to benefit much from that kind of instruction." He believes part of the reason this therapy does not work has to do with the fact that the child is pulled out of his natural environment and taught the social skills and then is expected to generalize them to non-treatment settings.

Dr. Barkley tries to circumvent this problem by training the child's parents and teachers to incorporate social skills training as part of what they do. He cited anger control as one social skill that lends itself well to parent- and teacher-initiated training. Dr. Barkley utilizes this method in the following way.

First, the child is taught in a small group setting how to stop and think before reacting to frustration such as being told he or she cannot do something. Then the parent is instructed to spend some time with the child each day to review a potentially frustrating situation. For an example, the parent may refer to one during the previous twenty-four hours where the child is seen getting angry. The parent then talks about what else the child could have done and role plays the situation again. As the parent walks through the situation, the child is reminded of other behaviors that are incompatible with getting angry. The parent might suggest that the child think about things that don't get him or her angry, or to count to ten, or tighten his or her lips, or keep his or her mouth closed. After the exercise, the parent rewards the child with tokens which can then be exchanged for special privileges or prizes. Dr. Barkley says, "It has been shown these children can pick up very quickly on controlling their anger, but these skills require rehearsal and practice."

Socialization groups prove to be another popular forum in which to teach ADHD children social skills. Betty Garver sent her son Joel to such a group because he was poorly coordinated and could not compete with the other boys. As a result, he tried to "one up" them or to boss them around, which only antagonized the other children. He did not know how to fit into a group. His mother said, "Recess for Joel was torture, like bamboo shoots under the fingernails."

Clinical psychologist Randy Mendelson, who practices in New Jersey, has been facilitating socialization groups for a number of years. He finds most children need this group therapy for at least six months to a year. According to Dr. Mendelson, a good socialization group should have four necessary ingredients; fun, structure, learning and reinforcement. In his groups, which run for intervals of ten week sessions, the children select the fun activity they want to use as a socialization exercise. These activities range from outside play such as tag to inside games such as "Uno." The children also make the rules to guide the activities. Just as in home behavior management charts, the rules are phrased in positive ways, e.g., "waits for turn" instead of "does not cut in front of others."

After the activity, the children sit in a circle and provide feedback to one another. The feedback is the learning part of the session. During this time, each group member hears what rules he or she has or has not followed and what type of playmate he or she has been. The reinforcement part of the process has two components. First, if a child gives honest feedback to a group member, he or she is socially reinforced. Second, the child receiving the feedback is rewarded (e.g., pretzels) when it is positive. In this way, both participation and prosocial behavior are encouraged.

During the preschool years, in the absence of an effective behavior management program such as the one described in the previous chapter, most ADHD children continue to be hard to manage. They tend to disobey rules and not do what is asked. They do not learn from experience. Discipline techniques, such as a reprimand, which work for most children, prove inconsequential for this child. Mothers become convinced they are bad parents and may begin to show signs of depression and low self-esteem. Disagreements between spouses over the best way to manage the child frequently arise.

Psychologist Dr. C. Keith Conners notes that, particularly during these preschool years, since the bulk of the childcare falls primarily on the mother, fathers often do not see the child as the master of his or her behavior. Ben Green, a father I spoke with, said he initially thought his wife somehow provoked their son's negative behavior because the boy behaved fairly well for him. Psychologist Dr. Russell Barkley feels, in general, that children are less oppositional with their fathers though the exact reason for this phenomenon is conjecture. Consequently, many fathers tend to think the behavior problems are the mother's fault for being either too strict or too lenient. Though Laurie Maxwell's husband did not find fault with her, friends often asked, "Why don't you spank the boy more?" She did not spank him more because physical punishment does not make an ADHD child behave better.

Because ADHD children are so hard to manage, most of their parents have great difficulty either finding or keeping babysitters. Liz Sacca once hired the daughter of a town councilman to watch her ADHD child and his brothers. When she arrived home later that night, Liz found the sitter in a heap in the middle of the floor crying because long after she put the children to bed, the ADHD child managed to wake his brothers and engage them in a game of toss with Mom's precious knickknacks. Other mothers, like Betty Garver, never hired babysitters because they worried that a sitter might underestimate their daredevil ADHD child.

Though ADHD children do not intend to be problematic, they create a great deal of parental frustration. Dr. Russell Barkley, who is highly regarded for his ADHD parent training program, explains, "ADHD children do not respond to the softer management techniques and subtle social consequences." Thus, most parents of ADHD children need to be trained as described previously in how to set rules, how to institute consequences, how to give commands clearly, how to follow through with appropriate consequences, and how to limit the amount of demands they make upon the child.

Before many of us learn appropriate ways to manage the hard-to-handle child, Dr. Barkley notes some common mistakes we parents of ADHD children frequently make. We tend to administer consequences in an extremely inconsistent way, he finds. The child on one day may have the roof fall on his or her head for a mildly inappropriate behavior. The next day, when he or she repeats the behavior, the parent may make little note of it or perhaps even find it a bit amusing. Also seen in ADHD families is non-contingent punishment by parents where the consequences are not contingent upon something the child does. The ADHD child becomes the family scapegoat and everyone's bad mood falls onto the child's shoulders.

In the talk/reason approach, parents try to ease the child into compliance by offering hundreds of reasons why a request was made. Most parents eventually discover that ADHD children make great lawyers. As Dr. Barkley explains, "With ADHD children, reason carries no weight whatsoever." Nor does excessive repetition of commands, another non-technique to which most parents fall prey.

These common mistakes are typically embodied in a pattern of interaction between the parent (usually the mother) and the ADHD child. It is called the Coercive Interaction Pattern. This pattern may also occur between teachers and students. According to Dr. Barkley, when it becomes the established manner in which the parent and child interact over parental demands made upon the child, the likelihood that the child will engage in future oppositional and hostile behavior increases.

As explained by Dr. Barkley, the pattern takes shape as follows: The parent places a demand on the child which the latter views as work and does not enjoy doing. At this point, the child either does or does not comply with the demand. In families where this pattern occurs frequently, Dr. Barkley notes that a lack of reward and/or appreciation is seldom given when the child does comply. When the child does not comply, in most instances the parent will repeat the command numerous times. This repetition postpones any consequence the child receives for his disobedience. By talking and repeating, the parent becomes less effective because the child sees that Mom or Dad's word is not backed up. By the time the child receives punishment, he or she has been allowed to continue to do things his or her way. Thus, the misbehavior is actually reinforced because the child wins at doing what he or she chooses and at waiting out the parent.

Usually, after about fifteen or twenty minutes, when the child does not comply, the parent makes threats. As the child ignores the threats, the parent becomes frustrated and then begins to make threats the child knows either will not be kept or will be modified in some fashion. For example, the parent might say, "you'll never see your bike again" or "I'm going to throw that Nintendo set in the trash." With each threat, both parties become more negative and frustrated and reach a point where both parties are out of control. At this point, in seventy percent of the cases, Dr. Barkley says, the parent acquiesces which means the demand is not met in the way initially specified. Either the parent actually steps in and does whatever is asked of the child, or the demand is simply not met at all. About twenty percent of the time the child is punished, but the punishment occurs too late in the transaction to be of value.

Another form of acquiescence which happens less often is the situation where the parent actually rewards the child for not complying. Dr. Barkley finds that when the parent acquiesces in this manner, the likelihood the child will engage in future oppositional behavior increases by four hundred percent. This type situation is seen frequently in instances where the child throws a loud and obnoxious temper tantrum. The parent not only stops making the demand, but may hold the child or stroke the child's hair in a calming effort.

To defeat coercive interactions, Dr. Barkley suggests that parents make the following changes: First, he advises them to limit the amount and type of demands they make upon the ADHD child. Before making one, the parents should also determine if the child is capable of meeting the demand. Once they do make a demand, parents must follow through on it and administer immediate consequences. Second, he instructs the parents in how to provide substantially more rewards, such as those suggested in the previous chapter, when the child does comply with a request. Dr. Barkley views the fact that many parents of ADHD children do not respond to the appropriate behavior as perhaps the biggest mistake they make in managing their child. Basic behavior management teaches parents to "catch the child being good." The best way to *decrease* good behavior is to ignore it. The best way to *increase* good behavior is to acknowledge and reward it.

Too often during the preschool period, the rewards prove few and far between for the ADHD child. From ages three to five, some ADHD preschoolers display temper tantrums, outbursts of rage, aggressive and destructive tendencies, often in public places. When asked to be accountable for their behavior, ADHD children commonly place the blame on someone or something other than self.

No one knows for certain what causes these aggressive and acting out type behaviors. They could be a part of the disorder itself, or a result of the manner in which the child and his environment interact, or both. I suspect the ADHD child is like a tumbleweed rolling over the desert where each movement gathers a little more dust and dirt. Though David as an infant evidenced a moody and irritable disposition, certainly my reactions to his ADHD behaviors served to make his symptoms and our overall situation worse. The ultimate irony of this disorder is that the child with the worst symptoms needs the greatest support, but receives instead a lion's share of negative feedback.

According to Dr. Barkley, the family histories of ADHD children often reveal other stressors in addition to the child's ADHD. He reports that psychiatric disorders are more common among parents of ADHD children, with the most common disorder being ADHD in the parent. Marital disputes exist with a higher incidence in ADHD families. Divorce is twice as common. Sixty percent of all mothers suffer from low self-esteem. About one-fourth of them become clinically depressed and require professional intervention. Fifteen percent of the fathers evidence alcohol or substance abuse problems.

Every member of the family realizes some negative effect as a result of ADHD. Jean Bramble, an ADHD case manager at the Learning Problems Clinic in Primary Children's Medical Center in Salt Lake City, explains that every family hits a crisis point when perhaps an illness or a loss of job or some such problem occurs that upsets the equilibrium of the family. Before balance is restored, each family member struggles. In families with ADHD children, Jean Bramble says that the ADHD child frequently disrupts the family's equilibrium to the point that the family is always out of balance and struggling.

Dr. C. Keith Conners, Duke University Professor of Medical Psychology, describes the effect that this disorder has on the ADHD child's siblings as "profound." He notes that siblings suffer because the ADHD child is so disruptive to family life, adding:

"Frequently, younger siblings feel terrorized by this child who does not know his limits and will actively avoid any contact with the ADHD child. Older siblings are usually more distant and don't spend much time around the ADHD sibling because they are embarrassed by his or her behavior."

Heather Flood, the sister of an ADHD boy, told me she often felt her parents were not fair and always gave her brother far more attention. Diana Stevenson, an older sibling I spoke with, said that whenever she had to go out to dinner with the family, she worried someone would say, "Look at the looney tune and his family. They're probably all like him."

Dr. William McMahon, Director of the Learning Problems Clinic at Primary Children's Medical Center in Salt Lake City, notes that siblings of ADHD children commonly place the blame for all their arguments and fights on the ADHD child. Some siblings do so with such skill they appear perfect. Dr. McMahon follows one particular family where the ADHD child's younger sister frequently sets her brother up so that the parents do not realize that she has caused the trouble. Ordinarily, when they play, she ends up screaming and the boy gets punished for upsetting her.

Melanie Hartsgrove, the mother of Sandy, an ADHD child, said, "Sandy became the family scapegoat. Whenever he and his sister had a fight, Sandy got blamed because I expected him to be the bad child. His sister instigated a lot of the trouble, but because Sandy is louder and can't cover up as well, he got in trouble."

Dr. Sam Goldstein, a clinical psychologist at the Neurology, Learning and Behavior Center in Salt Lake City, believes the siblings of an ADHD child need to be part of the treatment system. In counseling, Dr. Goldstein strives to make the siblings either positive or at least neutral toward the ADHD child. He recalls one case where both siblings, because they had such legitimate complaints about their brother's behavior, practically convinced him the family would be better off if the ADHD child moved away. In homes where great difficulties exist between siblings, therapists often deal with the problem using behavior management techniques for the siblings as well as the ADHD child. In the case cited by Dr. Goldstein, to get the siblings to stop picking on the ADHD child and vice versa, he used superordinate goals. For example, the entire family would be treated to a trip to the amusement park provided the parents did not hear one word about any fights or arguments between siblings.

Parents of ADHD children also suffer side effects as a result of this disorder and frequently fall into the guilt and blame trap. We feel depressed, ashamed, resentful and embarrassed because of our apparent failure as parents to raise a well-mannered and obedient child. Dr. Conners has observed that mothers of ADHD children will invariably cry if he says something to this effect. "I'm surprised you're still hanging in there. You must feel awful about yourself for some of the responses this child has elicited from you. But I really admire you, you must really care about your child to do as well as you've done with a child like this." He commented that these mothers feel a tremendous sense of guilt by thinking they have let the child down. Dr. Conners believes that parents of ADHD children need to understand "the disorder creates a great deal of stress and that they are only human."

According to Jean Bramble, the ADHD case worker at Primary Children's Medical Center, adoptive parents of ADHD children like biologic parents also feel guilty. However, she has observed that in some cases, adoptive parents feel an additional layer of guilt as well. This other guilt not only comes from feelings of inadequacy because of their inability to manage their adopted child, but arises out of their belief that perhaps they were never meant to have children. She said, "Indeed that is not the case. These parents are loving and readily seek help for their adoptive children."

In addition to feelings of guilt and blame, marital discord often arises as a by-product of this disorder. Dr. Conners notes, "Marriages are held together by the peace and quiet of ordinary times.

Those times are missing in most ADHD families." Both Brian Doyle and Chuck Maxwell said their marriages suffered because they and their wives were simply too tired at the end of each day to be social.

The effects of this disorder can be fought. Couples need to create the nice times which do not occur naturally in ADHD homes. Our psychologist insisted my husband and I go out socially without the children at least one night a week. Though at first we viewed this suggestion as trite, we found it worked. Parents, especially mothers who are at home with the ADHD child, need to spend some time each day engaged in their own personal activities. The time alone does not have to involve an exotic activity. Some mothers get renewed by taking walks; others like Laurie Maxwell find peace in the bathtub.

In terms of restoring the peace of the family, parents need to acquire behavior management techniques. Parents of ADHD children must be trained to make their rules clear, to set consequences, to institute those consequences properly, and to reward good behavior. A parent without these skills can usually slide by with a normal child. But an ADHD child finds every loophole a parent might leave open.

Though many parents find such rigidity a drudge, happy side effects do arise from good behavior management. Instead of losing both patience and face because the child does not obey, parents have the option to step out of the line of fire. They can apply a consequence immediately for their child's misbehavior and thereby place the responsibility for the child's actions where it belongs, on the child and not on the parent. After awhile, quiet peaceful moments return in ADHD households. Babysitters who in the past would not set foot through your front door prove willing to come back a second time.

Summary

- ADHD symptoms are highly visible at preschool stage and may affect the child at home, at school, with peers.
- In addition to impulsivity and possibly hyperactivity, the preschool pattern may be characterized by the following:
  1. inattentive and distractible,

2. easily frustrated,
3. temper tantrums,
4. aggressive and destructive behavior,
5. inappropriate behavior,
6. non-compliance.

- Social interactions are marked by poorly regulated behavior, immaturity and social insensitivity.
- Impulsivity prevents ADHD child from learning basic rules of fair play and socialization.
- ADHD children are often rejected by peers.
- Prosocial behavior may be developed through parental manipulation of the child's environment, social skills training, and socialization group therapy.
- Behavior poses a management problem for parents. Parents often disagree about the best way to manage child.
- Common parenting mistakes contribute to child's unmanageability.
- Many parents and children fall into Coercive Interaction Pattern.
- ADHD affects every family member.
- Siblings usually need to be involved in treatment.
- ADHD children often become family scapegoats.
- Parents report feelings of guilt, shame, depression and blame because of apparent failure to raise child properly.
- Married couples need to find quality time together and parents also need outlets apart from child and spouse.
- Use of behavior management makes ADHD children easier to live with and lessens the stress on the family.

CHAPTER FIVE

Diagnosis

The fall when David turned five, his dad and I decided not to launch his public school career. We both felt he behaved in too immature a fashion to succeed in that environment. Instead we placed him in the private kindergarten offered by his nursery school with the idea he could then begin the public school's kindergarten program the following year.

Where previously, David's blue eyes caught the nursery school staff's attention, his black and white world now cast him in a different light. David did not allow for the color gray. He related to everything and everybody in either/or, good or bad, yes or no terms. These same teachers who once assured me David just needed to mature, now asked me why he lagged behind.

By now, I realized David's nature had been extreme since day one and would more than likely remain as such. Half-heartedly, I joked with his teachers about the way his life would unfold. "David," I told them, "will either be a Rhodes scholar or an eighth grade drop-out, but he will never know mediocrity."

When the school's director administered some standardized tests in October, David's results bore witness to my comments. In most of the areas tested, such as listening comprehension and math concepts, David scored in normal to above normal ranges, but he performed quite poorly in the tests which measured simultaneous processing (the ability to discern parts from the whole), and visual discrimination. This score disparity led the director to believe that our son had a learning disability. She suggested a child study team evaluate David to find out "why this very capable child could not perform."

I felt threatened with the idea that David might not be able to survive on the basis of his intelligence. All along I told myself that his intellectual capabilities would compensate for his interpersonal difficulties. Now even that idea seemed unrealistic. My husband and I agreed to have our son evaluated by the child study team, though we did not have the vaguest concept of what such an evaluation entailed. As the evaluation process got underway, we learned that the form and function of child study teams fall under the rubric of special education. I had always assumed special education to be a service only for those with impairments like the mentally retarded, deaf and blind.

I since learned that, under the Education for All Handicapped Children Act and its implementing regulations, Public Law 94-142 passed in 1975, all handicapped children are entitled to a free and appropriate public education. Thus, PL 94-142 mandated the establishment of child study teams in every school district. These teams were instructed to evaluate any child suspected of having a learning disability and to develop an individual educational program for such children. Each state, in accordance with the federal law, then developed its own statutes to implement the rules and regulations governing Special Education. Thus, the actual evaluation and identification process of children with learning disabilities varies from state to state. In the state where I live, the child study team is comprised of a school psychologist, a school social worker, and an LDT-C, an acronym for Learning Disabilities Teacher Consultant—a teacher trained in the identification of and special teaching methods for children with learning disabilities. Other professionals (e.g., pediatric neurologists, speech/language pathologist, physical/occupational therapist) can be invited to submit consultative reports to assist the child study team in its deliberations.

For six months, from October 1984 through February 1985, we learned the nuts and bolts of a child study team evaluation. The process involved classroom observations wherein the LDT-C and the school psychologist visited David's classroom to observe how he performed academically as well as how he interacted with the teacher and his peers. These team members spoke with David's teachers to gather their comments and observations about him that might assist the child study team in determining the nature of his difficulties. The team members also spoke with David to determine what he thought and felt about himself. The social worker spoke with me for the purpose of gathering a social and medical history, as well as any factors I could think of which might contribute to his difficulties.

The LDT-C and the school psychologist also administered a battery of educational tests to determine David's intelligence, to assess areas where he did not perform to his ability, and to identify his learning strengths and weaknesses. They also sent David to outside medical consultants to rule out any physical causes for his difficulties. Fortunately, David Sr. and I reaped some benefits from marriage counseling and could be supportive of one another throughout most of the evaluation. Even relatives noticed the degree of harmony in our home.

When the team's social worker came to interview me about our family, I felt at ease. I wanted help for David and so I naïvely answered her every question, though I could not understand what our son's relationship with his grandfathers had to do with his academic performance. I also responded in great detail to the social worker's queries about our marriage, family relationships and social histories. By the time I finished my description, she knew everything there was to know about us.

In January, the team leader sent us a letter in which she requested we take David for a neurologic examination. I thought of neurologists as heavy duty doctors who only treated people with serious brain problems. When I asked the school's director if she knew why the team wanted this consultation, she too expressed confusion and concern.

The fact that a hospital housed the neurologist's office added to my fear. I conjured up visions of mad-professor-type laboratories where men in white coats hooked people up to masses of electrodes. When young David and I arrived for the exam, I soon saw that the office contained the usual equipment found in any doctor's examining room. But not all my fears subsided. I worried about what conclusions David drew to explain the reasons why he had become the subject of so much scrutiny these days.

When the doctor arrived, I grew very tense. This neurologist got right into the business at hand. The exam took thirty minutes. After he took a detailed medical history of David, the doctor questioned me about my son's personality characteristics and home behavior, and asked if I could think of any recent family stressors, such as a divorce that might account for his difficult behavior. But I could unhappily report to the doctor that David had showed such difficult tendencies since infancy.

After speaking with me, the doctor gave David a physical examination. He next asked David to walk, skip, touch his finger to his nose as fast as he could. David copied geometric designs, drew a crude picture of a person, attempted to complete two step commands. He functioned poorly on all these tests and could not repeat words in a sequence. The data gathered from these tests and exercises allowed the neurologist to inferentially determine how David's brain regulated his behavior. Some of these tasks, such as sequencing and drawing, provided data about David's motoric behavior. It also provided the doctor with insight into our son's ability to attend to task, and whether impulsivity prevented David from taking a careful and studied approach. Once all the tests were concluded, the neurologist turned to me and said, "David has Attention Deficit Disorder with hyperactivity." Though he explained what the term meant, I still did not fully understand David's problem.

When the doctor then proceeded to describe David as negative, aggressive and developing a poor self-image, I became very confused. I never viewed David as someone with a poor self-image. He always seemed so much in control, so much the master of his deeds, so selfish in his demands of everyone's attention, I felt certain David regarded himself too highly, that he thought no one else deserved as much as he.

"Not so," the doctor said. He then told me that David showed some features of anhedonia, which meant he did not derive pleasure or satisfaction from things and so might not respond to the reward systems generally used with ADHD kids. The full impact of this consultation took effect and my head began to spin.

Once I collected my thoughts, I pushed the neurologist for the prognosis for a child like David. In a clinical matter of fact voice, he said, "Your son might eventually abuse drugs or alcohol. He may do poorly in school. Treatment might help him." I tried to feel strong, but tears rolled down my cheeks for what seemed like a very long time.

Suddenly I became aware of David's presence. The entire time the doctor and I spoke, David had been in the room to hear every word. Though he probably did not understand such terms as anhedonic, or substance abuse, I'm sure he could not help but pick up the vibes. I became furious with myself for my insensitivity and stupidity. Once outside the office, I tried to explain to David that he need not worry, that everything would turn out fine. David yanked my arm in way of a reply.

I felt nauseous the entire ride home. So many thoughts raced through my head. Did I tell the doctor too much about David's history? Did I color his thinking? Did I exaggerate and make David's problems sound worse than they were? Did I cause David's problems? What did the doctor mean by "anhedonic"? David enjoys himself from time to time. That evening I told David's dad about the meeting. Though we actively sought an answer to explain our son's behavior, my husband and I were in denial about the severity of David's difficulties. So we dismissed the neurologist's prognoses and decided to wait for the child study team's findings.

When we met with the child study team two weeks later, each member handed us a typed report. In addition to my husband, myself and the child study team members, all of young David's teachers and the school's director were present. The social worker presented her report first. I quickly discovered that what I understood to be our private conversation had become my own personal book of revelations. Very little of what she wrote pertained to David's school situation. I learned after the fact to reveal to child study team personnel only the family information I want to see in print.

The next report came from the Learning Disabilities Teacher Consultant. The LDT-C spoke with David's teachers and observed him during class. She performed an educational and psychological evaluation, and administered a battery of tests to determine his I.Q., his learning characteristics, and his academic performance. Her less-than-stellar findings dashed my hopes that David did poorly in school because he found the work too mundane for his genius ability.

His teachers told the LDT-C that David behaved in a distractible and impulsive manner. With regard to social behavior, he functioned on a two- to three-year-old level. When she observed David's classroom performance, though he could follow directions, she saw how David could not remember to raise his hand or wait to be called on. He could not keep his place on a worksheet, nor could he form numerals with ease.

David approached the testing experience with the LDT-C willingly. However, when the tasks became difficult for him, David shut down and could not be redirected to complete the activity. When asked to throw a bean bag at a target, he became frustrated and wildly threw it around the room. She surmised, "In order to protect his self-image and decrease any embarrassment, David manipulates activities so that he appears successful." This sentence gave me great pause. I always thought manipulative implied shrewd or devious. Since David always overstated every thought and action, I never dreamed he could cast a smoke screen.

In this report I also discovered the word "perseveration." This behavior is somewhat akin to a phonograph needle stuck in the groove of a broken record. In David's case, perseveration meant that during testing he circled the first choice on an entire page of multiple choice questions which left an accurate appraisal of his ability to the whim of the wheel.

The school psychologist's report upset us the most. In general, she described David's behavior as immature for a five-and-a-half-year-old and said he repeated words, made nonsense statements and engaged in baby talk when she asked him questions about himself. Though David behaved this way with us too, we did not know he acted similarly in school. One teacher told the school psychologist that David showed no sense of humor and that he demanded perfection from himself and the other kids. The school psychologist assessed David's drawings of a tree, house and people as angular and distorted and she also saw signs that suggested neurological impairment. Before I could absorb what any of this meant, the school psychologist drew our attention to the next phase of her report.

I have no idea how my face looked when I read the part which described David's behavior during the testing. But David Sr.'s pallor turned a putrid shade of green. We read how young David lost his compliant manner and suddenly began to climb on the tester's lap. In his highest pitched voice he made obscene comments to this school psychologist who interpreted David's behavior as an attempt to avoid the work, to test his limits, and to get a reaction from the examiner. I sort of raised my eyes to check my husband's reaction, but quickly lowered them when I noticed the blank stares among the faces of all the people in the room.

The final paragraph of this report gave me a rare glimpse into the secret world of David's mind. The psychologist wrote, "The examiner tried reading incomplete sentences to David and asked him to verbally complete them. David could not attend to this activity for very long or very well. Two sentences he did complete were I wish I could stop . . . being bad, and I worry about . . . strangers. His comments about what he drew also suggested angry feelings. For example, he described his male person figure as liking to shoot people because he's a bad person when people bother him."

Though others said David had a poor self-image, until I actually read his words, I had no concept of the darkness that enveloped his world. By age five, David no longer possessed a child's capacity to herald in each day of life as though it were a huge gift-wrapped package waiting to be opened. He lost the joy and so did I.

With the reports finished, the team leader wanted David's dad and me to sign a form that would make David eligible for special education services. We were stunned to discover on the consent form the label which characterized David as Neurologically Impaired. My husband and I jumped to the conclusion that this label implied our son had brain damage. His teachers were so alarmed they advised us not to sign the consent form. In actuality, we all had been mistaken.

The team leader cleared our misconception with the explanation that this label meant that a child had a problem that was neurologically based which impaired learning. Since the services for David at this stage proved to be minimal, we decided not to accept them. Besides, David Sr. still had reservations about the entire process.

The school psychologist made attempts to bolster our spirits. She seemed to understand that when parents first learn their child is less than perfect, that he or she has a disability, the experience proves saddening, scary, disappointing, discouraging, humiliating, and guilt rendering. She suggested we seek private counseling and recommended a psychologist whose practice dealt mainly with children who had Attention-deficit Hyperactivity Disorder. Finally we met someone who could help us.

The diagnosis of Attention-deficit Hyperactivity Disorder is made on the basis of the child's symptoms. Often a school will initiate a child study team evaluation when the child evidences social, emotional and/or academic difficulty. However, the role of the child study team in the diagnosis of ADHD proves much like that of the general practioner who refers a patient to various specialists. Though frequently a parent, or teacher, or child study team might recognize a child's behavior as characteristic of the disorder, a clinician who is trained in childhood disorders should make the diagnosis and prescribe the indicated treatment. As in our case, if as part of the evaluation process, the child study team acting on behalf of the school district sends the child for a medical or psychological consult, that professional can make the ADHD diagnosis.

Parents and/or teachers who recognize the ADHD symptom complex have an advantage because they can use the services of a professional who understands this disorder when seeking a diagnosis. Thus, they avoid the misinformation and wrong diagnoses such as those which hampered our earlier efforts to get help for David. As mentioned in the second chapter, the practioner who does the assessment and diagnosis could be a pediatrician, pediatric neurologist, child psychiatrist, clinical psychologist or clinical social worker. The practioner who manages the diagnostic procedure will often refer the child to other specialists for the necessary assessment in their areas of expertise. For instance, a clinical psychologist might refer a child to a pediatric neurologist for a medical assessment to rule out other neurological problems and/or to determine if the child is a candidate for medical treatment of the disorder.

Guidelines for how to determine which clinician to use and how to find such a clinician are also included in chapter two. However, a basic rule of thumb is to use one who is highly trained in the diagnosis and assessment of learning disabilities and ADHD.

The process of diagnosis is much like solving a puzzle wherein the diagnostician must look at the child from many different angles. Thus, the examination should include a thorough family history; clinical interviews with the child, the parents and the child's teachers; personal observations; psychological tests, and a medical examination. In all instances, the diagnostician must first make a differential diagnosis to make the correct one and to determine the appropriate course of treatment. Such a diagnosis takes into account that the child's symptoms could be indicative of several different problems and so the diagnostician must differentiate the symptoms, rule out any other reasons for the child's problems, and consider the co-occurrence of other disorders.

Dr. Russell Barkley, Professor of Psychiatry and Neurology and Director of Psychology at the University of Massachusetts Medical School, reports that three disorders have a strong likelihood of co-occurring: ADHD, Oppositional Defiant Disorder (ODD), and Conduct Disorder (CD). Researchers do not know for certain why these disorders co-occur. As noted by Dr. Paul Wender, Director of Psychiatric Research at the University of Utah Medical School, "Hyperactive kids tend to be oppositional and have a greater than ordinary risk of being conduct disordered and learning disabled. We can identify pure forms of each disorder. One is not the other, but there is a higher probability that each will occur with the other than on a chance basis alone."

Dr. Barkley describes these behavioral disorders as such. ADHD is a developmental deficiency in several mental characteristics: attention, impulse control, regulation of activity. It is believed the child is biologically predisposed to the disorder and that it arises early in life. Oppositional Defiant Disorder is a group of symptoms characterized as negative temperament, hostile affect, aggression toward others and repeated intrusion and violation of the rights of others. Children with ODD evidence a persistent pattern of negative explosive mood, combined with a refusal to obey and aggression toward peers and other people. Conduct Disorder, diagnosed primarily in adolescence, is a repeated pattern of violation of social rules and the rights of others demonstrated by truancy from school, lying, stealing or vandalism of property, sexual promiscuity, cruelty to animals and people, the frequent initiation of fights.

Dr. Barkley notes that these three disorders sometimes evolve in a developmental fashion with a child evidencing ADHD first, followed by Oppositional Defiant Disorder and then, in later years, Conduct Disorder. His clinic samples demonstrate that children who develop Oppositional Defiant Disorder have a very high probability of later developing Conduct Disorder. However, ADHD children do not necessarily develop these disorders. Some clinicians maintain that Oppositional Defiant Disorder and/or Conduct

Disorder can develop in children from families where parental management can be characterized by excessive punishment and coercive interactions, while other children may develop these disorders without any mitigating factors. It is hoped that early diagnosis of ADHD and the multi-faceted management of symptomatology including parent training will thwart the onset of these other disorders in some cases.

With regard to making a differential diagnosis, Dr. Paul Wender, the author of numerous research studies about ADHD, says, "a good history is always the most important aspect of any psychiatric evaluation." He suggests the history be obtained from the parents and other people, such as teachers or grandparents who deal with the child on a frequent basis. In fact, Dr. Wender places great stock in the information supplied by teachers since they observe the child's performance in the major developmental tasks of the school-age child, namely academic performance and relationship with adults (teachers) and peers.

The history reported by parents also provides valuable clues about the nature of the child's problems. However, many parents are not aware of the importance of their observations. For example, when a pediatric neurologist based a diagnosis of Tom Sacca on a half hour examination and his mother's verbal picture of him, Liz Sacca felt skeptical. "I wondered how good the diagnosis could be. Everyone else thought Tommy climbed on mannequins in store windows and never listened to me because I was a bad mother." In Tommy's case, the telltale signs of ADHD proved so obvious, they could have been outlined with neon lights.

In addition to the child's developmental history, which is attained during the parental interview, current practice recommends the taking of a family history as well. The family histories of children with ADHD often reveal incidence of ADHD in other family members, learning disabilities, alcoholism, maternal depression, maternal feelings of low self-esteem, and the family pattern of reaction to stress. Dr. Barkley notes that fifty percent of the parents of ADHD children in his clinic need some form of therapy to treat their problems. In fact, he reports that nationally thirty percent of all fathers and twenty percent of all mothers require treatment as adults for their ADHD.

With regard to the parent and teacher diagnostic interviews,

Dr. Bennett Shaywitz, Professor of Pediatrics and Neurology at Yale University School of Medicine, and Director of the First Federally Funded Center for Learning and Attention Disorders, says that most experts agree that when a parent or teacher describes the child in terms of the constellation of symptoms characteristic of ADHD, then the child should be diagnosed with the disorder. He, like most investigators, uses instruments designed to obtain the parent's or teacher's assessment of the child's behavior.

One type of instrument used to determine a child's symptoms is a behavior-rating scale which the investigator asks the parents or teacher to complete. A number of different rating scales are in use today, but the principal behind them proves to be much the same. Basically these scales describe a number of common childhood difficulties; for example, sleeping problems or social difficulties. Generally the parent rates the child in terms of frequency of occurrence of certain behaviors, such as these which appear on Dr. C. Keith Conners' Parent Symptom Questionnaire: cries easily or often; doesn't get along well with brothers and sisters; is restless in the "squirmy" sense; has problems with sleep (can't fall asleep; up too early; up in the night). Dr. Conners explains that the investigator gets a good indication that a child has ADHD when the parents or teachers continually check those items which indicate a restless, inattentive, easily frustrated and impulsive pattern to the child's behavior.

Another aspect of the diagnostic process is the interview with the child. This interview allows the examiner to observe the child's behavior first hand. Dr. Conners cautions examiners about the ADHD child who in the first office visit will frequently behave like a model child, and calls such exemplary behavior the novelty effect. "On the third visit, that same kid will dismantle my desk if I let him," he explains. I also suggest that parents follow Paula Anderson's example. When she brought her daughter to see a clinical psychologist, instead of trying to control or manage Maggie's behavior, she let Maggie do whatever she pleased. This way the examiner saw the child's typical behavior.

Though Maggie's out-of-control behavior caught the examiner's attention, girls do not generally exhibit this type of behavior to the extent that ADHD boys do. Thus, girls go under-identified and consequently under-diagnosed. As Dr. Conners notes, "One has to be a really deviant little girl for someone to take her seriously."

As a result of research conducted by Dr. Sally Shaywitz, Associate Professor of Pediatrics, and Dr. Bennett Shaywitz, Professor of Pediatrics and Neurology, both at Yale University Medical School, the Shaywitzes concluded that girls do have ADHD. Dr. Sally Shaywitz explains that in order to have ADHD, girls must fulfill the same diagnostic criteria as boys. However, in general but certainly not in all cases, she noted that girls with ADHD tend to have more language deficits than ADHD boys. For instance, when they studied a clinic population of girls who had ADHD, Dr. Sally Shaywitz observed that their verbal I.Q.'s were much lower than in boys. Girls also evidenced a higher incidence of delayed speech. The Shaywitz research also revealed that ADHD girls are often more socially unstable than boys. Consequently, ADHD girls often have a history of social difficulties dating back to preschool.

According to Dr. Sally Shaywitz, the social difficulties and language problems may be intrinsically linked since ADHD girls may not have the sophistication in language that eases social interactions. As an example, she cited humor, being the most abstract form of language, as often eluding the ADHD child who tends to interpret language in a very concrete, literal manner. Consequently, on the playground, the child who does not interpret nuance and intonation will most likely not process social intent accurately, and therefore respond inappropriately.

Dr. Sally Shaywitz believes the reason ADHD often goes unrecognized in girls might reflect a bias in referral. "ADD with hyperactivity is so widely accepted as a predominantly boy's disorder that there may be a failure to even consider the possibility of ADD in girls and consequently a failure to identify all but the most severely affected girls," she says.

As part of the routine examination, many evaluators administer a battery of psychological tests. Some of these tests measure the child's social and emotional adjustment. Other instruments determine whether or not a child has another disability that impairs learning. One such instrument is an I.Q. test. Though it does not diagnose ADHD, an I.Q. test tells the evaluator whether or not the child can work to his or her potential. Dr. Conners feels that such tests and formal examinations also allow the diagnostician to observe the child during a structured intellectual demand and thus make note of the child's degree of frustration and ability to stay on task.

Research by Dr. Sally Shaywitz out of Yale University, using an epidemiologic sample, indicates that as many as ten percent of all ADHD children also have learning disabilities. Epidemiologic samples differ from clinic samples in that the population of children used in research studies drawn from clinic samples tend to have more severe forms of the disorder, while in the children used in epidemiologic samples drawn from non-clinic populations, the disorder ranges from quite mild to severe. Thus, the Shaywitz finding from an epidemiologic sample demonstrates a significant co-occurrence of ADHD and learning disability. As used here, the term "learning disabilities" applies to specific disabilities such as dyslexia, rather than the difficulty with daily scholastic performance experienced by nearly all ADHD children as a pervasive element of the ADHD disorder.

As reported by Dr. Sally Shaywitz, research studies currently underway of children diagnosed with ADHD reveal a significant incidence of learning disabilities which have gone undetected in these children because the appropriate in-depth educational evaluations had not been done. She believes the behavioral problems evidenced by these children, most likely the excessive motoric activity, caught everyone's attention to the exclusion of the appropriate educational evaluation. Dr. Sally Shaywitz agrees that a complete psycho-educational battery should be done as a part of the routine diagnostic procedure.

A pediatric examination is also warranted as part of the diagnostic procedure. The purpose of this examination is to rule out the presence of other physical problems that might create ADHD-like symptoms. In some instances, vision and hearing checks may also be indicated. Often times many clinicians, pediatricians included, will refer ADHD children to a pediatric neurologist for a neurological examination. During this exam, any gross neurologic problems, for instance epilepsy, are ruled out. Pediatric neurologist Dr. Bennett Shaywitz reports that in ninety-nine percent of the cases, the results of these exams are normal in so far as there are no gross neurological problems.

As part of the assessment, the pediatric neurologist also looks for "soft signs." Soft neurologic signs do not relate to any

particular area of the central nervous system. Instead, soft neurologic signs are those which are behaviorally associated with central nervous system dysfunction. Unlike paralysis, or cerebral
palsy or epilepsy which give hard evidence of neurologic dysfunction, soft signs are implied rather than definitive. For example, poor motor coordination is a soft sign. Dr. Shaywitz explains
that though soft signs prove a little more common in ADHD children, they are not diagnostic for ADHD. Many children without
ADHD present soft signs as well.

Unless a doctor finds evidence of a more serious neurologic
problem, Dr. Shaywitz advises against the use of sophisticated
and costly medical tests such as EEGs, MRIs and PET Scans
because they are not diagnostic of ADHD. Electroencephalo-
grams (EEGs) measure the brain's electrical activity and are very
useful for detecting seizure activity. Magnetic Resonance Imaging
is an X-ray based on the brain's magnetic fields that gives a picture of the brain's anatomy. Since ADHD is not an anatomical
problem, MRI's are of no diagnostic value for ADHD. Positron
Emission Tomography, otherwise known as PET Scans, has
demonstrated value for research purposes.

As explained by Dr. Bennett Shaywitz, these tests involve
injecting the child with a radioactive isotope compound and then
using a geiger counter to track the flow of the isotope and thereby
determine how the brain regulates behavior. He points out that
not too many people would want to have their child injected with
a radioactive isotope.

Once the evaluation process is completed and the ADHD diagnosis made, education about the disorder and its manifestations
proves to be the first step of treatment. As explained by psychologist Russell Barkley, who has conducted more than 450 seminars
about ADHD, when parents realize the child has an underlying
problem, their view of his or her behavior changes. When Dr.
Barkley educates parents about ADHD, he discusses the
disorder's general characteristics, its developmental course, and
the risks associated with the condition. He hopes such information
will enable parents to view the child's problems as a handicap,
and in turn, come to view the child as a handicapped individual.
Having accomplished the development of this perspective, Dr.
Barkley has accustomed parents to expect less from the child and
so become less frustrated themselves. Therefore, they do not

punish or come down on the child nearly as much.

"We don't wish to overwhelm parents with grief," Dr. Barkley says. "If I had to choose from all the childhood disabilities one could have, I'd choose this one. ADHD is by far the least disabling."

Diagnosis raises a question for most parents. Generally they ask, "What should I tell my child and when?" The explanation Dr. Barkley provides depends on the age of the child. For the older child, he will spend up to an hour on the matter. However, with younger children, he suggests a brief explanation. He tells them, "Some kids are good at bike riding, others are not good at art. You have a hard time concentrating on things that are boring and we understand you can't help that."

The ADHD diagnosis often brings a sense of relief for both parents and child. The clouds of confusion that surround the whys and wherefores of a child's behavior lift with the knowledge that neither the parent nor the child caused the problems. Guilt and blame become replaced by hope and help.

Summary

- ADHD is a medical syndrome and diagnosed on the basis of symptoms a child exhibits.
- A professional knowledgeable about ADHD should coordinate and make the diagnosis, though special education evaluations often reveal the symptom complex.
- The evaluation for the diagnosis of ADHD includes:
  1. a thorough medical and family history,
  2. interviews with the parents, the child, and the child's teachers,
  3. observations by the evaluator,
  4. a physical examination,
  5. other medical, psychological and educational tests.
- Sophisticated and costly medical tests such as EEG's, MRI's and PET Scans are of no value in the diagnosis of ADHD.
- In all cases, a differential diagnosis, which considers the possibility of other causes for symptoms or co-occurrence of other disorders, must be made.
- Oppositional Defiant Disorder, Conduct Disorder and

learning disabilities often co-occur with ADHD.

- ADHD is a developmental disorder characterized by deficits in attention, impulse control, and regulation of behavior.
- Oppositional Defiant Disorder is characterized by a persistent pattern of negative explosive mood combined with a refusal to obey and aggression toward peers and others.
- Conduct Disorder, generally diagnosed in teenagers, is a repeated pattern of the violation of social rules and the rights of others.
- ADHD is frequently undiagnosed in girls.
- Girls with ADHD have the same symptoms as boys, but they have more language deficits and tend to be more unstable in social situations than boys.
- Ten percent of ADHD children also have learning disabilities, such as dyslexia.
- Children diagnosed with ADHD should receive an in-depth educational evaluation to determine any co-existing learning disabilities as routine practice.
- Education about ADHD becomes the first step of treatment.

CHAPTER SIX

Management: A Multifaceted Approach

Once we had a diagnosis for David, I hoped we would have smoother sailing. But after the first visit with Dr. Burke, our new child psychologist, both David Sr. and I learned that no magic exists to cure ADHD. In fact, a lot of counseling would be required to restore a smile to David's face. Results from a test administered by the psychologist pointed to David's excessive worry and self-criticism as an indication that our son had become depressed.

Both his Dad and I made the assumption that only David would be counseled. However, this child psychologist insisted the entire family be present at the sessions. He explained that a family is a system of reciprocal emotional relationships. Thus, David's behavior affected us and ours affected him in a cyclic and ongoing way.

Before any positive changes could occur, David's dad and I needed to unlearn the behavior management techniques which fell into our use. Our inconsistency, criticism, rejection and physical punishment proved to be the worst possible responses to the ADHD child's behavior, and only served to heighten David's sadness. Like most ADHD children, he had no idea why his world turned out to be such a capricious place.

Neither did I until after an ugly scene erupted between young David and myself. Like Pavlov's dog, David responded to the ring of a bell, only in his case, the ring of the phone sent him into action. When he was a toddler, he took this cue as the time to make mischief. As a preschooler, he dropped whatever he might

90

be involved with and demanded my undivided attention. On the occasions I chose to ignore his peskiness, David disconnected the phone plug and left me to hang in mid-sentence.

In his latest strategy to end my conversations, David played mummy and wrapped himself in the cord. As in the past, I ignored this obnoxious behavior, but in order to continue my talk, I had to exert untold pounds of pressure so the phone receiver would not recoil from my ear. One day I became fed up. In an attempt to unravel David, I gave the cord a Herculean tug. I not only sent him reeling to the floor: the cord left a five-inch burn mark across his neck. Whenever anyone asked him about the mark, young David, who is not prone to go into great detail, simply replied, "My mother pulled a cord around it."

With David's neck still red and raw, we could not help but bring this incident to the psychologist's attention at our next appointment. Though Dr. Burke counseled David about his inappropriate behavior with the phone cord, he made certain that both young David and I understood that a neck burn could never be a natural or logical consequence. Instead he suggested time-out as an alternative. Dr. Burke explained, "When David is annoying or disruptive, time-out will interrupt him and give everyone a chance to cool down."

In earlier years, our attempts to use time-out failed. After the psychologist walked us through his method, I could see why we had been unsuccessful. He first told my husband and me to select a safe, quiet, unstimulating place to send David when he misbehaved. We had tried to put David in a corner in the kitchen, but he never stayed. Dr. Burke explained that in light of all the activity, the kitchen proved the worst possible place because most ADHD children react to the stimulation and do not get the essential message that time-out is a punishment for misbehavior.

David's dad and I also thought the length of time our son stayed in time-out should be in direct correlation to how ticked off he made us. But Dr. Burke told us to set a timer for no longer than five minutes. Aside from the fact that this punishment is designed to be a brief consequence for inappropriate behavior, Dr. Burke warned, "If you keep David there too long, he might forget what he did to get sent to time-out in the first place."

Even with such expert advice, I continued to have reservations about this method's success. I figured David would refuse to go to the time-out spot, or leave it before he should, or come back and continue his misbehavior. When I raised these concerns, Dr. Burke told us that initially we might have to escort David to time-out and force him to stay there. In those instances where his behavior did not change, David would be sent back to time-out and told he would continue to go back until he complied. Dr. Burke included David in the time-out discussions, and when situations warranted this procedure, he did not resist us. However, in the beginning, his dad and I frequently forgot to use time-out as the first resort.

After our third session, the child psychologist requested that David's dad and I note the times our son behaved inappropriately. Our next meeting revealed this startling fact about our assessment of our son's behavior. Both David Sr. and I did not always know when behavior was inappropriate. For example, though we agreed disrespect should never be tolerated, we sometimes interpreted a disrespectful comment as okay when David couched his remark in truth or humor. Where young David's world proved to be black and white, ours proved to be excessively gray. We did not look at an action for its face value.

The behavior modification charts Dr. Burke taught us to design and implement soon improved our inconsistent approach to managing our son's behavior. As a starting point, he asked us to select the three behaviors which bothered us most from our rather extensive list. We settled on David's horrible behavior during mealtimes, his refusal to obey us, and his nasty treatment of his brother. When the psychologist asked what behavior we would like David to display instead, I found the question simplistic. However, I answered, "I want him to be nice and to behave well."

"Does David know what behave well means?" he replied.

I always said to young David, "You'd better behave." I assumed he understood what I wanted perfectly well. But Dr. Burke explained that behaviors need to be specifically stated because such broad terms as "behave well" are not clear to the child. That made sense, so I suggested that on David's chart we put, "Does not hit brother."

Dr. Burke agreed this sort of behavior should be discouraged. However, he explained that since we really wanted to encourage David's use of appropriate behavior, these behaviors should be phrased in positive terms. He suggested that we write, "Treats other family members in a polite, respectful, gentle fashion, i.e., no hitting, yelling or running away." Also, because of the pervasive day-long nature of this behavior, he felt that we pick a manageable time period to focus on initially, like two hours in the afternoon.

"This time limit is not to say that polite, respectful behavior is not important at the other times, too. As we get positive results, we'll gradually extend the time period to require such behavior all day," Dr. Burke said. The other two behaviors we targeted for reward were, "Cooperates with the morning routine: washes and dresses self, eats neatly, ready on time, no yelling" and "Is well-mannered at evening dinner table: comes on time, sits and eats meals without complaint or hassle."

Ever mindful that I had two children close in age, I wondered how David would react to Jonathan's free agent status. Until Dr. Burke suggested we also use a chart for Jonathan, the thought had not occurred to me that a child need not have a problem to benefit from good parenting techniques. After all, my husband and I wanted to encourage these behaviors in both children.

After we had targeted the behaviors, Dr. Burke showed us how to construct the chart. He drew a rectangle on a piece of paper and then divided the rectangle horizontally into one large section and seven smaller but equal-sized sections, and then vertically into four equal-sized sections so that the rectangle ultimately resembled a grid. In the first and largest horizontal section, Dr. Burke listed the target behaviors separately one below the other. At the top of each of the next seven sections, he wrote the days of the week Sunday through Saturday one after the other. In the remaining bottom section below the list of behaviors, he wrote "total daily score." When children are young—preschool through kindergarten—it is often best to use a "star" or "sticker" chart. One star is given if the behavior is done spontaneously by the child or immediately upon first request. No stars are given for noncompliance or if constant or repetitive commands are given.

Later, when the boys were older, Dr. Burke had us rate each behavior on a numerical scale of three (excellent), two (good), one (needs improvement), and zero (poor). Throughout a given day, David received feedback about his behavior by earning or losing points toward the total daily score. This way, appropriate behavior was reinforced immediately. On the other hand, when David behaved inappropriately in one of the three target areas, he lost a point in conjunction with being sent to time-out. Then at the end of each day, we sat down with David and watched while he tallied the scores for each behavior and then the total daily score. Thus, the chart became a visual record for David to see concretely where he met with success or failure.

Dr. Burke had also established score ranges to denote excellent, good and poor behavior days with consequences positive and negative set ahead of time for each outcome. The positive consequences came in the form of rewards. In selecting rewards, Dr. Burke made sure we understood one of the cornerstones of behavior modification, specifically "a reward is only successful if it has meaning for the child." Since both boys bargained for additional time before they went to bed, we made extended bedtime something they could earn. Normally, they went to bed at 7:30, so we decided that for a good behavior day, they earned this regular privilege. For an excellent behavior day, the child was allowed to stay downstairs with us until 8:00. Similarly, on a poor behavior day, the child went to bed a half hour before the regular time as a predictable consequence for lack of cooperation and effort during the day.

Beyond that, we also sweetened the pie with a daily monetary reward of twenty-five cents for an excellent day, ten cents for a good day, and nothing for a poor day. In addition, at the end of a good week, each boy could receive a bonus such as a pack of baseball cards or a trip to Dairy Queen, and for an excellent week a video rental or special time with Mom or Dad.

Dr. Burke began each counseling session by studying the weekly charts. Rather than criticize David for the bad days, he offered his condolences and said, "Gee, Chief, sorry you had a problem here." With our child psychologist as the purveyor of this system, David soon saw that we took both the charts and time-out seriously. Eventually David learned not to blame us for his low scores and accepted the responsibility for his behavior. We never concentrated on more than five types of behavior at a time. Throughout the months, we added new behavior patterns and dropped others that no longer proved problematic.

Over the course of the summer of 1985, life in our home improved measurably. David was nearing six years of age and

Jonathan had just turned four. I attributed this change to the home management techniques we now employed and the child care program both boys attended for six hours a day. Initially, I opposed the idea of sending the boys to a summer program, but Dr. Burke emphasized the importance of structure in David's day and advised us not to expect him to make good orderly use of free time.

When fall arrived, we moved again. After I enrolled David in the public school kindergarten in this new town, I agonized about whether to tell his teacher he had ADHD. Even though David evidenced problems in nursery school, I still viewed his behavior as primarily a home management problem and conned myself into believing he would not meet difficulty in school. Besides, I worried that David might be stigmatized as that "pain in the neck kid" if I drew attention to his problems. Despite the child psychologist's recommendation, I decided this situation could best be handled in the privacy of our home.

By mid-October, David's dad and I noticed a change for the worse in our older son's behavior. His frustration level lowered and he angered quickly whenever any task presented a slight challenge. He had difficulty keeping himself in control. He talked incessantly, "dolphonized," screamed and hollered. When he began to constantly clear his throat, we rationalized that his change in behavior had been prompted by some form of allergy.

Though we still went to the child psychologist and used the behavior charts, nothing could stop the course of his behavior or the chain reaction that ensued as a result. Since I no longer worked outside the home, I spent every afternoon with David. By evening, after a full five hours of his argumentative, negative, angry, nasty ways, my nerves rattled. I, too, slipped back to the argue, yell, holler and scream mode.

Dr. Burke felt certain the source of David's frustration grew out of the demands the school made on him. But I could not understand how a mere two-and-a-half-hour program could create this much distress. Besides, whenever I casually asked his teacher how well he was doing, she never gave a negative report.

However, when the long awaited first report card arrived home, our six-year-old son's performance seemed totally lackluster. David earned "satisfactory" as a mark in most areas, but work habits and social development had been checked "needs improvement." Under comments, the teacher wrote, "David must work on following directions given once. Criticism of peers continues to be a problem. Good knowledge of beginning sounds." At the parent/teacher conference, I learned that David seldom participated in class activities and apparently "tuned out." During free play, he stayed by himself.

Not all the teacher's comments proved negative. She drew my attention to David's picture of a house. Though I saw a crude structure, the kindergarten teacher said that in all her years of teaching five- and six-year-old children, David was the first student to include a basement on the house drawing, which she thought indicated that he was a divergent thinker. She assured me David was a bright child who would do well when he "clicked in."

By mid-November, our quasi-docile home environment deteriorated into a bad dream. The child psychologist suggested David needed medication to help treat his ADHD symptoms. The pediatric neurologist, who a few months earlier assessed David's symptoms to be mild, witnessed the change in behavior first hand. David could not contain himself during any part of the examination. The doctor rated as severe our son's Attention-deficit Hyperactivity Disorder.

In addition, the neurologist said that David's constant lip licking and throat clearing noises represented involuntary motor actions called tics. This information surprised David's father and me. We figured David's scarlet cracked lips to be a sign of cold weather. This physician felt David could not be a candidate for psycho-stimulant medications, the medicines of choice in the treatment of ADHD, because this class of medicines is contra-indicated when tics are present. The neurologist informed us about alternative medications, and though he did not want to prescribe them at this point in time, he suggested we consider their eventual use if needed.

Three weeks later, David was placed on one of these medications—Mellaril. He acted in the irritable manner of an over-tired child. When we went back to see the doctor after the Christmas holiday, he noted David's aggressive and emotionally unstable mood and my distraught feelings. The doctor raised David's dosage of medication and we kept our son on it for the next two months.

During this entire time, we continued to use behavior modification and went as a family to the sessions with the child psychologist. He continued to teach us about the disorder. How we came to understand the extent to which this disorder affected David and the family proved much like the process of peeling an onion. We needed to get through layer upon layer to reach the center.

We first had to learn that ADHD children need a calm, quiet, predictable atmosphere. Changes in the routine promote changes in behavior. As a family, we continually went on spur of the moment outings or undertook major home projects. We seldom thought to keep these things to a minimum or to prepare David for any necessary changes.

We constantly subjected David to large group activities despite the fact such situations sent him into a frenzy. We thought "the more the merrier," but for David too many people meant an unhappy time. We missed this point over and over again in our desire for normalcy. We wanted David to be like all the other children. When he balked about playing soccer or going to birthday parties, we forced him to participate, until the child psychologist raised our level of awareness. He advised us to "avoid large group activities as much as possible. David will do better in one-to-one situations that are short in duration, structured and well-organized."

During the course of these sessions, David Sr. frequently identified similarities between young David's behaviors and his own. When Dr. Burke said things like, "David prefers to play with younger children because he may be a more desirable playmate to them and can be more in control of events," David Sr. responded, "So did I." Eventually dad realized he had been very much like his son, not a problem child, but rather a child with a problem.

By the end of January 1986, David's classroom difficulties escalated. The kindergarten teacher said he tried on many occasions to take charge of the class and became verbally aggressive with peers. When he did not meet with instant success in a task, he became extremely upset. During playtime he wandered around the room and withdrew from all social involvement.

The child psychologist spoke with the teacher and observed David in class. He instituted a behavior modification program. A month later, the teacher reported an improvement in David's attitude and effort. At home, his behavior seemed to deteriorate.

Lately, the thought crossed my mind that David would be better off if I left home. When Dr. Burke asked, "Why do you think he behaves the worst with you?" I could only surmise that something about me brought the worst out in my son. But the psychologist offered another possibility. He thought that David stored all his frustration until he came home from school because he trusted my commitment to him and felt safe enough to act on his feelings. Though intellectually his explanation made sense, emotionally I felt like my guts were on a platter.

By the end of February, we faced another dilemma. After three months of taking Mellaril, David could no longer tolerate this medicine and needed to be weaned from it. The pediatric neurologist recommended another medication often used with children who exhibited tics. The child psychologist, who still held hopes that David could take psycho-stimulant medication, prodded us to see another pediatric neurologist highly regarded for his work with ADHD children. Though this doctor charged $350 for an evaluation, David Sr. and I had grown accustomed to the fact that answers for David were expensive, and we made the appointment.

The waiting room of the specialist's office contained a jungle jim, a slide, and a slew of toys. Six-and-a-half-year-old David became so excited at these prospects, his voice level went beyond "dolphinizing." As he attacked each new toy, he yelled to his five-year-old brother to come and play, but these days Jonathan withdrew from that kind of heavy-handed activity. Instead of joining his brother, he sat next to his dad and quietly read a book. When the time finally arrived for David to be examined, his activity level had reached the fever pitch we knew so well.

As the nurse ushered us into the doctor's office, she looked rather tentative. The doctor introduced himself and told us as long as David could be controlled, he would prefer to examine him without us. We no sooner got halfway back to the waiting room when we heard young David make a pronouncement. "I'm the boss of this office," he insisted. I thought for certain a summons would follow, but we did not see either David or the doctor for over an hour.

Much to our surprise, when the neurologist finally delivered our son, he remarked about the good manner in which David behaved. Before he brought us into the office, he said to David, "Please wait here while I talk to your Mom and Dad."

David quietly replied, "Oh yes, I'll wait here."

I often joked that a lobotomy might do David some good and wondered what the doctor had done.

Once inside the office, the doctor told us David's waiting room behavior had been the worst his nurse ever observed. Thus, the doctor thought he would have a difficult time with David's exam. Though initially David had been highly distractible, his ability to concentrate "improved remarkably during the individualized attention." This evaluation did not reveal any new information. The doctor advised us to follow the guidance of our regular neurologist and give David a trial on a new medication named Haldol.

David began that medication in mid-March. In early May, the neurologist saw him in a follow-up examination. Though his vocal tics stopped, David's hyperactivity and impulsivity showed no improvement. The doctor increased the medication but no positive result occurred, so he stopped all medicines in June. David ended the school year with improvement noted in that environment. The teacher commented on the final report card, "David's effort in reading, although sporadic, is much improved. His interaction with peers has improved but continues to be difficult for David. I look forward to hearing of his continued success in first grade." We headed into the summer with David's behavior somewhat under control.

In most cases, a number of interventions are required to effectively manage the ADHD child's symptoms. Health care professionals refer to these multiple interventions as the multimodal treatment approach. Basically, this approach employs various strategies designed to alter the course of the disorder so the child can lead a fairly normal life. The nucleus of the multimodal approach consists of four major therapies: education about the disorder, behavior management and parent training as discussed in earlier chapters, modified school program, and medication. Individual or family psychotherapy sometimes proves necessary as well.

Which of these strategies are used and the extent to which they are employed depends, of course, on the severity of the child's symptoms. Jim Hopkins, for instance, evidenced difficulty mainly in school, so his treatment primarily addressed that problem. Maggie Anderson needed both home and school management, but no medication, whereas my son needed all the treatment modalities.

Dr. C. Keith Conners, Professor of Medical Psychology and Director of the ADHD clinic at Duke University Medical School, says, "One aspect of treatment is not enough. The parenting behavior is not going to diminish the vigor of the abnormal biological system in the child. On the other hand, diminishing the vigor of the abnormal biology with medication is not going to teach the kid the rules of the game or his ABC's."

Since no single approach can accommodate most ADHD children, the treatment program generally requires a professional to oversee the case management. As mentioned in earlier chapters, this professional might be a pediatrician, child psychiatrist, pediatric neurologist, child psychologist, or clinical social worker. Jean Bramble, a case worker at the Learning Problems Clinic at Primary Children's Medical Center in Salt Lake City, says this professional must be well trained in the treatment of ADHD children, knowledgeable about the biological, social, environmental and educational aspects of the disorder, and helpful to the parent and child in whatever way possible.

To begin treatment, the parents, the ADHD child, the grandparents, teachers and other people significant in the child's life should be educated about the disorder. To this end, the practitioner responsible for the child's treatment will explain the disorder's symptoms, manifestations, developmental course and prognosis. ADHD parent support groups can also help in the education process since most of these groups offer presentations on various aspects of the disorder as well as suggestions for how to cope with it.

Parent training in behavior management techniques is the second step in treatment. In addition to learning how to give commands clearly, how to follow through with appropriate consequences, and how to use behavior charts, many parents also find they must modify the home environment. Colleen Paterson recognized her daughter Allison's need for structure and routine. Thus Colleen scheduled an activity for Allison every day after school.

Her dinner, homework, bath and bed time occur around the same time each evening. Colleen has also learned not to make her structure so rigid that she pushes her daughter to a point of frustration, so she frequently allows Allison to take a five minute break during homework time if she is finding the work difficult.

Most ADHD children also need a modified school environment. The changes Dr. Russell Barkley of the University of Massachusetts Medical School recommends do not require a great elaborate effort on the part of the teacher. He suggests that the teacher reposition the child's desk to monitor him or her closely, use effective rewards and less punishment, reduce the length of assignments and the amount of written work. Even with these modifications, many ADHD children will also need the assistance of special education services. The school program will be discussed in greater detail in subsequent chapters.

The use of medication proves to be another form of intervention which produces significant positive results for many ADHD children. For most parents, the decision to employ this treatment is difficult to make. Unlike an antibiotic for an ear infection, the medication used to treat ADHD must be taken on a long term basis, because medication does not cure the disorder. Instead it controls the child's ADHD symptoms.

Only a physician can prescribe medication. However, often a non-physician with primary responsibility for the ADHD child's treatment program will advise the use of medication. When making a determination of if and when to use medication as a form of treatment for an ADHD child, psychologist Sam Goldstein, author of a textbook about ADHD for clinical use, says that most practioners follow this basic guideline. Medical treatment is recommended when other interventions do not meet the hoped for results.

However, in cases where the child's behavior is out of control, medication may be started before any other treatments. Dr. Russell Barkley reports that at least sixty percent of ADHD children need medication in addition to other interventions. I caution parents to discuss the use of medication thoroughly with their child's doctor before deciding for or against its use.

Dr. Bennett Shaywitz cautions parents about the use of medication as a sole treatment. In fact, he will not prescribe medication unless a child has an optimal educational program and unless the parents understand the implications of the ADHD diagnosis. Said Dr. Shaywitz, "ADHD is a chronic problem which the child will have throughout life. You just don't write a prescription for medication without making changes in the child's school and home situations. Besides, without the right kind of support, the medication probably won't work."

No predictive test exists to determine if a child will benefit from medication. Dr. Paul Wender feels that one can think about a trial of medication for ADHD children in much the same way a physician prescribes medication for a patient with hypertension. In actuality, no one knows for certain if the blood pressure medication will lower Mr. X's blood pressure, but the physician knows that medicine has been researched extensively and proven safe and effective for this purpose, and therefore recommends that Mr. X try the medication to see if it helps. However, Dr. Wender cautions that with all prescription drugs, physicians must weigh the cost-benefit issue and determine if the advantages of treatment outweigh the disadvantages. Many studies show about 75% of ADHD children have a favorable response to stimulants.

Once a child is determined to be a candidate for medical intervention, the physician must choose which medicine, in what dose, and under what circumstances it should be administered. The psycho-stimulant medications prove to be the first choice in medication therapy. The most commonly used stimulant medication is Methylphenidate (trade name Ritalin). Other stimulant medications less frequently used are D-amphetamine (trade name Dexedrine) and Pemoline (trade name Cylert).

Dr. Wender says when deciding which stimulant to use, "The rule is anybody might get better on anything, and that for a given, the only way to tell whether Methylphenidate or D-amphetamine is better for a given child is to try both. However, if the child responds well to the first medicine tried, then that's great."

Treatment guidelines advise against the use of stimulant medications with children who evidence tics or Tourette's Syndrome. However, Dr. William McMahon, Medical Director of the Learning Problems Clinic, Primary Children's Medical Center, Salt Lake City, finds that in cases where other therapies have been tried unsuccessfully, the guidelines provide exception for "the careful use of stimulant medications with informed parental consent and a comprehensive treatment program."

For children who cannot take stimulants because they are contra-indicated or ineffective, medicines which belong to the class of drugs called anti-depressants become second choice. The anti-depressants most commonly used with ADHD children are Imiprimine (trade name Tofranil), and Desipramine (trade names Norpramin and Pertofrane).

No one knows for certain why stimulant medication helps ADHD children. Nor does anyone know why some ADHD children are not helped by these medications. The commonly accepted theory regarding the neurological basis of the disorder is that ADHD children produce too little of a neurotransmitter called dopamine. Consequently, in ADHD children, the areas of the brain responsible for impulse control, regulation of motor behavior and concentration are not aroused to the extent they need to be in order to function efficiently. Thus, even hyperactive ADHD children, though their motor movements appear to be traveling upwards of 100 MPH, are actually not functioning to capacity.

Dr. Gabor Barabas, a pediatric neurologist and Associate Clinical Professor of Pediatrics at Robert Wood Johnson University Hospital in New Brunswick, New Jersey, explains that neurotransmitters are chemicals in the brain involved in the regulation of brain cell function. In order for the brain to regulate behavior efficiently, an appropriate balance of neurotransmitters is required. The exact manner in which stimulant medications work is not known. However, researchers think stimulant medication might enable the ADHD child to produce more of the neurotransmitter dopamine so the child's brain cells have the necessary balance of neurotransmitters. As a result, the abnormal biology is altered to a more normal state and the ADHD child, with or without hyperactivity, is better able to concentrate, to control impulses, and to regulate motor behavior.

Ritalin, the medication most widely used in the treatment of ADHD, has been prescribed for over fifty years. This medication has also been one of the most widely studied of medicines given to children. In 1988, in a report to Congress, the Food and Drug Administration wrote, "We continue to believe that Ritalin is a safe and effective drug if used as recommended in the approval labeling suggested by the FDA in the treatment of ADHD."

Ritalin is prescribed more than the other stimulants because of the relatively low cost/high benefit results of the medication. By low cost, I mean that the use of Ritalin in properly diagnosed ADHD children seldom results in any serious side effects. The side effects most commonly reported are: slight loss of appetite, mild insomnia, irritability, headache, stomachache. Those effects are often minimized by adjustments in the dosage. Many people believe growth suppression to be a side effect. However, Dr. Russell Barkley, President of the Section of Clinical Child Psychology of the American Psychological Association, wrote an article about Ritalin which appeared in the Spring/Summer 1989 issue of *CHADDER,* a newsletter produced by CHADD, an ADHD parent support group association. He said, "Growth in children on medication is not typically impaired, and, where reduction in growth is noted, often resolves with the first to second year of treatment."

When a patient begins any stimulant medication, the physician starts with the smallest dosage possible. The dose is then titrated or raised in small increments until the desired clinical effect is achieved. Dr. William McMahon finds that the correct dose is determined by the patient's clinical response and in the absence of severe side effects. Physicians generally use a guideline of 1 mg Ritalin per kg of the child's body weight as a maximum daily dosage. ADHD researcher Dr. Paul Wender says, "The simple fact about stimulants is they don't work before you take them and they stop working when they wear off." Ritalin wears off in a matter of hours, so the child's ADHD symptoms reappear like clockwork. Since Ritalin is usually in and out of the body within three to four hours, children will often take a morning and afternoon dose and some will even require a late afternoon or early evening one. Some children take a longer-lasting sustained release form of Ritalin which lasts approximately eight hours.

When initially placing the child on medication, the prescribing physician will often monitor the child's therapeutic response frequently, and once the proper response is achieved, will usually examine the child twice a year. Many physicians will also stop the medication once or twice a year to reevaluate its need. Parents who are concerned the dosage is either too high or too low need to discuss their concerns with the prescribing physician, or in some cases seek a second opinion.

After a child is determined to be a candidate for treatment with medication, the prescribing physician must determine the circumstances under which a child needs it. Most physicians agree the ADHD child who needs medication will require this form of treatment in the demanding school environment where he or she must be able to sit still, pay attention, think first-act later. However, some practioners believe that all ADHD children should have drug holidays, and therefore do not prescribe medication for after school, weekends or summers. Yet the ADHD child can have the same difficulties in the home and with friends as they do in school. So the decision with regard to the circumstances under which medication is needed as an intervention must be made on the basis of each individual child's symptoms, not, as Dr. Goldstein points out, in an arbitrary fashion, "based on old wives' tales."

When faced with the decision to use stimulant medication, particularly Ritalin, many parents receive input from "well-intentioned" friends, relatives, neighbors, and in some cases, total strangers. Some of these people are misguided and wonder why medication is given to children "who obviously just need more discipline." Others are misinformed and think the medication has dangerous side effects.

Before the child goes on medication or even afterwards, most parents hear comments similar to these: Do you really think your child needs drugs? Gee, he (she) doesn't seem that bad. If you give your child drugs, won't he (she) become a drug abuser?, Couldn't you provide more activity and tire him (her) out instead?

Some parents have even been accused of giving their child medication to make family life easier. Many wrestle with the notion that if they were better parents, they could control the child's behavior.

Such misguidance and misinformation does little to help the ADHD child or the parent. I believe that as parents of ADHD children, we need to be aware of all the treatment options available and to have correct information about those options so we can make intelligent and informed choices. We all need to know that medication is not administered to make a bad child into a good child or a poor student into a better student. ADHD is a biologically based condition. Consequently, the medication used in its treatment is given because it effectively alters the abnormal biology into a more normal state.

In fact, for the child in need of medical intervention, such therapy is often the kindest help. Nineteen-year-old John Brett told me that when he began medication in sixth grade, his life turned around. The years he spent off medication between eighth and tenth grade, he called "a living hell." John was taken off medication for those years because of two common misconceptions. The first being ADHD symptoms disappear with puberty, and the second being the medications used to treat ADHD no longer work after the child reaches puberty because of physiological changes in the body.

Current research demonstrates the effective use of medication for the treatment of ADHD in both adolescents and adults. At the age of fifteen, John Brett went back on medication after home circumstances and his ADHD symptoms proved so intolerable he entertained thoughts of suicide. Today, his attitude is optimistic and he asked me to tell every person with ADHD, "If you put your effort into something, you can get what you want out of it."

The use of stimulant medication with ADHD children tends to be more effective when parents and the ADHD child understand the basis for it. As he told me and as he wrote in his book *The Hyperactive Child, Adolescent and Adult, Attention Deficit Disorder Through The Lifespan,* with consideration given to the age and sophistication of the child, Dr. Wender will frequently explain the ADHD medical treatment in this fashion: "Not being able to sit still or concentrate happen because there are chemicals in the brain. Some people make too much of them and some people make too little. Maybe you make too little." Dr. Wender then tells how the medicine can help the patient to compensate for the lack of chemicals. However, he emphasizes the point that while the medicine might be very helpful to the child, it is not a mind controlling drug. The patient still has free will and must exercise his or her autonomy. For instance, the medication will facilitate the child's ability to focus attention while studying for a test, but the child must choose to study. The medicine will help the child control his or her temper, but only if the child wants to. The medicine does not control the child.

Many children are not even aware of the manner in which medication has helped them. Because ADHD children characteristically lack insight about their behavior, according to Dr. Wender, they will frequently report that medication has had no effect even when the child's parents and he note a big therapeutic change. When Dr. Wender asks the child to account for why he or she has not been to the principal's office in three weeks, or why sleepovers and birthday party invitations are pouring in, the child will respond, "Just lucky I guess." The assessment of the positive effects of medication through the use of behavior rating scales and clinical observation often give an accurate appraisal of the treatment benefit.

Some children resist taking medication. When this situation arises, each parent, child and physician must deal with it on a case by case basis. Dr. C. Keith Conners finds that a common reason why a child would resist this treatment has to do with the social disapproval demonstrated by the various names other children assign to Ritalin such as "stupid pills," "smart pills," and "spaz pills." For the ADHD child, these unfortunate labels, and/ or even having to take the medication, become guilt by association. Thus the child equates not taking the medicine with not having a problem.

In addition to education about the disorder, parent training, modified school program and medication, a few other treatments exist which Dr. Russell Barkley feels have promise but are still in the experimental stages. Social skills training, self-instruction, and self-control training fall into this category. He suggests that parents first utilize the proven treatments in this category which offer the greatest results.

A number of purported remedies exist which Dr. Barkley cautions against because they have no validity for the treatment of ADHD. He mentions high doses of vitamins, scalp massages given by chiropractors—which he notes incidentally may have some associated risks—visual perspective and ocular motor training, allergy treatment, and dietary treatments such as sugar restriction and Feingold diet.

A number of mothers I interviewed told me they tried the Feingold diet which theoretically eliminates hyperactivity by restricting additives, preservatives, salicylates and sugar. The only thing this diet produced proved to be the placebo effect which is typified by Liz Sacca's experience. Initially, Liz thought the diet had some positive result because she expended such a huge effort and the diet proved to be the first action she felt she could take to help her son. Later, she realized her feelings about herself as a mother improved, but her little boy's symptoms did not get better. According to Dr. William McMahon, "Any treatment carries a tremendous placebo effect. But generally, this effect does not last over time."

With regard to dietary treatment, no expert suggests that children be given a lot of additives, sugar or preservatives. However, people need to realize that these elements do not cause ADHD and thus their elimination cannot cure the disorder. In addition, Dr. C. Keith Conners, author of *Feeding The Brain, the Effects of Food on Children,* cautions against diets which are unreasonable and exclude a lot of the essentials needed by children. He explains, "We found on the Feingold diet kids developed vitamin C deficiencies because they missed all the vitamins that come in fruits."

A common misconception among some parents and professionals is that allergies cause ADHD symptoms. Dr. Russell Barkey warns parents about the "visit to the clinical ecologist who does the huge three day workup of allergies." He says that no evidence supports the treatment of allergies as a significant part of the treatment of ADHD, though allergy treatment may help a child's allergies. According to Dr. Conners, about twenty-five percent of all children have some form of allergy. However, the incidence of allergy is slightly higher among ADHD children. He says, "There is evidence to suggest that ADHD kids have less functional immune systems and therefore have more allergies. However, it is very unlikely that allergy causes the disorder."

The symptoms of ADHD prove to be highly responsive to treatment. Child Psychiatrist William McMahon strongly believes that the larger the system of people involved in the treatment of this disorder, the more likely the treatment will be effective. In the behavioral training program employed by his clinic, a price break is given if Mom and Dad come as a couple because experience demonstrates that when both parents are trained, attempts to manage the child's behavior have more success. Sometimes involving both parents in the treatment of the child's ADHD is not always possible, particularly in single parent homes. However, other people involved with the child can become part of the system. For example, in cases of single parent or two parent homes, Dr. McMahon often uses grandparents as part of the system because their presence and contribution frequently prove to be a great reinforcer to the child.

In our case, our psychologist proved to be an extremely important part of the treatment complex, though we do not need to see him regularly these days. As Paula Anderson said, "I'm comforted by the fact that I can call him whenever a problem comes up that I don't know how to handle." When the various treatments take effect, fewer and fewer circumstances arise that parents can't handle.

Summary

- ADHD children function best in a calm, quiet, structured, predictable atmosphere.
- Multiple interventions are required to treat ADHD symptomatology.
- The multimodal treatment approach includes:
  1. education about the disorder,
  2. parent training in behavior management strategies,
  3. modified school program,
  4. medication.

  Other therapies may be employed when indicated.
- Treatment is managed best by health care professionals knowledgeable about all aspects of the disorder.
- Medication alters the abnormal biology to a more normal state.
- The need for medication is determined after other interventions have produced only limited success, and/or on the basis of severity of symptoms.
- Medication should never be the sole ADHD treatment.
- No predictive test exists to determine who will benefit from medication.
- Psycho-stimulant medications are first choice for treatment of ADHD. Methylphenidate (Ritalin) is most widely used.
- Medication is used to control the child's symptoms; thus when to use it depends on the individual child.
- ADHD is believed to result from too little of a neurotransmitter chemical called dopamine. Stimulant medication is thought to possibly increase the amount of dopamine so that the attention span increases, and impulsivity and, where

present, hyperactivity, decrease.
- Some ADHD children resist medication because of social disapproval.
- Clinical effects of medication can be evaluated through behavior ratings scales and clinical observation.
- Other therapies which have promise as possible effective treatments but are still experimental include:
  1. training in social skills,
  2. self-instruction,
  3. self-control.
- Therapies which have no validity for treatment of ADHD include:
  1. megavitamin therapy,
  2. visual perspective and ocular motor training,
  3. chiropractic manipulation,
  4. allergy treatment and dietary treatment.
- The more people involved in the child's treatment, the more effective the results.

CHAPTER SEVEN

Self-esteem in the ADHD Child

An odd occurrence happened in our home for the second summer in a row. Life improved. Without the stress of the school environment, David's symptoms became reasonably manageable. Sure, both my husband and I felt as though the effort required to keep David within limits often compared to pedaling a bike uphill, but we coped fairly well, as did Jonathan. Though David constantly lorded control over his younger brother, fortunately Jonathan had a very calm, quiet disposition and seldom balked when David insisted on running his life. Provided Jon did not get hurt, we ignored most of David's actions.

During this summer of 1986, David even developed friendships with a couple of the neighborhood children which allowed me some breathing space. Interestingly, Jonathan gravitated to a little boy who behaved much like his brother, while David became best friends with a little girl who proved as mellow as Jonathan. With the other children as suitable distractions, David no longer demanded my constant attention.

Even the two week visit by David Sr.'s seventeen-year-old son Mark did not upset the status quo as it had in the past. Though young David adored his older stepbrother, until this summer, he could not handle the change in routine. Within a matter of hours after Mark arrived, David's voice grew intolerably loud and he became frenetic and overly emotional. As a consequence, the tension level for the entire family increased, and instead of a pleasant visit, Mark became subjected to the worst his other family had to offer. But this July 1986, my husband and I knew how to keep a lid on David's behavior, and Mark finally enjoyed a happier atmosphere along with the constant attention enthusiastically showered on him by his younger brothers.

When September rolled around, I felt ambivalent about the arrival of school. For years, I anxiously anticipated the peace and quiet I would have once David attended a full-day program. Now I wondered if the school pressures might once again mean a change for the worse in my son's behavior. Over the summer, the child psychologist tried to alert both my husband and me to the potential risks for David in the primary grades. However, until the final hour drew close, we both chose to bask in the sunlight of David's improved disposition. When our son charged through the door at the end of the first day of first grade with a smile stretched from ear to ear, both the psychologist's concerns and my own seemed foolish. David had a wonderful teacher who wrote "I love you" on every paper. In turn, he fell in love too.

During these happy days, David nicknamed me "Kitten." I am not the kitten type. In fact, I prefer dogs. But David loves felines of any type. When he called me "kitten," I accepted this name as a demonstration of his love, as a sign I had gotten my seven-year-old son back. This nickname and the stuffed animals he brought to my pillow each night acted as booster shots and helped me through the bad days.

In mid-September when I brought David for a follow-up visit to the pediatric neurologist, he proved to be a mere shadow of the former wild fellow this doctor had seen a few months earlier. While we sat in the waiting room, David picked up a copy of *Marvin K. Mooney Will You Please Go Now* and began to read aloud. He finished the story while the neurologist and I stood by in total amazement. David had neither read an entire book nor sat still in a doctor's office. In a report to the child psychologist, the doctor wrote, "David is neurologically stable at this time. He is doing well in school and I noted a significant improvement in his attentional problems from previous examinations."

I should not have been fooled by David's apparently reformed behavior. Just as the return of the swallows to Capistrano heralded the spring season and the promise of happier days in our home, the arrival of David's birthday at the beginning of fall meant a change for the worse in his behavior. This year when he turned seven, the only difference from previous times was that the change caught me off guard. Our son's dark side crept into our lives subtly.

I first noticed David's mood had become negatively transformed when he began to take issue with my driving. He insisted I tell him where we were going, what roads I planned to take. Heaven help me on the occasions I made a last minute decision to take a different route without first informing him. David would carry on as though I had violated a sacred oath.

To make matters worse, my car had a speedometer like a digital clock which read out the exact rate of speed in brightly illuminated numbers. Whenever we drove anywhere, David eagle-eyed the speedometer and yelled at me if the number exceeded the posted speed limit. I had no idea why this child turned out to be so inflexible. To David, driving at 37 MPH in a 35 MPH zone meant speeding. No matter how many times I tried to explain that a slight variation could be acceptable, this boy would not listen to my explanation, and I, in turn, caught his full wrath and fury.

One day, I gave up trying to explain myself to him and yelled, "I am the boss, not you." I then proceeded to warn my son about the terrible fate that would befall him if he did not learn to mind his business. I did not hear a peep about my driving until a week later when David arrived home after school. With a shaky voice but nonetheless firm resolve, he announced, "Now you're in trouble. I stopped the police car and told him that you speed all the time." I could not believe he turned his own mother into the authorities.

Here stood proof that once David set his mind to an idea, he never let up. The child psychologist explained to us how our son's propensity to get stuck on a topic, his inability to adjust easily to change, his short attention span, impulsive behavior and poor social skills could really create a miserable existence for him in school. Again Dr. Burke, the psychologist, urged us to ask David's teacher to initiate a child study team evaluation so he could receive an appropriate school program.

After our first experience with this procedure, I felt reluctant to go through an evaluation again. Besides, both my husband and I now felt fearful of "the system" and worried about the repercussions of having David labeled. When we voiced these concerns to the psychologist, he explained that without the proper school recognition and program, David could very likely be tagged as the "kid with the ability who refuses to do the work." We were told that teachers might come to view David's failure to perform as either his voluntary choice or the result of some underlying emotional difficulties.

Dr. Burke then bluntly added that ADHD children label themselves as bad kids with behavior problems. "Which label would you rather David have?" he asked. Well, we knew we'd rather have our son understood as a child with special needs which made certain aspects of learning and socialization difficult for him. The following mid-October day, I spoke with David's teacher.

When the conference began, I told the first grade teacher about our home situation and the tremendously hard time David had been through as a result of this disorder. She listened intently to this information and to my concerns that David meet with success in school. Since all of David's papers came home with stickers that read "Super," "Good Going," or "I Love You," I was surprised that she had already recommended David for the school's basic skills program which did not require an evaluation.

Still, this program did not address my son's other problems. As in kindergarten, David had difficulty paying attention and could not seem to follow directions. Because he rushed through most of his work, it looked very sloppy. She assured me that David tried very hard, that many first graders have similar difficulty, but when I looked around the room at the other children's drawings and papers, I could not help but see that David's work did not measure up to theirs.

Nor were his work habits the only problem. Just as in kindergarten, David bossed his classmates and reprimanded them whenever they made a mistake. The first grade teacher told me David tended to be a very serious little boy and she felt his intensity level interfered with his ability to make and keep friends. "David's a nice little boy. He's just very hard on himself and his classmates," she said.

We ended the conference in agreement that a child study team evaluation for David would be warranted. I knew my son had a chronic problem. But now that I realized parental determination could not alleviate his problem and that the results of the child study team evaluation might offer him more help, I found the evaluation process palatable.

After eighteen months of our periodic visits to the child psychologist, some of the finer points of home management became a part of my repertoire. For instance, David needed to be prepared for all changes in routine, so when Halloween arrived, this seven-year-old had been well rehearsed for the events of the day. In the afternoon, David and his five-year-old brother would participate in a Halloween parade and play at school to which parents and grandparents were invited. That evening, the entire family along with two friends would go trick or treating.

This first grade year, David opted to be a witch. Jonathan now in kindergarten, had grown so accustomed to being in David's shadow, he chose entirely of his own accord to be the witch's black cat. For Jon's costume, I found a black sweat suit, whiskers, a tail and cat's ears. David would don a black robe, a cape, a witch's hat and broom, a ratty brown wig, a wart-covered nose and green face makeup. I felt so good about their costumes that I could hardly wait for the boys to come home at lunchtime to get ready for the school parade.

At the stroke of noon, David flew through the door and screamed in horror, "Witches are girls. Get me another costume. I'm not being a witch." I felt panic. We did not stock a cache of costumes ready for any whim. David began to lose control and started to yell, and scream and call me names for "being a stupid mother." Even time-out could not get him calmed down.

He did, however, stop his tantrum the moment the idea dawned on him that his little brother could be the witch. "I'll be the cat," he proclaimed. Jonathan who had been subservient to his big brother's spell for so long, picked this day to take a stand. He would not hear of a change in costume and I supported his decision. Recognizing defeat, David slipped back into his nasty temper.

I felt like a genius when the obvious solution came to my mind about twenty minutes later. I told David he could be warlock. "What's that?" he yelled. "A male witch," I replied. But David did not buy this brilliant idea and continued his tirade. Only ten minutes remained of the lunch hour and David, who had not even begun to get dressed, started to criticize Jon's costume, at which point I almost sent him to school as the fabled headless horseman.

Fortunately, my mother arrived on the scene and convinced

him that Halloween costumes knew no gender. David put on his costume. I applied the final red blotches on his green face and brought him to school where all his classmates already sat at their desks. When we opened the door, the entire class cackled and shrieked. "Look at the witch." He did look great.

David ran out of the room and ripped the wig off his head and the warty nose from his face. "They're laughing at me," he screamed. Though his teacher and I tried to explain that the kids just thought his costume looked so real, this seven-year-old witch could not make the distinction. He only agreed to rejoin the festivities after I wiped every smudge of green paint from his face.

As I sat in the audience and watched all the little children, including my son Jonathan, enjoy themselves and regale in their costumes, I became overwhelmed with sadness. This celebration proved to be anything but a party for my son. David's disorder still prevented him from being like all the other kids. Once again my denial tricked me. This witch had been there since his first Halloween. I fled the scene because I could not stop crying.

David came home from school no longer dressed in his costume, but relatively calm that afternoon. I, on the other hand, felt stretched to my limit. When the time arrived to get ready for trick or treating, I soon discovered this evil spell would not quit. David acted up again and when I snapped and screamed unmercifully at him, Jonathan joined forces with his brother and began to yell about his costume.

By the time my friend and her two children arrived to go out trick or treating, I felt like an emotional basket case. I had no idea what could have possessed mild-mannered Jonathan to act up that Halloween Day. Normally, Jonathan played a very passive role. At times, I could even fool myself into thinking that my younger son took all the family stress in stride. This horrible scene proved to be the precursor for many bad days to follow.

At our next appointment with the child psychologist, I recounted the horrors of Halloween Day. He explained that the holiday had all the makings for a blowup; too much stimulation, too much change in the routine, too much excitement, and for David, in particular, too little self-esteem. The constant negative feedback from his parents and peers, the frustration he felt from not being able to perform to his ability level in the classroom, and his socialization problems carried a high price. David could in no way handle being the center of all that attention. The psychologist reminded me that scenes like Halloween would become exacerbated if I responded less than matter-of-factly to my son's behavior. As a result of this nightmare, David experienced yet another blow to his already damaged self-esteem and I again felt like a terrible mother.

For the next couple of months, both my husband and I searched for ways to help David feel better about himself. We tried sports like swimming, gymnastics and basketball at the Y.M.C.A. but David balked about these activities. He put a great deal of pressure on himself and could not tolerate the fact that he did not do these sports perfectly. Eventually, we did not force him to go. At least three days a week, I encouraged David to have a friend over to our house after school. David bossed these children so much that I felt embarrassed for my son and uncomfortable for them. After a couple of months, only one little boy who never challenged David remained on the social scene. Then, I did not know how to help David build friendships.

By December, the school work load increased. Now that homework had been introduced, David had spelling words to study and sheets of math problems to do. He could barely control himself long enough to sit still and do this work. The moment a task presented the slightest challenge he fell apart. He'd scream for my help and then he'd complain about my input. After a few blood baths, the child psychologist suggested we add to David's chart, "Completes homework on time without argument." Though the chart helped, I began to feel as though the load we had to carry to keep David on track had grown too heavy.

Despite all the behavior management both my husband and I used, we could not get a semblance of normalcy in our home. Our efforts proved to be only a partial solution. In January 1987, both young David and I crashed and burned as a result of the stresses this disorder placed upon us.

The actual circumstance which brought us to our knees began quite innocently. David had a story to write for homework and I tried to help him with it. He behaved so nastily that I threw up my hands in disgust which made him extremely angry. The more he mouthed off, the angrier I became. Pretty soon the scene approached near Halloween proportions. I had the presence of mind to pull out of the fight. However, the next day, I insisted he take a note to his teacher in regard to the problems we had with the assignment.

Throughout the entire school year, David's teacher and I communicated by note, so when no reply came home that day or the next, I questioned David. He developed a guilty posture and avoided answering any of my five hundred questions until I grabbed his face, looked him straight in the eyes, and demanded to know what he did with my note to the teacher. By the time he admitted he never delivered it to her, I was in a fury. I ranted and raved so much that David probably thought he committed a violent crime.

I could not get control of myself. Practically every ounce of frustration I'd stored over the past seven-and-a-half-years gushed out. Later that evening as David changed for bed, I continued to fume about the note until I ultimately threatened him. I hollered, "Tomorrow you will take another note and that note will tell the teacher what the first note said and that you did not give it to her."

All the color drained from this little boy's face. David covered his ears and began to scream, "I hate myself. I'm going to climb up a tree and touch an electric wire and die." I felt horrible. I lifted him off the floor and while I rocked him back and forth I told him over and over again, "Mommy was wrong to yell at you David. You're a good boy. I love you very much. You didn't do anything so bad. Forget the note. It's not important. You're teacher always tells me what a good boy you are."

After awhile, his sobs stopped and he went to bed. Then I fell apart. My son, though still a small child, felt so much misery, he wanted to die. I knew he fought hard to fit, to belong, to feel loved. Yet he stood alone, a ring-master forced to keep the lions of the world at bay lest they swallow him up. Maybe this night when the lion became his mother, the effort proved too much.

The next day, we had an emergency appointment with the child psychologist. Even though David's emotional state stabilized that evening, guilt, shame and fear overwhelmed me. I thought I must be the worst mother ever, but Dr. Burke said I too had become a victim of this disorder. He explained that I had reached the point of emotional overload and suggested I go away for the weekend to calm down and recharge my batteries, which I did. When I returned, I felt better, though still unsettled.

A few days later, we also saw the pediatric neurologist. After I described our family situation of the past few months and the ultimate crisis, the doctor said the time had now arrived to try stimulant medication, specifically Ritalin. Before now, the neurologist did not want to prescribe this medication because David evidenced tics. Since the tics were no longer evident, the doctor now viewed the problems created by David's ADHD to warrant a closely monitored trial of medication. Finally, we would be able to try the treatment approach which had worked so well for so many children before us.

The medication did not promise to be a magic cure. But for our son, this treatment provided the missing puzzle piece. The medication enabled David to regulate his own behavior, emotions and impulsive decision making. His hyperactivity diminished. His attention span and ability to concentrate increased along with an improvement in his organizational skills. Use of the medicine in conjunction with behavior management techniques, family therapy and school program allowed David to experience the world as a kinder place where he could be quite successful and well-liked by others.

Three weeks after David began medication, we went on vacation to Mexico. These ten days we spent together turned out to be the most wonderful time we had ever experienced as a family. Mexico requires much adjustment, yet David maintained a positive attitude, and for most of the trip, acted as resident cheerleader. We came home on Valentine's Day, and that evening I found this note on my pillow. "To cat meow. I love you kitty cat. The best cat in the world." How the tide had turned in one short month. Even Jonathan now sought out his older brother as a playmate.

As a family we continued to work in therapy for the rest of the year. David's behavior grew consistently better and so we now addressed some of the bad patterns our family had fallen into over the years as we wrestled with his condition. The most difficult one for us to break proved to be using David as the family scapegoat. Jonathan had subtly become a master puppeteer who knew precisely how to pull his brother's strings. Whenever any disturbance erupted, David got blamed to such an extent, he confessed to sins he never committed. We concentrated our efforts toward raising our little boy's self-esteem.

In order to make this change, our psychologist told us we had to take certain actions. First, his dad and I had to look and listen at all times before we reacted. We had to learn to view a situation through David's eyes. Oddly enough, when we did put ourselves in David's position, many of our perceptions changed. Above all, we needed to learn not to yell or say damaging things to our child. Dr. Burke told us, "ADHD kids really test your patience and so it's understandable that you lose your temper. But you have to understand how hard life is for them, too."

We learned in therapy that David could not help himself and did not understand why we got angry with him, hit him, or yelled at him. The psychologist said we had to step back a bit, and not take the child's behavior personally. Even though Dr. Burke acknowledged how difficult such steps could be, he reminded us that since the child cannot stay in control of his or her emotions, the adults had to do so.

"ADHD must be managed thoughtfully, not emotionally," the psychologist taught us. Eventually we learned that the goal of any encounter is to teach the child what behavior is and is not acceptable. With all honesty, I must add that even today David's dad and I still fall back into old patterns of response. But never do we or our son David slide as far down as in the dark days.

The darkness of David's first grade year occurred because his self-esteem bottomed out. Though not all ADHD children experience the loss of self to the extent that they feel despair, not feeling good about oneself runs rampant in children with this disorder. Given the factors which contribute to the development of self-esteem, that ADHD children prove to be at risk to have a poor self-image is not surprising.

As explained by private therapist Judy Welch, the development of self-esteem is a lifelong process. Furthermore, our sense of self changes in response to our feelings of self-worth, self-confidence and self-reliance. Young children do not know how to nourish their sense of self, so they look to others for support, acceptance and approval. Initially parents nurture their child's self-esteem, then significant others such as teachers, siblings, peers and coaches play a role in the child's feelings about him or herself. According to Ms. Welch, teachers play a vital part in the development of self-esteem in children because they are the main providers of feedback in academic areas. This feedback not only communicates ability level; it tells the child how he or she compares to peers.

In the workshops Judy Welch conducts on self-esteem, she informs parents and teachers about the manner in which a child's self-image can be elevated based on the opinions the child holds of himself or herself. These opinions, she says, are formed by the messages the child gives himself, those received from others, and how the child interprets the messages from others. Children who receive positive feedback develop an inner confidence and can therefore nourish their own sense of self. They generally grow into happy, well-adjusted adults. Unfortunately, many ADHD children often largely receive negative input from family, peers and teachers. Therefore, they develop an extremely poor sense of self and eventually prove unable to perceive a message as positive when it is intended as such. ADHD children also become patterned to give themselves negative messages.

Judy Welch defines self-esteem as an unconscious, emotional reflection of a child's judgment about himself or herself which is always characterized by actions and attitudes. She notes that children with high self-esteem take pride in their accomplishments, act independently, assume responsibility easily, tolerate frustration well, approach new challenges enthusiastically, and feel capable of influencing others. Children with high self-esteem make comments like: "I can handle that job." "I made this picture all by myself." "Wow! I'm going to learn long division." "I really like this story I wrote about dinosaurs."

A child with low self-esteem expresses a defeatist attitude a great deal of the time. He or she avoids anxiety-producing situations, demeans his or her talents, feels others don't value him or her, blames others for his or her weaknesses, is easily influenced by others, becomes defensive and easily frustrated, and feels powerless. The child with low self-esteem might make statements like these: "I'm not going to school today. There's a hard test in math." "Nothing I draw looks any good." "I flunked the test because the teacher did not give me enough time to study." "I can't find the scissors." "I don't have an atlas." "Now I'll never finish my social studies homework."

In the case of Susie White, her mother Lynn recognized Susie's lack of self-esteem when she asked all the little girls in her

Brownie troop to draw a self-portrait. Susie did not draw a bold picture and use most of the paper like the other little girls. Instead, she drew her self-portrait, the size of a pea, in the lower right hand corner of the paper so that it was barely discernible. At this point in time, Susie's ADHD disorder had not been diagnosed, and Lynn carried the burden of responsibility for her symptoms.

According to Dr. C. Keith Conners, "being effective is the basis of self-esteem." He says there are a million ways that kids can be effective. For instance, they can dress themselves, play with other children, succeed academically, and experience a sense of accomplishment through sports or the performing arts.

Dr. Conners explains that most ADHD children do not have the means to feel effective. Their symptoms usually make everything they attempt a hassle. Even their special talents often go unrecognized or undeveloped because many ADHD children prove unable to practice or sustain interest in their individual milieus. Thus, the normal means by which most youngsters receive boosts in self-esteem do not exist for ADHD children.

Based on his clinical experience, Dr. Conners says, "Most people either write off ADHD children as miserable little beings who deserve the negative responses they get, or else they ignore these children." Such responses do much harm to the child's self-image. Dr. Conners reports that long-term, follow-up studies of ADHD children reveal almost a uniform deficiency in self-esteem. Though the academic and behavioral deficits tend to persist, he says that as adults, the ADHD person's low self-esteem becomes a far more serious deficit because success in life is determined by a person's motivation, belief in self, and confidence.

Therapist Judy Welch notes that many ADHD children become battered by a steady stream of failure, frustration and disappointment, resulting in badly bruised egos. The degree to which the child experiences this emotional beating depends on the degree of severity of the condition. For Peter Rothman, every environment represented a struggle. Even the day camp counselors perceived him as uncooperative. Since he had difficulty going from one activity to the next, ten-year-old Peter turned out to be the last child to get to the starting line and the last one to cross the finish line every day. His mother Donna often mistook his uncooperative behavior as obstinacy.

Undiagnosed ADHD children often suffer blows to their self-esteem because of the mythology developed to explain why they do not "get with the program." Many parents and teachers, faced with a child who does not comply, often draw the conclusion that the child has control of his or her behavior, but chooses to act in a way contrary to the rules which have been prescribed.

As a result of this "he - or - she - could - do - it - if - he - or - she-wanted-to" myth, many ADHD children become subjected to a great deal of punishment. Dr. Russell Barkley observes that these children do not want to behave the way they do. By the age of eight or ten, many show signs of poor self-esteem because they really want to behave well. After they are punished for mis-behavior, they make great promises to change, which of course, they cannot keep because, Dr. Barkley says, "they are at the mercy of their characteristics."

Yet ADHD children come into the world with the same desires as all other children. They want to be loved, liked, accepted, and so, like other children, they want to please. Unlike other children, they experience failure so frequently, their self-esteem gradually erodes. This sense of failure becomes compounded in those cases where parents, unaware of their child's underlying disorder, accept that their son or daughter is out to drive them over the edge. In actuality, a frustrated parent often sends the ADHD child's sense of self on a downward spiral.

Parents often find that they compromise the very standards of decency they set for themselves. For example, Judy Woodruff's daughter Karen frequently exploded in fits of temper. Like her daughter, Judy always had difficulty with self-control and pun-ished herself for years with the assumption that if she tried harder to be a better person, her problem would go away. One night when Karen displayed a temper outburst, Judy raised her hand to smack her daughter and unintentionally made Karen's nose bleed. The next day, both mother and daughter went for help. Evalua-tions determined they both had ADHD.

The message here is not that every person who loses his or her temper has ADHD, but rather that people with the disorder often spend years trying to explain why they cannot stay in control of their behavior. As with Judy Woodruff, the explanations in most cases employ guilt and blame and consequently foster poor self-esteem. Parents who come from this emotional place, have few coping mechanisms to deal with the problems presented by their ADHD child's symptoms, and thus a mantle of negativity falls upon the ADHD child's shoulders.

Furthermore, when parents and teachers do not understand the dynamics of this disorder, they often have unrealistic expectations. Judy Welch, a former teacher and school psychologist, explained how many parents and teachers get stuck in the old belief system that if they really push a child, that child will straighten up and do what is asked. Sometimes when the parents and/or teachers push, the child does perform well, which gives rise to the opinion that if an ADHD child does something once, he or she should be able to perform accordingly at all times.

By the way, the child with ADHD oftentimes proves equally as baffled as to why he or she can get it together sometimes but not others. This "he-could-do-it-if-he-tried-hard-enough" myth and the aforementioned "he-could-do-it-if-he-wanted-to" myth, are closely related and reinforced by the inconsistent nature of the ADHD child's symptoms.

Pediatrician Melvin Levine, Professor of Pediatrics and Director of the Clinical Center for Development and Learning at the University of North Carolina in Chapel Hill, believes inconsistency to be the biggest roadblock to children with attention problems. Many people act as though the inconsistency of the ADHD child's symptoms means that he or she really does have self-control because occasionally the child does conform.

Yet Dr. Levine points out that many chronic conditions in medicine are inconsistent in their manifestation. For instance, people with asthma do not wheeze all the time, and people with arthritis may have swollen joints one day and not the next.

But the misunderstandings about the inconsistent nature of ADHD symptoms takes a toll on the child's self-esteem. Instead of allowing the ADHD child to feel effective for the times he or she does perform well, these myths signal the message that the child is incompetent.

Unfortunately, the most consistent aspect of the ADHD disorder proves to be that most ADHD children receive this "incompetency message" regularly. In fact, this message is so consistent, the child often incorporates it into his or her own belief system. Sometimes the incompetency message is delivered overtly by negative feedback and punishment. Other times, parents in particular develop a demoralizing pattern of response which becomes so subtly ingrained, they do not realize the messages they send to the child.

Dr. William McMahon reports that parents of ADHD children frequently fall into a condescending pattern of response to the child which in turn reaffirms the "incompetency message." In his practice, for instance, Dr. McMahon has noted some parents who identify the ADHD child as a social and emotional cripple and overprotect him or her because they feel responsible for the youngster's every move. In other situations, the parents cut the ADHD child a very wide swath and everyone walks on egg shells around him or her. This response not only deprives the child of normal consequences for his or her actions, but such condescending treatment sets the child apart from everyone else. ADHD children often feel they do not fit.

Fortunately, for ADHD children, self-esteem changes when the child's circumstances improve. According to therapist Judy Welch, the most effective remediation of poor self-esteem is to change the child's belief system in himself or herself. In order to effectuate a positive change, significant others, particularly parents and teachers, need to alter their belief system about the child. When the parent, teacher and the ADHD child acquire knowledge about the disorder, they all have a basis upon which to begin a change in their point of view.

To change their belief system, parents and teachers must dispel the myth that the ADHD child is willfully non-compliant. Dr. Sam Goldstein says that once parents and teachers come to view the child as "the kid who can't," rather than "the kid who won't," they feel less angry about the child. As a result, they become able to help the child because they feel less stressed. Attention-deficit Hyperactivity Disorder affects everyone the child interacts with to some degree or another, therefore everyone must learn to cope with the disorder. Parents need to make changes in their approach to the child if they want to nurture the ADHD child's sense of self.

Behavior management, of course, proves to be the most beneficial method of changing parenting behavior. These methods, described in earlier chapters, also help parents to cope better with frustrations created by this disorder. Teachers, as well, often find behavior management tools have an important place in the classroom. Many parents and teachers tend to view effective management techniques primarily as the use of behavior charts and explicit rules followed by predictable consequences. Once these techniques are employed, most parents especially find they cannot live without them. And though these techniques certainly lessen the amount and type of punishment used, and in addition, enable the child to take responsibility for his or her behavior, they do not, in and of themselves, promote good self-esteem.

According to Dr. C. Keith Conners, the goal of all interventions is to make the child feel good about his or her abilities and to feel effective. To do this, he says those involved with the child "need to catch the child being good." Throughout the course of most days, children behave appropriately in many instances which parents can show approval of; for instance, when the child remembers to do his chores or to bring home all the necessary homework materials. The child might share a toy or perhaps politely asks for a snack.

None of these behaviors are above and beyond the call of duty. But even though we expect a child to behave a certain way as a matter of course, we still need to reward the child for meeting expectations. Praise becomes the greatest sculpting tool a parent or teacher has to help the child carve a positive self-image. In younger children, Dr. Conners finds that blunt forms of praise, such as "excellent job" and "that's wonderful," work surprisingly well. He also finds older kids to be sensitive to such blunt statements and so praise must be subtly delivered in remarks such as "it looks like you put a lot of work into this."

At the conferences she gives on self-esteem, Judy Welch tells parents and teachers to check the child's self-esteem bank account to make sure there are more assets than debits. She advises parents and teachers to monitor the number of withdrawals they make through negative feedback, and to make numerous daily deposits of praise, encouragement, recognition and positive attention. To this end, Ms. Welch made a list of phrases parents and teachers can use, *52 Ways to Say "Good for You."* Among those included are: "I appreciate your help." "That's a good point." "That's certainly one way of looking at it." "Good thinking." "Nice going." When the acknowledgments are varied in expression, they let the child know the praiseworthy behavior really received consideration.

Judy Welch believes realistic expectations on the part of the parents, teachers and ADHD child provide the backbone upon which a child can gain self-respect. Thus, the child's strengths and weaknesses need to be determined. In her clinical experience, she has found that the more information parents, teachers and the ADHD child know about the disorder, the greater their sensitivity to the child's strengths and weaknesses. Knowledge is like the white plaster cast worn by a child with a broken arm. The cast conveys the message "I can't write with this hand, but maybe I can type with the other one." Once everyone understands the child's problems, they can revise their expectations, look for constructive ways to overcome his or her difficulties, and not make unreasonable demands on the youngster's limitations, just as they would not demand that a child write with a broken hand.

In addition to providing parents with a great sense of relief, knowledge about the disorder affords the child and the significant others the opportunity to maximize the strengths and compensate for the difficulties. For instance, often the diagnostic evaluation provides teachers with information about the child's learning characteristics. The teacher can use this knowledge to formulate judgments about how long the child can work on a task, how much homework the child can handle, and how the child processes instructions.

Instead of a haphazard existence, parents as well can plan around the ADHD child's strengths and weaknesses. When Paula Anderson and her husband learned that their daughter Maggie had no control over her inability to sit still, they stopped expecting her to remain quiet for an hour while the family ate dinner at a restaurant. Even ADHD children can compensate for their difficulties. For example, ten-year-old John Golding learned to ask his teacher if he could go to a study carrel in the back of the classroom when he could not filter out distractions.

In John's classroom, his peers also have been taught ways to help assist him with class projects. Judy Welch stresses the important effect peers and siblings have on the way the ADHD child feels about himself or herself. Thus, peers and siblings should be encouraged to participate in the boosting of the ADHD child's self-esteem by offering positive feedback and not criticism.

Ms. Welch believes that children with ADHD, their parents and teachers need to look beyond the problems associated with the disorder to the positive aspects that accompany ADHD. These children have many assets they can play to the hilt, but often need the help of parents and teachers to tap their natural resources. The ADHD children she has come to know exhibit creativity, a burning curiousity about life, an energy level and tireless drive which can be channeled toward a productive end.

Parents and teachers can encourage the ADHD child to develop a special interest. Children feel good about themselves when they find something they can master. Psychiatrist and researcher Dr. Paul Wender notes that ADHD children often perform superbly well when given a task of high interest to them. For instance, he finds that ADHD boys tend to be interested in dinosaurs, or earthquakes, or tidal waves, or other miscellaneous catastrophies, and the ADHD boy will read voraciously on those subjects.

Parents and teachers can build opportunities for success in the child's environment. Children feel good about themselves when they feel effective, competent. They develop confidence when they receive positive feedback, meet with success and fulfill their responsibilities. Since ADHD children often have difficulty taking and meeting responsibility, parents and teachers need to structure the situations for the child in this area. For example, since John Golding turned seven, he has had the responsibility of feeding the family pets. Lack of organization poses a problem for John, so his mother puts the food he will need on the kitchen table every morning before breakfast. John proudly reported to me that not one pet, not even a goldfish, has died under his care.

There are a hundred different ways parents can build opportunities for their child to experience success. Below are some suggestions which many parents have found to work well. I have arbitrarily divided these suggestions into four categories: special jobs, special interests, extra-curricular activities and play. Some of these ideas may work well for your child. Others might be totally disastrous. When selecting or devising strategies to build his or her success, the individual child's age, strengths, weaknesses and interests must be taken into account. At times even the best laid plans fail. In such instances, don't be discouraged and don't assume that you or your child are at fault. These suggestions, many of which apply to either boys or girls, are intended to be catalysts to spark your imagination.

Special jobs can be a cross between chores and fun and provide an excellent way to develop a sense of responsibility. When presenting a child with the opportunity to do such a task, perhaps we all would do well to recall the example of Tom Sawyer. Because Tom made the whitewashing of Aunt Polly's fence appear to be so much fun, the other kids became so eager and highly motivated they even paid Tom money to be allowed to do his task. Special jobs can involve such daily tasks as setting or clearing the table at mealtime, saying grace, emptying the trash, feeding the pets, or making school lunches. On a weekly basis, the child can put away groceries, plan and/or prepare a meal, water plants, and/or sort objects for recycling. The child can also be responsible for the decorating of the home for the different holidays, and for helping plan a family outing. He or she can also be the family historian by taking family photos and/or placing photos in albums.

Children usually love to be helpers. They can be encouraged to assist in special home projects such as building a book shelf or training a pet. Whenever I wallpapered a room, my children participated by taking the scraps and wallpapering a cardboard box.

Children tend to be naturally curious and often develop special interests. The parent can help the child build self-esteem by encouraging him or her to become expert in an area of interest. Many children like to start collections of any number of items such as dinosaurs, sports team memorabilia, stamps, dolls, rocks or sea shells. For a child interested in birds, the parent can help him or her build a bird feeder and be responsible for keeping it stocked. Solar system enthusiasts would enjoy a trip to a planetarium and a telescope to study the night skies. Other children might like to plant flowers and tend gardens.

Parents can also foster good feelings in the child by regularly playing with the child. Dr. Russell Barkley explains that play can take two forms: directive or non-directive. He describes directive play as developmental skills teaching type play in which the parent tries to teach the child something through the use of a game or construction kit like Legos. Dr. Barkley says, "Directive play basically involves a lot of teaching and this type of play with ADHD children just gets parents in trouble."

Instead he advises the use of non-directive play. In this style of play, the child is given full control over what the parent and child will play. The parent also follows the commands given by the child. Rather than act as the leader, the parent has the task of observing, commenting, describing the child's play, and periodically giving positive feedback.

I accidentally fell into non-directive play with my children when they acquired a Nintendo set and I, of course, could not get past the first board on Super Mario Brothers. Whether playing Monopoly, checkers, chess or cards, the parent does well to structure the game so the child can win.

Extra-curricular activities frequently reported as successful and of high interest to ADHD children include team sports such as basketball, soccer, hockey, football and baseball. Parents can play a crucial role in helping the child develop self-confidence by practicing the skills needed for these sports with him or her. For instance, throw the child balls he or she can catch. Some children might prefer to participate in sports that require little to no interactions with peers such as swimming, skiing, weightlifting, track and field, martial arts or gymnastics. The performing arts, such as children's theater groups or dance classes, offer yet a third type of alternative. Regardless of which activity the child selects, parents need to support him or her by attending practices, contests and performances.

John Brett, an ADHD teenager I spoke with, said, "I think when you have ADHD, you need an outlet." He advised parents to find something their ADHD child can do that makes him or her feel positive. For John, weightlifting boosted both his physical strength and his sense of self. He says that when he lifts weights, he also develops his ability to concentrate, because he knows if his mind wanders, he could seriously hurt himself. John also asked me to tell parents that even if their kid is failing every class, they should not take away the outlet which often proves to be the only thing in the kid's life that makes him or her feel good. Otherwise, says John, "He'll get more screwed up."

ADHD children do not have to be beaten down as a result of their disorder. Judy Welch says, "We can help resurrect a new self-image in our children with feelings of pride, security, and a sense of I-can-do-it-ness through encouragement and praise." In order to assure a positive outcome for the ADHD child, Dr. Conners offers this advice:

"Parents need to view ADHD as a chronic disorder. Good things and difficult things about the child will come and go. So you better develop your own sense of equanimity and not give up on the kid, because he will make it eventually, unless the toll along the way proves too high."

Through a concerted effort to boost the ADHD child's self-esteem, the miserable effects of the condition can be thwarted.

Summary

- ADHD children often suffer from low self-esteem.
- Self-esteem develops and changes over the course of a person's lifetime.
- Self-esteem has three components:
  1. the messages we give ourselves,
  2. the messages received by others,
  3. the way we interpret the messages from others.
- Parents and teachers play a vital role in the child's development of self-esteem. Siblings and peers also have an impact.
- The child's actions and attitudes reflect his or her self-esteem.
- The basis for self-esteem is feeling effective. ADHD symptoms often make the child feel ineffective.
- The "he-or-she-could-do-it-if-he-or-she-tried-hard-enough" myth and the "he-or-she-could-do-it-if-he-or-she-wanted-to" myth, along with unrealistic expectations, contribute to the child's poor self-image.
- The inconsistent nature of the ADHD child's symptoms support the myths created to explain the behavior.
- ADHD children often receive the message that they are incompetent.
- Self-esteem is boosted when parents, teachers and the ADHD child change their belief systems about the child.
- Knowledge of the disorder, effective management, and positive reinforcement of appropriate behavior with praise and encouragement help change the belief system.
- The goal of intervention is to enable the child to feel good about his or her abilities.
- The child's strengths and weaknesses must be determined.

- Parents and teachers must build opportunities for the child to be successful.
- ADHD children need to have an outlet.
- ADHD children do not have to suffer from low self-esteem.

CHAPTER EIGHT

The Elementary School Years: The Parent as Advocate

In May 1987, I met with our school's child study team to learn the results of the evaluation requested the previous fall. Since David's dad and I had already been through this process two years earlier when David had been diagnosed, I thought the conference would be quite easy to handle intellectually as well as emotionally. Yet, the formality of the proceedings caught me off guard, and I felt tense and upset with what I perceived as the dehumanizing nature of this meeting. Except for his teacher, no one seemed to speak about my son David as a living, breathing soul. Instead, he became a summary of tests results.

As a result of the child study team evaluation, David would, indeed, be eligible for special education services. In most states, because there are so many different learning disabilities, children who receive special education are assigned labels which denote classification categories rather than their specific learning disability. In some states, for example, dyslexic children are labeled perceptually impaired. At the child study team conference, I learned that David would have to be labeled "neurologically impaired" if my husband and I wanted our son to have a special educational program designed to meet his individual needs. His dad and I both preferred no label be used at all. After all, "neurological impaired" did not reveal any specific information to the teachers about our son's particular learning difficulties.

A few days after the conference, my husband and I received in the mail, a copy of each child study team member's written report about our son. Of all the reports, the social worker's interview with David, then seven-and-a-half, proved to be the most revealing. She wrote:

"David describes himself as American. When pressed to describe himself as a person, he says he is nice. David likes that he has a new puppy, Mollie, and that he takes care of her well. He states that he is happy most of the time. David does not like the way his brain makes him get into trouble. It tells him to do bad things and when he does them, he gets into trouble. David also doesn't like that his brain does not think too well. He hardly ever gets a 100 on his spelling test. David likes to play games or build things. He does not like to run or do work. David's three wishes were: one, have all the money in the world; two, own this world; three, could have magic."

Based on David's comments, the social worker drew the following conclusions. "David spoke of his brain in the third person, as though it were separate and apart from him, but very much in control. David did not see that he could alter his perceptions, or the work of his brain either by studying harder or concentrating on his behavior. David appears to behave in a certain manner and relinquish blame for his behavior to causes other than himself."

I always knew my son to be very intelligent, but until I read this report, I did not realize his intuitive abilities. In actuality, David described to the social worker, and consequently anyone who read her report, the neurological manifestations of his ADHD disorder. He talked about his brain in the third person because, he, more than anyone else, knew how little control he had over his behavior. Though he desired to succeed, to be accepted, to have his intentions properly executed, David could not will his brain to do what he wanted. Before the necessary treatment interventions, most times David had only limited power to regulate his behavior, while at other times regulating the functioning of his brain proved to be a force beyond his control.

A week before school ended that first grade year, I received one final note from my son's teacher. "Dear Mary," she wrote. "Wasn't David great today in the play? I'm so proud of him. In fact, his overall behavior has changed in school. His attitude is very positive lately, and several times he has complimented some of his classmates (a real first!). The gym teacher has also noticed the change—and the smiles! I'm just delighted for him. I hope you are experiencing this 'new David' at home, too." Thanks to the behavioral interventions and medication we used to manage our son's disorder, our entire family did reap the benefits of David's improved condition.

Now I don't mean to imply that all our problems ended. David still needed to learn how to behave appropriately. For instance, one summer evening, he threw a stick into the air which accidentally landed on his brother's head. Jonathan ended up in the emergency room. I had fully intended to be lenient and forgive David for his mistake, but he did not show any remorse for the consequences of his impulsive behavior. Instead, he bounded in the door and screamed at the top of his lungs. "It was his fault! I told Jon to move and he didn't do what I said. You should punish him."

Maybe my tightly clenched jaw and glowering eyes persuaded this boy to change his tack. Whatever the reason, David, a survivor, realized this occasion did not lend itself to "the best defense is a good offense" approach. He did not even balk when I sent him to his room for the day, and I felt particularly pleased that my temper did not flare and make things worse.

However, I continued to be disturbed by the thought that maybe David's impulsive behavior would someday push him across the line which separated the horizon and the end of the world. Unlike in his toddler days, I could not watch him like a hawk every minute to keep him from going too far. So at our next session with the child psychologist, I decided to bring up this stick incident with the hope that perhaps he could get David to realize that impulsive acts can lead to serious consequences. I still had not fully accepted that David often had no control over his impulsive acts.

After I recounted the details of that afternoon, the psychologist commended me because I gave David an immediate consequence for his action and did not get angry with him. But rather than lecture David about the evils of impulsivity, he asked, "Did you expect the stick to hit your brother?"

"No," replied David in a very soft voice.

The psychologist then queried, "What could you have done

differently?" Dead silence.

After fifteen seconds or so I offered, "You could have looked around first to make sure nobody would be in the way."

I did not realize the extent of my poor judgment until the psychologist immediately told David he should never throw sticks or rocks or anything for that matter. I had missed the point that this ADHD child who could not readily or thoughtfully control his impulses needed strict limits. "No" for David actually proved to be much kinder than expecting him to use appropriate judgment.

That summer between first and second grade, David attended day camp. Since social interactions remained difficult, David continued to isolate from his peers. Though he did participate in team activities, David spent most of his free time with his twenty-year-old group counselor. Until the winter came, neither my husband nor I realized how the camp experience had benefitted our son.

David, now eight years old, signed up for swimming and tennis at the Y.M.C.A. Such initiative and participation had never before been part of David's style, and in the past, we forced him into sports activities. These efforts resulted in disaster. For example, we pushed him to play tee ball. During the first game of the season, our pride and joy sat in the middle of the field and proceeded to repeatedly yell, "This is boring." He did not play ball after that morning, and his dad and I no longer made emphatic suggestions purportedly for our son's own good.

When school resumed in September, David left the house each morning eager to begin his day. He returned a happy spirit. One of his first papers to come home showed a rocket blasting toward space. Underneath, David wrote, "When I grow up I want to be an astronaut. I want to do that because it is fun." He neatly formed each letter and spelled all words correctly. I felt such joy to see my son happy. Finally, he shed the difficult skin that bound him like a tightly wrapped coil ready to spring when slightly jarred.

Second grade obviously agreed with David. In addition to the care and concern of his morning and afternoon teachers, our son also had the support of the program designed specifically for him under the aegis of special education. When the school year began, David received supplemental help in the school's resource room for two half-hour periods a week. But by mid-October, both his teachers noted the difficulties following directions presented for David every day. If a worksheet had multiple directions, David generally read and followed only the first directive. Though he understood the concepts being taught, his inability to follow directions seriously affected his performance.

Disorganization proved to be an equally formidable opponent. The inside of David's desk looked as though a family of ferrets had taken up residence. Whenever the teachers asked the class to take out a workbook or hand in a homework paper, our son could not find what he needed amidst the varied assortment of crumpled papers and books. When he had more than one worksheet to do independently in class, David often forgot to do them all. Sometimes he brought the wrong materials home for homework. Other times, he forgot his assignments all together.

Since I made habit of communicating with David's teachers on a regular basis, I learned about his school difficulties and frustrations very early in the year. Both second grade teachers and I agreed that the special education program designed for David at the end of first grade needed some adjustments. We spoke with the person assigned to manage David's program. She devised a solution where each morning a basic skills teacher came to my son's classroom to help him, along with four other children identified with similar difficulties. The teacher went over the directions for the day's work, answered any questions the children had, and made a daily schedule for each child to follow. As the child completed a task, he or she crossed it off the schedule list.

At mid-day, the basic skills teacher followed the same routine for the afternoon session. At the end of the day, she returned to the classroom and checked each child's backpack to make sure that all the necessary materials went home. If the children evidenced difficulty in any area of instruction, the teacher also gave them tutorial help during the day. The program worked wonderfully and gave David the necessary support. Because the other children were involved as well, David felt "unspecial" which for his self-esteem proved to be quite important. David wanted very much to fit in with the gang.

In addition to the support from the basic skills teacher, David's resource room teacher devised some creative interventions geared to help him meet success in the regular classroom environment.

For instance, our son showed an interest in the computer so the teacher developed tutorial computer games for his use at home. Not only did she make game discs for each week's spelling words, but the second grade teachers told her what tests they would administer and she made study guide games as well.

Both of David's second grade teachers also played important roles in his academic and emotional development. They took a special interest in him and communicated with me on a regular basis. Yet even with such care, occasionally unanticipated glitches arose. The worst one proved to be the creative writing project the afternoon teacher assigned in honor of Thanksgiving. She asked each child to "imagine you are a turkey and you have just found out you are going to be Thanksgiving dinner. How do you feel and what are you going to do about it?"

When David's turkey-shaped booklet came home with the smiley sticker pasted on the bird's plumage, I couldn't wait to read his response. Before I even opened the cover, I assumed he probably created a scenario where the turkey escaped by some ingenious method. And so I joyously dove into his "Turkey Talk" wherein David wrote, "I just found out I'm going to be Thanksgiving dinner. I think I know what to do. I will bite the farmer. And I'll stab him in the head and put him in a cage and fry him over a fire. And I'll injure his wife . . ." His story line followed this violent tack. As I read on, I wondered what possessed my little boy to such extreme anger.

As luck goes, the next day his father and I were scheduled to meet with David's teachers at the annual fall teacher's conference. As soon as we sat down, I said "That was some story David wrote." The afternoon teacher called it "quite descriptive" and she said that because of the descriptive violence, she showed David's story to the guidance counselor.

"What did she think of it?" I said swallowing rather hard.

In reply, the teacher whispered, "The counselor thought it was—um—a little much, unusually violent, quite intense." With that comment, everyone fell silent.

Long pauses have always made me uncomfortable. After fifteen seconds or so, I found the silence so loud, I slipped into my "crack a joke" mode and, in an attempt to lighten the moment, rhetorically asked, "Gee, do you think Edgar Allan Poe started out this way?" Everyone sort of smiled. A moment or so later,

David's morning teacher said she discussed different Thanksgiving rituals with the class just before they wrote their turkey stories. One little girl enthusiastically gave a detailed account of her mother's experience growing up on a farm, and how each Thanksgiving, her grandfather slaughtered a turkey for dinner. Much to the great disgust and horror of the other children, this classmate described the bloody scene as the headless turkey ran around after it had been decapitated. The teacher reported that eight-year-old David had been quite upset by this information.

Now the violent nature of David's story did not seem quite as inappropriate. In fact, it made great sense to me. This child cried for days when a goldfish died. On occasion, he still mourns the loss of two stuffed animals he left in a taxi cab when he was six. He even said to his brother Jonathan, who has been asking for a hamster, "Why would you want a hamster? It will just die and you'll be sad." I could now understand how my son got caught up in the emotion of the moment as he sat at his desk writing about how he would avoid the evil farmer's butcher knife.

The remaining months of second grade proved to be a happier time for all of us. David's teachers called me every Friday to report about the events of the week. They informed me about any special projects that might be scheduled so I could monitor their completion and thereby avoid the 8:00 P.M. bedtime "what-do-you-mean-you-have-a-book-report-due-tomorrow?" fights.

These second grade teachers also recognized David's lack of self-esteem and made efforts to boost his opinion of himself. Since he loved science, they tried to encourage him in every way. One night, his teacher even called to tell David to go outside and look at the sky because Venus would soon pass in back of the moon. That phone call went a great distance to let David know how highly his teacher regarded him.

Besides the genuine and special interest they showed David, the teachers also had regard for my input. When I called one day because David walked out the door in the morning knowing all the answers for his Social Studies test and came home in the afternoon with a failing grade, the teacher thought he might have encountered difficulty with the process of selecting multiple choice answers and offered to retest him. Orally, he scored 100. The teachers understood that the mechanics of writing often interfered with David's ability to get spelling words down on the paper correctly, so each week after he had taken the written test, they asked him to orally spell the words he misspelled. Orally, he usually spelled all the words correctly. David received an "A" for the year. I think these teachers would tell you that the special efforts they made for David took planning and sensitivity, but they did not take a great deal of time.

I admired these teachers because they openly evaluated their methods and found ways to make the school environment successful for my son. They accommodated his special learning characteristics and worked to develop his positive qualities. The teachers never chastized him for his poor social skills or his demands on the other kids. Instead they complimented him when he behaved in a polite and courteous fashion. They understood his need for structure and so they made his day as predictable as possible. They even gave him special jobs to do. When the final report card came home from school that June 1988, David received four A's and two B's, and "Outstanding" for effort. But more importantly, young David came home smiling.

Due to the severity of our son's Attention-deficit Hyperactivity Disorder, David Sr. and I knew the nature of his developmental disorder at the outset of his public school career. We had been alerted to the potential learning difficulties David might face in school as a result of his ADHD symptoms. With this knowledge, my husband and I could take steps to insure that our son would not have to succumb to years of demoralizing academic failure. However, usually the average age of diagnosis is around eight years. By then, many of these children have established a pattern of poor school performance. Others, even less fortunate, go undiagnosed well into the later elementary, junior or senior high school years having experienced a steady stream of academic failure and social rejection resulting in low self-esteem. The older a child is when diagnosed, the greater the amount of remediation needed.

In general, ADHD is manifested in elementary school-aged children as follows. They may exhibit inappropriate activity unrelated to task, poor ability to sustain attention and to concentrate, difficulty inhibiting impulses, organizational problems, attentionseeking behaviors, low frustration tolerance, low self-esteem, interpersonal difficulties particularly with peers, and learning difficulties, especially under conditions of partial reinforcement.

Such characteristics account for the reason ADHD children are at high risk for, at best, poor school performance marked by underachievement, and at worst, for academic failure. Unlike their non-handicapped peers, the education promised to all Americans is much harder to come by for ADHD children who cannot sustain attention, filter out distractions, organize themselves and think before acting.

Dr. Melvin Levine, Professor of Pediatrics and Director of the Clinical Center for the Study of Development and Learning at the University of North Carolina, Chapel Hill, believes the inconsistency of symptoms and the unevenness of development further adds to the woes of ADHD children. Often teachers and parents view the ADHD child as just not trying hard enough. After all, they rationalize, if Susie can remember to bring her book to class one day, she should be able to remember every day. If Johnny can do well in math and spelling, he should be able to do well in social studies. If Susie and Johnny did not have a handicap, these assumptions might be correct.

To understand why many ADHD children fare so poorly in school, we need to be aware of the ramifications of their symptomatology in the school environment. According to Dr. Richard Zakreski, a therapist in private practice with a special interest in ADHD and learning disabilities, academic productivity problems are the hallmark of the disorder. ADHD children are often unable to regulate their behavior without a teacher closely supervising them. Therefore, they often cannot heed formal classroom rules such as raising their hands, remaining quiet and paying attention. In addition, they often fail to complete their work under independent or semi-supervised situations.

Homework proves equally difficult for many ADHD children. Not only is homework a fairly independent task, but it also requires the ADHD child to perform after an entire day of trying to energize himself or herself to regulate behavior so as to follow rules, concentrate and pay attention in school. For parents and ADHD children alike, homework is their nemesis. It creates so much tension and frustration that Gene Conlin, a father I interviewed, called it "a confrontation." Gene explained, "Every night, I used to spend three or four hours yelling at my son until I was red in the face because it took him that long to complete a fifteen minute homework assignment." This experience is not unique to the Conlin family. Many ADHD parents reported similar frustrations.

In general, ADHD children also tend to be disorganized. Not only do they forget to bring the necessary materials to and from school, but they also lack a systematic approach to tasks. They may have difficulty following sequences in four and five step processes. Furthermore, impulsivity often prevents ADHD children from getting all the directions for an assignment, and/or from doing their work carefully. As Dr. Zakreski says, "Children who have difficulty paying attention, organizing and concentrating will not learn efficiently or reliably."

As ADHD children progress through school, many are compromised by this inability to process information reliably and efficiently. Beyond the primary grades, the tasks build on previous assumed skills and become more complex. Dr. Zakreski observes that ADHD children have difficulty with complex behaviors like study skills. He explained that most children acquire study skills when, as younger children, either they are shown techniques by teachers or parents, or they develop techniques on their own. However, ADHD children exposed to the same patterns and models as their non-handicapped peers, do not acquire these skills without very concrete and deliberate instruction. Since study skills are seldom taught in this manner, when asked to read a chapter independently and/or study the material for a test, ADHD children frequently have no idea of where to begin or what information is salient.

Furthermore, a large portion of the ADHD children Dr. Melvin Levine treats have trouble with memory. Though many parents report their children have fantastic memories and can recall particular events in their lives in intricate detail, Dr. Levine labels that episodic memory, which he says is quite different from "the memory needed to memorize a list of vocabulary words, or to remember in April what was learned in Social Studies in October." That type of memory requires the ability to retrieve information. To do that the child has to have a pretty organized mind because he or she first needs to file the information and then be able to find it when asked. Dr. Levine notes, "If you are very disorganized and very impulsive, these traits have a bigger impact the higher the grade in school. No matter how smart you are, it is pretty hard to reason out in what year a particular battle was fought."

These information processing problems also explain why many ADHD children will leave for school in the morning knowing all the answers for a test and return home in the afternoon with a failing grade. According to Dr. C. Keith Conners, Professor of Medical Psychology at Duke University Medical School, "We often see a distinction between what the ADHD child knows and what he or she can produce." Dr. Conners explains that when taking a test, the ADHD student mentally has to organize the material and then produce what he or she knows. Because many ADHD children have difficulty with this skill, Dr. Conners notes that teachers often think the child has a short term memory problem because it appears that the information stored is very fragile and only available for a short time.

However, Dr. Conners believes, the problem is more a function of the ADHD child's inability to focus on the material as it is being retrieved. While this same child will be disorganized on the playground as well, Dr. Conners says that this characteristic will not be as apparent in that setting. "But in school the structure is much tighter and reveals the extent to which he or she is unable to adapt to that structure. Under the proper circumstances, perhaps a Socratic dialogue between the teacher and student, the ADHD child would be able to reveal what he or she knows."

As children advance to the upper grades, they are required to work independently to a large degree. For instance, students may be asked to read an entire chapter and be responsible for knowing and understanding the content in that chapter, often without teacher reinforcement. Dr. Zakreski explains that ADHD children usually have difficulty reading independently because their minds wander. Consequently, they do not assimilate the reading material in a cohesive manner. Instead, they must continually redirect themselves to task and try to pick up the thread of where they left off. As a result, continuity is lost and they do not learn the material efficiently.

Another common problem for many ADHD children is handwriting. Many parents I spoke with reported that teachers frequently complained about the child's messy work. In fact, poor handwriting often compromises the ADHD child's performance. For example, numbers illegibly formed or not arranged carefully in columns will lead to math computation errors.

According to Dr. Levine, there are around four different reasons why an ADHD child might have difficulty with handwriting. First, impulsivity prevents some children from taking special care. Second, to write well, children need to have coordination between the flow of ideas and the flow of motor movements, and in some children, the flow of their ideas is too rapid for their fingers to keep pace. Third, writing is very much a memory task, and the children have to simultaneously remember letter formation, punctuation, grammer, capitalization, vocabulary, directions, and their ideas. Finally, some children have fine motor dyspraxia which means they have trouble knowing which muscles to use and in what particular order to employ them to form the letters. Dr. Levine notes, "It is important to pinpoint which particular pathway of writing difficulty is affecting the child, because it will have bearing on which remediation is used."

So far the learning problems I have described are those that arise primarily from the symptomatology associated with ADHD. These difficulties result in academic productivity problems and in information processing problems, the latter being particularly germane to older age school children required to perform more complex tasks. Clearly, these problems create much difficulty for many ADHD children in traditional school settings. In the next chapter, interventions geared toward helping the ADHD child's academic productivity problems will be addressed.

In addition to the aforementioned learning problems, Dr. Richard Zakreski notes that some ADHD children also have learning disabilities. The most common ones in ADHD children are language processing problems. To process language effectively, people must be able to manipulate the symbols of our language to read and write and spell. According to Dr. Zakreski, these processing problems probably result from the diffuse way language is distributed throughout the cortical areas in our brain. In order to process language efficiently, a lot of areas in our brain have to work in consort. For ADHD children who have difficulty with self-regulation, there is a greater chance for a disruption in the coordination of all the diferent cortical areas required to process language reliably and efficiently.

Think for a minute about how a symphony orchestra produces a piece of music. A conductor leads a group of musicians all of whom have different functions but at times play the same notes and at other times play different notes. A musician who does not play efficiently and who is not able to respond to the conductor's signals can disrupt the entire piece of music.

Now think about language, particularly as it pertains to reading. A child who has neurologically based difficulties with self-regulation will not be able to call all the language musicians into play efficiently. As explained by Dr. Zakreski, reading is a complex behavior built upon a hierarchy of skills beginning with decoding. Perhaps the child has difficulty decoding symbols. Thus, when reading the child may put so much energy into making a reliable association between sound and symbol, that meaning, the second skill, goes by the boards. If the child puts a lot of energy into understanding the words, he or she may not remember the content, or what was read in earlier passages, the third skill. Then, the child may be asked to make inferences based on the reading, the fourth skill. Because he has had so much difficulty with all the prerequisite skills, the child's understanding is very tenuous. Even without language processing difficulties, ADHD children, because they have trouble with organization and sustaining attention, will also evidence performance problems with academic tasks which require complex processing.

Clearly, most ADHD children need some type of modified educational program to compensate for their academic productivity problems and their information processing problems. Dr. Russell Barkley, Professor of Psychiatry and Neurology and Director of Psychology at the University of Massachusetts Medical School, reports that roughly half of the children with ADHD can function in the regular classroom environment provided appropriate classroom management and curriculum implementation modifications are made. Other children whose ADHD significantly impairs their educational performance will require special education and related services. Unfortunately, both regular education and special education help often eludes many ADHD children. "The majority of ADHD children fall through the cracks in the current educational system," according to Dr. Barkley.

He explains, as many parents know all too well, that no adequate educational guidelines exist to thoroughly and efficiently deal with the ADHD child's learning problems. In many states and school districts, ADHD children are excluded from special education services. Furthermore, often teachers and school administrators know very little about the disorder. Dr. Barkley says, "For the most part, the parents of ADHD children have to shop around for the best school district or the best teacher they can find who is willing to be flexible enough to use some of the interventions which work for these children." Fortunately, many teachers and school districts are willing to try to help the ADHD child. But the point here is that the ADHD child's right to a free and appropriate public education should not be relegated to the luck of the draw.

In order to understand why ADHD children fall through the cracks, and why they are often excluded from special education, we need to have a basis of knowledge about the laws currently governing special education. I spoke with Fran Rice, a child education advocate who previously served on the Executive Committee of the National Board of the Learning Disabilities Association, formerly the ACLD. As you might expect, the educational services available to children whose handicapping condition is ADHD are not clearly defined. Otherwise, parents would not have to shop around for sympathetic teachers and school districts.

However, Fran Rice explained that two federal acts, The Education for All Handicapped Children Act, 1975, and Section 504 of the Rehabilitation Act, 1973, do offer protection for ADHD children. When advocating for your child, bear in mind the adage "knowledge is power." The more you know about your rights and your child's rights, the better chance you have to see that he or she receives an appropriate educational program.

Be advised that sometimes negotiating the system can be difficult and tricky, especially because each state has its own equivalent laws to comply with the federal requirements for special education. Parents who are experiencing problems with obtaining a free and appropriate public education for their children might do well to discuss their individual situations with trained advocates or other individuals with knowledge and expertise about the education rights of handicapped children. In the appendix, I have included a brief discussion of legislation under which the ADHD child might receive educational services, along with the names and addresses of some of the agencies which might be able to direct you to trained advocates. ADHD parent support groups might also have such information.

Most parents of ADHD children first seek educational intervention for their child under the aegis of the Education for All Handicapped Children Act (EHA) 1975. In this act, Congress mandated every educational institution in receipt of federal monies to provide a free, appropriate public education designed to meet the individual and unique needs of all handicapped children between the ages of three and twenty-one, and to assure that the rights of handicapped children and their parents or guardians were protected. A free and appropriate public education (FAPE) means that children with handicaps have the right to attend the public school system and to have a meaningful education.

Congress then passed Public Law 94-142, the implementing rules and regulations created to insure that all handicapped children receive a free and appropriate public education as stipulated by the EHA. In addition to protecting the rights of the mentally retarded, deaf and blind, this law also made the same provisions for children with separate handicapping conditions, other health impairments and specific learning disabilities.

As absurd as it may seem, ADHD children are often denied special education services because ADHD is not specifically defined in the EHA and its implementing rules and regulations, PL94-142. In many districts, in order for ADHD children to receive needed interventions, they have to be "blessed" with another disability. Yet Dr. Sally Shaywitz, Associate Professor of Pediatrics at Yale University Medical School and co-author of the report on ADHD given to the National Conference on Learning Disabilities, told me, "In terms of interfering with a child's ability to benefit from an education, ADHD can play a significant role."

It would seem to me that those who would deny special and needed educational services to ADHD children are really doing a great disservice to a significant group of ADHD children whose handicapping condition is such that it seriously impairs the child's ability to benefit from an education. By no means do I intend to cast aspersions on all school districts and all teachers, because many do take a special interest in the educational needs of ADHD children. Those of us fortunate enough to have such districts and teachers are grateful to these people. However, many children are less fortunate and not being served appropriately.

For instance, Hope Clark's son Tom has a 138 I.Q. Because of his symptomatology, Tom is very distractible and disorganized. He scores on grade level in achievement tests, yet in sixth grade, Tom failed three subjects. After a thorough medical and psychological examination at his parents' expense, Tom was diagnosed by a qualified physician as having ADHD. When his mother asked her son's school district to either modify Tom's school program or offer him special education services, she was told that Tom was lazy and that she should withdraw all her support, so that he could learn from the experience of failure. That stupidity is akin to throwing a diamond in the rough down a sewer drain because the stone requires polishing.

As an ADHD child not "blessed" with an additional disability such as dyslexia, Tom falls into the approximately sixty to seventy percent of ADHD children to whom Dr. Russell Barkley refers as being able to function in the regular classroom with a modified program. In the cases where no other learning disability exists, Dr. Richard Zakreski says, "If ADHD children can be helped to produce the work, in many cases their academic adjustment can be like that of their non-handicapped peers." Perhaps if Tom could be helped to produce his work, he might be able to achieve success in the regular classroom, and maybe even in programs for the gifted which certainly would seem to be indicated for a child with a 138 I.Q.

Whether an ADHD child needs special education services or a modified program in the regular education classroom, teachers of students whose handicapping condition is ADHD need to be trained in much the same way parents of these children are trained. First, the teachers need to be educated about the disorder and its ramifications in the home, school and social environments. They need to know the characteristics of students with ADHD, as well as their educational, psychological and social needs. In absence of a clinical diagnosis, teachers should also be instructed in methods of identifying children who display characteristics which might indicate ADHD, so that those children could receive the appropriate diagnostic evaluation.

Such education could take place through school staff in-service programs, recertification programs, and college curricula for teachers in training. For diagnosed ADHD children, teachers can play a vital role in the network of physicians, mental health professionals and parents as part of the multi-modal treatment plan for ADHD children. Teachers also need to be taught techniques and strategies for effectively teaching ADHD students. Some of these interventions will be discussed in the following chapter. In general, currently the only training and/or education teachers receive about ADHD is if their district chooses to offer an in-service on the topic, or if they attend seminars, which some of them do, usually on their own time after school hours.

Understanding your child's rights and your rights is the first step in helping him or her to receive an appropriate education. The next step is knowing how to advocate for your child. As parents, we know our child better than anyone else. We also have a vested interest in his or her well being, and so we are our child's most important advocate. We must work to assure that he or she receives needed services, and at the same time, we need to be certain that our expectations for our child are realistic. As our child's advocate, we need to be assertive, to ask questions, to question answers that do not make sense to us. However, being assertive does not mean being aggressive. As parents of handicapped children, we have to be consistently involved in our child's education. In fact, studies demonstrate that handicapped children with involved parents make the most progress in school.

Being involved with our children's school program is not an easy job. Not only does it require time, effort and energy, but it makes many parents feel intimidated by school personnel. Furthermore, we sometimes worry that if we make requests on behalf of our child, that the school personnel will come to view him or her as that pain-in-the-neck-kid with that pain-in-the-neck-parent. In fact, many of us are afraid our efforts will backfire, and our child will be made to suffer because we are "bugging" school personnel. Because we have rights guaranteed under the law, should our worst fears come true, such situations can be dealt with.

But I am impressed for the most part that schools and teachers really do have the child's best interests at heart. Parents should not be intimidated when they have to speak to school personnel. This is not to say that there are not unreasonable teachers and administrators, just as there are unreasonable parents. Try not to make unreasonable demands. For instance, I know of one parent who felt the school should be responsible for providing her child with after school social activities because he had socialization problems.

Be advised that school personnel can also feel intimidated by parents. Diplomacy goes a long way in avoiding many disputes. When we parents have to meet with school personnel, keeping a good attitude and a courteous demeanor are really important. Sometimes we parents of ADHD children are just so tired and frustrated, we have a hard time maintaining a calm and collected posture. But we really serve our child and ourselves in the most productive way possible when we remain non-confrontational with the school staff.

Though we often think that the teacher should know how to manage our child in school, we need to remember that few teachers have had any formal training in regard to ADHD. Besides, in absence of a diagnosis, often they are equally as frustrated and in the dark as we parents are about why the child behaves poorly or does not perform in school. Thus teachers may make the same false assumptions that we parents might make. That is, he-or-she-could-do-it-if-he-or-she-wanted-to or if-he-or-she-tried-hard-enough. Even when teachers know the child has this disorder, they, too, often feel helpless and confused about how to help. Teachers usually make great students. Rather than complain or get angry, try to work with the teacher to be a problem solver. Give them literature to read about ADHD. Give them any helpful suggestions you may have picked up along the way. Some suggestions are included in the next chapter. Since many ADHD children are served in the regular education classroom, you could even suggest that your district use one of the teacher in-service days to present a program about ADHD to the entire staff, not just the special education staff.

Many parents find meeting with school personnel to aid in the selection process of their child's teachers very productive. Parents of ADHD children, like Jan Lawes and Barbara Chapman, often are heard to say, "My child had a wonderful teacher who really understood him (her) and he (she) did great last year. This year the teacher is not so willing to help and he's (she's) doing rotten." Rather than wait until the school year begins and the child is placed, teacher selection should be made before the end of the previous grade. ADHD children need teachers who are structured and organized but not rigid, and who are patient and willing to take a little extra time to understand the nature of the child, and to make a little extra effort to help the child succeed. The ADHD child's teachers also need to use a lot of encouragement and praise, because, as we know, ADHD children perform well when they are reinforced for appropriate behavior.

Making an appointment with the child's teachers at the beginning of the school year is also a wise move. At this meeting, we parents need to discuss the concerns we have for our child, as well as the child's strengths and weaknesses. We want to encourage team work and let the teachers know that we will support their efforts at home. Suggest frequent and open communication throughout the year, but not just to keep abreast of how the child is doing, or to determine if further interventions are needed. We also want to keep track of any special assignments or projects looming in the future. A parent who approaches a teacher in a non-threatening way, who shares information and tries to be supportive, will be appreciated by most teachers. If your child's teacher resents parental involvement, then the child has not been placed appropriately.

Parents of ADHD children also need to become good record keepers. Guidelines for establishing your child's record are included in the appendix. Basically, you should keep a file on your child and include in it any communication from the school, copies of communication from you to the school, copies of all reports about your child, copies of all report cards and achievement tests scores, and records of any phone calls or meetings including date, time and person or persons with whom you spoke. I also save all my son's school papers until the end of the school year so I can look them over before IEP conferences to identify any problem areas. By keeping good records, should disputes arise, you will have a better chance to protect your rights and your child's rights.

Summary

- Signs and symptoms of ADHD in elementary school-age children may include:

1. inappropriate activity unrelated to task,
2. poor ability to sustain attention and concentrate,
3. difficulty inhibiting impulses,
4. organizational problems,
5. attention-seeking behaviors,
6. low frustration tolerance,
7. low self-esteem,
8. interpersonal difficulties with peers,
9. learning difficulties, particularly under circumstances of partial or no reinforcement.

- ADHD symptoms seriously impair the child's ability to learn. Children are at risk for academic failure.
- Inconsistency of symptoms leads teachers and parents to mistakenly believe the child could do better.
- Academic productivity problems stemming from inability to complete work, disorganization, impulsivity and inability to follow directions are hallmarks of the disorder.
- ADHD children have more difficulty as school tasks build on prerequisite skills and become more complex.
- ADHD children have information processing problems.
- Handwriting is a problem for many ADHD children.
- Most ADHD children need a modified school program.
- Parents need to know their rights and their child's rights to obtain appropriate education for the child.
- The Education for All Handicapped Children Act and its implementing regulations, Public Law 94-142, and Section 504 of the Rehabilitation Act govern the rights of all handicapped children to a free and appropriate public education. See appendix for discussion of how these laws do and do not pertain to ADHD children.
- Both laws dictate criteria for eligibility for services.
- Parents are the child's most important advocate.
- To advocate for your child, a parent must:
  1. know your rights and the child's rights,
  2. be involved in the child's school program,
  3. develop a good working relationship with school personnel, particularly the child's teachers,
  4. have realistic expectations for the child,
  5. make reasonable requests,
  6. communicate regularly with teacher,

7. be a problem solver not a problem maker,
8. be a diplomat,
9. maintain thorough and accurate records.

CHAPTER NINE

The ADHD Child
in the Classroom

David's first eight years of life were not the care-free wonder years we associate with childhood. Instead, David's wonder years were filled with tension, with negativity, with not fitting. But as he entered his ninth year, it was as though he emerged from a chrysalis at peace with himself. David's affect had changed and this once unhappy child who had been described as anhedonic— the inability to experience happiness—now smiled most of the time. He acquired an enthusiasm for life and a sense of humor, but most important, he liked himself. This change I attribute to his early diagnosis, treatment and incredible resiliency. Though the entire family has had to deal with the effects of this disorder, the struggle mostly is borne by David. He is on the front lines every day.

In July 1988, I brought David to the pediatric neurologist for a follow-up visit. After the doctor examined my son, he sat me down in his office and said, "What a wonderful change. You know, I used to worry about the both of you and wonder how you were ever going to make it. David's symptoms were so severe. You should be very pleased."

Well, I was more than pleased. I felt such gratitude and such relief that my little boy's symptoms had stabilized.

But the relief did not come from a sense that David had been cured. By now, I had come to understand that this disorder has no cure. The neurologist also told me that day in his office there would always be new issues to deal with, new problems which would arise. But the doctor knew and I now knew our entire family had the tools to handle them. One of the tools proved to be the ADHD parent support group a few of us formed with the aid of Dr. Burke, our child psychologist. Through this group we helped and encouraged each other to learn how a family can live comfortably with this disorder most of the time.

By no stretch of the imagination did our family walk off into the sunset, hand in hand, a perfect Fifties sit-com family. Coping with ADHD requires a lot of hard work and constant effort. Nor was ADHD our only struggle. Shortly after Jonathan, our younger son, entered first grade, we learned he was dyslexic. As a result of his learning disability, Jon, too, experienced frustration in school. At times, he acted out behaviorally. He made such comments as "I'm stupid." "No one likes me."

Clearly, six-year-old Jonathan needed to have his self-esteem bolstered. His dad and I had to find some avenue where Jonathan could excel which was totally separate from any activity in which David participated. We enrolled him in tennis lessons. At the first lesson, the instructor said, "Put the racket in your right hand, put your left hand over your right, put your left foot forward, then pivot on your right heel and swing the racket."

By the time Jon finished following these commands, he looked like a Haitian contortionist. I did not insist he take another lesson. Instead of tennis, Jon, this dyslexic child who wrote all his letters and words backwards and upside down, decided to write and illustrate stories. By the end of first grade, he had a portfolio. Through the help of special education, he also read on grade level.

In addition to his academic struggles, Jonathan needed to assert himself in the family. For years he watched David command center stage. He accepted his supporting role so passively, it appeared he adapted quite well. In fact, Jon behaved so responsibly, he often seemed like the older brother rather than the younger sibling. But between first and second grade, Jonathan no longer would accept this role of peacemaker. When David tried to monopolize toys, games, Jon's friends and/or family members, Jonathan began to fight back. He has emerged into his own person.

In September 1988, David entered third grade. I assumed his school experience would be as wonderful as the previous year.

But in our district, third graders move to a different school. The teachers in this new school did not know David. They hadn't watched him struggle and grow during his primary school years. Nor did they know his capabilities. They did not know me either. So not only did I have to introduce the teachers to my son, the child with ADHD, I had to introduce them to his mother, the woman who watches her kid like a hawk.

As in previous years, I had to make appointments with his teachers to explain my son's handicap, his strengths and his weaknesses. Despite the fact that I hated this task, experience has taught me that good and frequent communication between home and school is a necessity. This third grade year such communication proved to be crucial. For the most part, David's teachers have been wonderfully supportive.

Children in our district change classes in third grade. They are grouped by ability in math and reading. David had four teachers. Despite the fact that his second grade teachers had great faith in David's ability, the third grade ones gave their own placement tests in early September. Though David's body was present, his mind had not yet fully reported to school. Thus, he did not perform well and was placed in groups below his ability level. David came home from school angry, because as he said, "I did this stuff last year." With David's teacher advocating on his behalf, the school staff was willing to rethink the situation which resulted in a change in placement for him to groups more in keeping with his capabilities.

No fault lies here. Finding the appropriate placement for David is not an easy task. My son's ability is not just a measure of his scores on intelligence or achievement tests. As a child with ADHD, David juggles many balls. So when placing him, we have to make certain he is presented with material commensurate with his ability, but not challenged to the point where he experiences so much frustration that he shuts down or feels badly about himself because he is not achieving. David is a perfectionist who sets very high goals for himself. Innate ability and the ability to perform are often separated by a very fine line.

In this third grade year, though the major battle had ended, new skirmishes developed. David did not want me to be so involved with his school. He resented the extra set of books I kept at home for the times he forgot his homework materials. He did not want the teachers to make any modifications in his program. He just wanted to be like all the other kids. But some of them were calling him "loud mouth." David did not always feel that he fit. My husband and I made special efforts to help David develop some friendships. By the middle of the school year, we often had a house full of boys.

Over the course of time, David's confidence grew to the point that he became less guarded about sharing his feelings with us. He even told my husband and me about goings on in school. The day he came home and said, "Mom, I did something in art today that no one has done in eleven years," admittedly I became a little queasy. I managed to muster some strength and asked, "What was that dear?" To my relief he answered, "I drew a triangle in a triangle." It seemed the art teacher had not encountered too many third grade students who could draw two-dimensional triangles.

In May 1989, when I went to the parent teacher conference, I was non-plussed. His teachers opened the meeting by telling me, "You have some smart kid there. I wouldn't worry about him. He's going to run a corporation some day. He just needs to get through school first."

I always worried that David would fall through the cracks, but this comment reassured me that his teachers had taken the time to get to know my kid and to appreciate him.

And thanks to the results of his treatment, David made great strides at home too. The scales have tipped, and the days when David cannot control his behavior are few. Sure new or unanticipated problems arise. There are times when he does not remember to stop, look and listen before acting on impulse. For example, we went on vacation to an island where farm animals roam freely. David was swimming when suddenly this huge black beast on the beach caught his eye. He excitedly charged out of the water toward the animal. Fortunately, David made a great racket which caught my attention, because the beast he was about to throw his arms around turned out to be a bull who did not appreciate this enthusiastic attention.

But what do bulls know anyway? Both my husband and I have now come to appreciate David's zest for life, his boundless energy, the enthusiasm he brings to tasks which interest him, and the battles he has fought. Though sometimes our son still spins a little, he stays on course, and so do we.

The year I began to write this book, David announced he wanted to be an astronaut. Though I had hoped he would pick a career closer to home, I now felt certain he was not trying to get as far away from me as possible. I even knew he was not playing on my fear of heights and trying to get me riled and scared. When I asked David if he minded that I wrote this story, his eyes lit up and he danced around the room chanting, "Oh wow. I'm going to be famous."

As the manuscript progressed, David stole glances at bits and pieces of the text. He became less than thrilled. He was reading from the earlier parts of the story. What met his eyes was contrary to his emerging sense of self. David was just beginning to feel as though he belonged. He was beginning to believe that he was a pretty terrific kid and worthy of fame.

To think that Mom might make him infamous was not his idea of great literature. Often he came to my desk early in the morning, before I was awake, and penciled comments into the manuscript. Two particularly compelling notations were "Stoopid" and "Why are you writing this junk?" I tried to explain, but David did not seem to understand. When I referred to the toddler as "a monkey on a mother's back," he scribbled, "you're a monkey on your own back." After that, I quietly sat with nine-year-old David and asked him if he would like me to stop writing this book. He quickly and emphatically told me he did want me to write it and then added, "but if you only put the good parts." After a two day pause, he added, "And I want to read it before anybody else does, because I might have to edit it."

I could understand how David felt. He is a gutsy kid. He has had to fight very hard to protect himself in environments which are not always user-friendly. On top of that, I sometimes run too much pass interference. I try to overprotect David which does not help him to feel effective and competent. When I told him I would rather he not sign up for football because I was afraid he might get hurt, David just sighed and said, "Mom, how do you expect me to make the N.F.L. if I don't practice and play?" Who could argue? Today, I know that David will land on his feet.

Other ADHD children and their families are not as fortunate. "I've never felt successful in school," seventeen-year-old Louisa Christianson told me. Louisa's ADHD was not diagnosed until she was sixteen. For most of her academic career, Louisa thought she was dumb. She says she is not motivated by much and hates school "because they don't let you take the classes you're good at." Louisa can't take a test if the classroom door is open. She even gets distracted by her own thoughts.

Louisa is just one of many ADHD children whose school experience has been predominantly negative. Even children diagnosed at earlier ages often feel like failures because they experience such difficulty in the school environment. Ten-year-old John Golding's classmates call him "stupid." One of his teachers told him he was a "daydreamer." His art teacher marked him down a grade on a drawing because she felt he did not try hard enough, yet John's classmates all said that his drawing was better than anyone's picture. John felt he did the best he could. Though that teacher made him angry, John also gets angry with himself because he often knows the correct answers to test questions, but since he is so disorganized and distractible, he usually marks the wrong answer box.

Before his son was diagnosed, Gene Conlin and his wife were advised by the school to take a parenting course. Gene said, "The teacher was convinced that Frank could produce if I exerted my authority as a father and gave him a kick in the pants." The Conlins did take a course and found it helpful, but not for Frank's school performance. When another teacher complained that Frank did not concentrate, did not pay attention, and never finished his work, Gene recalled teachers making similar comments to his own parents. He felt overprotective of his son, explaining, "It was so painful to have people yell at me and discipline me all the time. I thought it was so unnecessary and I did not want Frank to go through all that unnecessary pain. I did not want my son to repeat my life because my life was filled with loneliness, self-doubt, negativity, and the feeling that I just did not fit."

Much of Gene Conlin's frustration rose out of an overwhelming sense that, as in his life, Frank's teachers did not realize Frank wanted to succeed but could not. Gene Conlin is not unusual. Often parents complain that teachers do not seem to understand or acknowledge their child's ADHD problems. But, as Dr. Sam Goldstein, a school psychologist and author of guides for teachers of ADHD children, says, "It is awfully hard to fault the teacher because he or she is a product of the system that educated him or her." Dr. Goldstein points out that regular education teachers, and often special education teachers, do not have any background in basic neurological processes. Universities do not teach them how students learn, or why they learn or why they do not learn.

Dr. Goldstein maintains that teachers need to identify the skills needed for a child to succeed in their class. Having done so, they then need to identify which children are missing those skills and provide a range of interventions to assist the child deficient in these skills. Like their non-handicapped peers, ADHD children, Dr. Goldstein says, need to focus on relevant stimuli, to sustain attention, to maintain a reasonable level of emotional control and to inhibit bodily movement. When presented with a student who looks perfectly normal, who has ability, who performs sometimes but not always, and who appears to choose to misbehave, understandably teachers draw false conclusions. Nonetheless, when teachers are educated about ADHD, its effects on the child's learning, and ways to intervene, ADHD children will have a better chance at achieving success.

ADHD children should not have to go through school experiencing frustration and failure. Those ADHD children who primarily have academic productivity problems and information processing problems can be helped to achieve success in school through interventions which manipulate the learning environment. According to Dr. Richard Zakreski, a clinical psychologist in private practice who specializes in the treatment of ADHD children, their ideal school program would include smaller class sizes, more individualized instruction, motivational programs using materials of high interest to the child, and daily school to home scholastic productivity and behavior charts. In the cases indicated, special education services and medication to alter the child's abnormal biology also prove helpful.

Admittedly, smaller class sizes and individualized instruction are not generally possible in regular classrooms where teachers have twenty-plus children. Besides, ADHD children come in all sizes and shapes. Some ADHD children can perform in the regular classroom setting with teacher assistance. Some might need resource room assistance for part of their day for support in their areas of weakness. Other ADHD children will need to have extensive modifications made in the curriculum, particularly those who have multiple disabilities. This group of children may need to be in a self-contained classroom where the teacher-pupil ratio is quite small and the instruction is of a highly specialized nature.

Given that variations in individual needs exist, still for many ADHD children, the regular classroom environment can be manipulated to help them achieve success. Often, placing the child with a teacher who can deal with the youngster's special needs makes a huge difference in how the child feels about himself or herself, and how he or she performs. A good teacher for an ADHD child is one who understands the nature of the disorder, who appreciates the child's struggles, and who welcomes parental involvement. Equally important is the manner in which the teacher behaves toward the ADHD child, or what I call the teacher's affect. After speaking with teachers, parents and professionals, and reading various materials, I have compiled the following suggestions for ways in which a teacher might interact with an ADHD student.

In general, the ADHD child does best with a teacher who is loving and kind and has a supportive attitude. Often physical contact, such as a pat on the back or a hand on the shoulder, lets the child know the teacher cares for him or her. After recognizing the child's strengths and weaknesses, teachers must be firm and consistent in requiring the youngster to perform tasks commensurate with his or her ability while at the same time providing lots of encouragement. Ridicule should never be used. ADHD children can try anyone's patience, but teachers who remain calm, who do not show anger, irritation or rejection toward the child, and who show him or her respect, will cultivate a classroom atmosphere where he or she feels safe.

The ADHD child's learning environment needs to be as free from distractions as possible. In general, the ADHD child's desk should be close to the teacher, and away from doors, windows, heaters and air conditioners. Seating the ADHD child in the front of the room and next to a well-organized student also proves helpful. Most ADHD children will also need assistance to keep their desks neat and organized so that necessary materials can be readily located. Desk tops should contain only the materials required for the task at hand.

The style of teaching can have a strong impact on the academic productivity of ADHD children. They require an organized teacher who provides a highly structured environment where expectations are specifically stated and understood. Many ADHD children fail to start or complete work because they do not know what is required. When giving directions or instructions, the teacher is advised to use clear and concise directions, to establish eye contact, and to assign only one task at a time. Complex directions need to be broken down into smaller steps. The teacher will probably also have to help the child organize his or her work.

Many ADHD children do not ask questions when they do not understand the material being taught or the requirements of a particular assignment. Instruction needs to be very concrete, and the teacher must determine if the child understands the lesson. Furthermore, before the ADHD child begins to work, the teacher needs to make certain he or she understands the demands of the task. Once a task is assigned, the teacher may need to help the child structure the task in a step-by-step manner. The teacher might also have to redirect the child to the task when he or she has difficulty completing it. ADHD children tend to take longer to complete their work carefully, so sometimes they may need more time than their non-handicapped peers.

ADHD children frustrate easily. Rather than push the child to the point of frustration, at times the teacher may need to reduce the amount of work assigned, or alter the manner in which the work is done. For instance, some children have such difficulty with writing that their teachers cut down on the amount of written work, or allow them to dictate their written assignments to their parents to write down, or to use the computer. Some teachers reduce the amount of problems or worksheets the ADHD child has to do in class or for homework.

In some cases, the manner in which the ADHD child is tested also needs to be modified. As Dr. Zakreski explains, tests should be a measure of what the child knows. If a child has difficulty, for instance, putting his or her thoughts into writing, or using correct punctuation or spelling, perhaps oral tests would be better. The point is to allow the child to demonstrate his or her knowledge of the material in a way that assesses subject matter proficiency, rather than the child's ability to take tests.

Under the guidance of a thoughtful teacher who tried different strategies to help her son, the mother of Steven White reported that Steven, whose favorite book was *Leo the Late Bloomer,* bloomed. He earned straight A's in second grade. In third grade, he floundered. At the mid-year conference, the teacher reported to his mother that almost every day, twenty minutes after she had handed out an assignment, Steven's page was blank. Both the teacher and his mother told Steven that he simply had to do his work. One day after the conference, Steven came home from school teary-eyed. "Mommy, I'm trying. I just don't know what to do." Now in fourth grade, Steven is receiving the necessary support, and once again, he is achieving.

So far, the modifications I have described are fairly simple. Albeit, they require extra time and effort on the part of the teacher, but they do produce positive results. These fall into the category of teacher-centered interventions. According to Dr. Sam Goldstein, many teachers get frustrated because they do not see any long term changes in the child's performance when they stop using these types of interventions. But as Dr. Goldstein explains, teacher-centered interventions manipulate the environment. They do not change the child. Still, Dr. Goldstein says they are very helpful to the ADHD student and their success should be determined while the intervention is occurring. After all, we cannot cure ADHD. We can only manage the child's symptoms.

In addition to these techniques, Dr. Zakreski notes that often ADHD children need behavioral interventions to help them compensate for their short attention spans, disorganization and inability to complete their assignments. He strongly advocates the use of daily school charts which are both a teacher-centered and child-centered intervention. There are many different style school charts.

But Dr. Zakreski believes a well designed school charting system will have the following components: The child should know ahead of time what behavior is expected. He or she has the choice to decide to meet or not meet the expectation. Feedback is then provided about how well the child met the expectation. Finally, the child receives consequences, either good or bad, depending on how well he or she met the expectations. Usually the consequences are meted out by the parents, but school based responses can also be used.

Sample school charts are included in the appendix. The charts not only provide the child with feedback about the child's school performance, but charts also are an effective way for parents and teachers to work as a team, and to communicate frequently.

Besides the valuable feedback charts offer, Dr. Zakreski explains, school charts serve other useful functions. First, they help the child to overcome the characteristic inattentiveness associated with the disorder by providing motivation to attend to task and complete work. Desirable outcomes in the form of rewards which have meaning to the child (e.g., extended bedtime) are tied to work completion which may not hold much intrinsic value for him or her. For instance, a primary grade child who finishes all his/her seatwork on a given day might earn a trip to the park. An elementary aged boy might opt for a pack of baseball cards.

Second, the school chart helps organize the child. Most of these charts include a space for the child or teacher, if need be, to record homework assignments. The child, preferably with teacher supervision, can then use the chart as a guide to gather the necessary homework materials before leaving school at the end of the day. Once at home, the parents review the chart to check the daily progress and that evening's assignments. Since forgetting to bring completed homework back to school happens quite frequently with ADHD children, he or she, with the help of the parent, can use the chart to reorganize his/her book bag so the completed work, perhaps placed in a special folder, gets back to school.

Besides teacher-centered interventions and charting, medication often proves to be another valuable intervention for ADHD children. In fact, according to Dr. Zakreski, the use of medication has been associated with improved academic performance though not necessarily with improved learning. This is not to say that all ADHD children should be given medication. As explained earlier, this decision must be made by a competent physician on an individual case basis. However, by altering the child's abnormal biology, often the ADHD symptoms which interfere with his or her ability to perform appropriately in school are lessened.

Dr. Zakreski believes that before an ADHD child takes medication, a chart system should be used for a few weeks to a month to assess what he or she is able to do on his or her own when provided with a program designed to motivate, structure and organize the child. Once this baseline is established, it can be used to guide the decision about whether to use medication and, later, to evaluate its impact. Should medication be warranted, Dr.

Zakreski says, "some type of rating scale such as the Conners Teacher Symptom Questionnaire should be used to document the effects of the medication and what dosages prove most effective."

Though medication can be an enormous benefit to many ADHD children, some caution needs to be observed so that the child is not given the wrong message about the medication. First, we do not want the ADHD child to develop the belief that the medicine alone is making him or her function appropriately. These children need to know that medication is only a support and that they have control over their behavior. Second, teachers should not publicly ask these children whether they have taken their medication that day. Not only does such an insensitive question single the child out and humiliate him or her, it also verifies to the youngster that he or she is different from peers and is incompetent.

One of the nicest aspects of summer vacation for many parents of ADHD children is that they do not have to think about homework. Without question, this task has driven many parents of ADHD children and the children themselves to utter desperation. Donna Rothman told me that night after night her son Peter sat in the kitchen chair spinning around while she tried to help him get his work done. She would say, "Peter, pick up your pencil." But he would just spin some more. Then she'd plead, "Peter, please pick up your pencil and just write the answer down. You just told me the answer. Now write it down." When the interchange reached the yelling point, sometimes Peter would scream back and other times he would be passively defiant. Donna would get to the point where she started to shake. Then she gave up and told Peter to pack up his books. Many days he went to school without his work completed.

Dr. Russell Barkley utilizes the following interventions to modify the homework plan and thereby assist the ADHD child, his or her parents and teachers with the homework burden. The modifications Dr. Barkley recommends depend on the child's age and attention span, but these are his general guidelines.

First, he believes the amount of homework assigned should not be excessive, but rather appropriate to the child's ability to attend to task. Thus, he suggests a meeting with the teacher to reduce the amount of homework and to determine if it is legitimate homework and not uncompleted classwork. He explained that the

ADHD child should not be asked to make up in a few hours at home the work that he or she could not get done during the majority of the school day.

Second, once the homework assignment is of an appropriate length, Dr. Barkley teaches the parent to break the work into smaller units. Thus, the child works for a period of time, takes a break, and then comes back to finish. The units of work time depend again on the age and attention span of the child. A timer is set during the work period so that the child knows there is a limit to the amount of time he or she has to complete the task. If the child completes the work on time, he or she earns tokens (chips, points or stars, etc.) which can be used as currency and applied toward a particular reward, such as a trip for pizza or extra television time. If the child does not finish on time, he or she loses tokens.

During the first few weeks of this homework program, Dr. Barkley says the goal is to increase productivity. Once the child meets this goal by completing homework assignments, the program then focuses on accuracy. At first, the child is rewarded when seventy percent of the homework is done accurately. After that, the accuracy standard is increased in slight increments until the child receives an accuracy rate of eighty-five percent.

In addition, some children also receive a checklist to keep alongside their homework. This checklist offers a step-by-step procedure for the child to recheck his homework. For instance, the child would be redirected to look over the instructions for an assignment, reread the action words, and then check to see that the directions were followed correctly. By the way, in keeping with the ADHD child's positive response to structure and routine, a specific place and time should be established for the homework task.

With adolescents, Dr. Barkley also modifies the homework plan. However, he notes that they have longer attention spans than younger children and therefore can do more homework. Still, it needs to be legitimate homework and not unfinished classwork. Timers are also used, but they are set for six periods so the child can move around between assignments and not get frustrated or bored. The checklist is individualized for each child. Again, the list directs him or her to double check the work and make sure the directions are correctly followed.

Dr. Barkley also suggests that with older age children, a second set of books be kept at home, because in junior and senior high school, both their lockers and thinking are not terribly organized. Consequently, often necessary materials are left at school. Dr. Barkley acknowledges that most teenagers are not thrilled with these interventions, but as he says, "our goal is not so much happiness as success." With both younger and older children, parents are asked to check the completed assignments against the assignment sheet to make certain he or she has accomplished the tasks given.

The systematic approach to homework can work for many parents. But Dr. Barkley says, "At least a third of the parents of ADHD children are not good at supervising homework. They might be equally as temperamental, impulsive, quick to upset, or perhaps overstressed by other circumstances." In these cases, he suggests that parents use a tutor whenever possible. Dr. Barkley notes that tutors can be arranged through direct hiring, particularly of a special education teacher interested in tutoring. Additionally, many areas of the country have tutorial centers. For children who go to a school aftercare program, homework tutoring can be done there. Finally, Dr. Barkley has even placed children with teachers who stay after school to do paperwork. Though these teachers do not necessarily tutor, the child is at least afforded a structured environment in which to work.

Dr. Barkley also acknowledges that not all teachers will be amenable to modifying the homework program. In those instances, he informs the teacher that "the child is unlikely to get that degree of work done." He then instructs the parent to write a note to the teacher when in their judgment the amount of work on a given day is too great. In these cases where the teacher for whatever reason does not believe the homework program should be modified, sometimes the teacher's supervisor needs to be called upon to arbitrate. Sometimes the child needs to be placed in a different classroom. And, says Dr. Barkley, "sometimes the parents have to move to a better school district."

When I was a teacher in training, a popular poster found in many classrooms read, "Give me a fish and I eat for a day. Teach me to fish and I eat for a lifetime." Dr. Zakreski believes "teaching ADHD children study skills is a wise investment." Often these children will need the help of a resource room teacher in developing study skills because, unlike their non-handicapped peers, ADHD children do not pick up these complex skills without highly concrete, simplified, individualized and supervised instruction. With the help of a special study skills program, most ADHD children will be able to learn how to organize a book report or an essay and how to study content for the various subject areas.

In addition to the above mentioned interventions which have been proven to help the ADHD child succeed in school, Dr. Goldstein notes that there are also some child-centered interventions which might be useful. However the use of such interventions and the type of intervention used depend on the child involved. As explained by Dr. Goldstein, the following child-centered interventions attempt to alter the child's cognitive processes. For instance, when faced with a problem to solve, ADHD children, because they are impulsive and do not think a situation through, will often make the wrong choices in solving that problem. So the child might be taught a problem solving strategy whereupon he or she learns to identify the problem, think it through, identify the possible options to solve it, and then base a course of action on this carefully planned approach. The problem with cognitive training strategies, however, is that the kids tend to utilize them effectively under controlled circumstances, such as in the resource room, but then do not generalize the approach to all tasks.

Another child-centered intervention which Dr. Goldstein finds interesting is teaching children to monitor themselves through the use of tracking. For example, he or she might be given an audio tape which gives off a random beep. When the child hears the beep, he/she marks a chart to note whether he/she was on task. Dr. Goldstein reports, in the research literature, tracking has been documented to be an effective intervention in the setting where the child is being cued with the beep or whatever monitoring device is used. However, tracking does not generalize well to non-controlled settings.

Many ADHD children go through life feeling as though they do not fit. And yet, as parents and teachers, we do have strategies which can help the ADHD child feel a sense of belonging, of success. ADHD children can be helped to achieve in school. They do not have to go through life as the kid with potential who never made it. A Zen master once said, "To give your sheep or cow a large, spacious meadow is the way to control him." But ADHD children when given a large, spacious meadow wander aimlessly, and as their parents and teachers, we cannot leave them to their own devices. Since ADHD children have such a hard time fitting into the environment, we have to change the environment to fit the child. The school environment can be successfully adapted to meet the needs of the ADHD child.

Summary

- ADHD children can be helped to experience success in school.
- School personnel need to be educated about the disorder and how it affects the child's ability to learn.
- Teachers and parents need to communicate and work as a team.
- ADHD children need to be placed in academic programs suited to their individual needs. Many ADHD children will function successfully in the regular classroom with modifications. Others may require resource room assistance and a small percentage need highly specialized instruction in self-contained classrooms.
- Interventions include:
  1. manipulating the environment by modifying teaching style, methods of instruction, and physical placement of the child,
  2. use of school charts,
  3. modifying task requirements both in class and home-work,
  4. use of medication,
  5. developing a formal homework program,
  6. teaching study skills,
  7. use of cognitive training strategies.

CHAPTER TEN

ADHD in the Adolescent and Adult

As my son David enters his second decade of life, I once again feel the optimism I had when this newborn child came into the world. The early diagnosis and treatment of his Attention-deficit Hyperactivity Disorder have paved the way for David to have a near normal, happy and well-adjusted life. I do not mean to imply that problems do not exist. As David meets new challenges, faces greater demands, his ADHD symptoms flare. Furthermore, how our family, a system of reciprocal emotional relationships, responds to the stresses and strains of ordinary and extraordinary times also affects David. All problems considered, knowing about this disorder and how to effectively live with ADHD have helped the entire family.

For David Sr. in particular, our son's diagnosis has been a blessing in disguise. My husband did not view young David's behavior to be out of the ordinary. To the contrary, David Sr. often commented that our son behaved much better than he himself had as a child. For many years, David Sr. thought of himself at worst as a "bad seed" and at best as "just not good enough." But never until the diagnosis of our son did Dad realize that he, too, had been at the mercy of the symptoms of ADHD.

By the age of ten, David Sr.'s life was darkened by a steady stream of frustration and failure. In elementary school, he could not concentrate, had difficulty following instructions, persisted in doing the first thing that came to his mind, and could seldom sit still. Yet at times, he would "ace" a test which led everyone to believe that he just did not apply himself. Though most adults viewed him as polite, well-mannered and articulate, problems with peers proved to be a constant source of disappointment.

My husband's academic and social problems stayed with him into adolescence. He continued to show poor judgment and never really thought about the consequences of his actions until he landed in the thick of trouble. Sometimes his impulsive actions were viewed as just the exuberance of youth. Yet, most times he felt remorse and bewilderment about what might possess him to behave so poorly. Nonetheless, his difficulties led to harsh consequences. By his teenage years, David Sr.'s sense of self hit an all time low and he always felt depressed.

In early adulthood, David Sr. was still immature. He wanted immediate gratification and often felt "bored" with life in general. He changed jobs and relationships frequently. Many times his significant others questioned why this nice, capable guy did not live up to his potential. Now, in his mid-forties, David Sr. has an answer. The following pages are his story as he told it to me:

Elementary school is a blur, but I do remember that my parents moved a lot and I never attended the same school for any substantial period of time. I can remember not grasping what was going on in class. As early as kindergarten, I got into trouble for doing things like walking on tables, wandering off during recess, having problems with the other kids. I remember being unhappy when I had to go to school and I used to stall by not eating my breakfast. School was a fearful place for me. I felt scared by the size of the place and the authoritative teachers who disciplined me because they had to, I guess. I knew I didn't do well and did not like feeling that humiliation. I got left back in kindergarten.

Life at home was not much better. Even as a real young kid I got into a lot of trouble. I actually remember playing with matches and accidentally lighting some curtains on fire in my mother's room when I was five. In that same house I also pushed my older sister through a glass door which cut her wrists and scarred her. I never meant to do any harm. For some reason, I either did not or was not able to operate within the rules. I felt very much like an outsider, even in my own family. I was very lonely.

My two sisters were successful students and people. I was the boy with a lot of promise who was going to be a late bloomer. In fourth or fifth grade, my parents sent me to some special classes after school for reading and writing. I had to spend hours writing on a blackboard to try and improve my penmanship.

In junior high school, my good experiences were few and far between. How afraid I was of the teacher determined whether I pretended to pay attention. With a teacher who cut any slack, I behaved like a real wise guy trouble/maker. Some teachers hated my guts because as soon as they turned their backs I threw something. I usually behaved that way with the teachers who gave me no encouragement.

But I did do well with some teachers. They understood me as being a sharp kid and allowed me to express the things I knew. And I knew a lot. My seventh grade geography teacher was a jazz buff who always hummed jazz songs in class. One day he said, "Does anyone know what song that was?" Of the entire class, I was the only kid who knew it. I not only knew that song, I knew as much about jazz as the teacher. From that day on, he and I talked jazz. We developed a rapport and I did pretty well for a couple of marking periods, but I could not sustain the effort.

During the time I did perform well in his class, that teacher realized I had a lot going for me. So I had a good experience with him and with a few other teachers as I went along. But for the most part, I met with alienation, with comments like, "Why aren't you more like your sisters?" "Why don't you try harder?" "You're bright, but you're just lazy."

I have a short attention span. In those days, unless something really interested me, my attention span was horribly short. I knew the batting averages of every baseball player, and every singer and song on the charts. I did not necessarily have an interest in the things other people liked, but still I could sit and study those things that interested me for a long time and understand them. To this day, if anything I don't have a terrific interest in goes on longer than a short period of time, I'm lost. That holds true from cocktail party conversation to lectures. I can tune in with the best of them for the short haul, but I cannot stay with it.

During junior high school, my group of friends and I began to get in trouble. This group I hung around with didn't have any wimps. It didn't have any Rhodes Scholar types either. We use to let the air out of tires, and rip antennas off cars. We even went as far as to break into the houses of people we knew. We'd find a window or door that could be opened and raid the refrigerator.

We never took more than a can of Readi-whip. I never thought about the consequences. It just seemed like fun.

Eventually the police caught up with us. No charges were pressed. But the embarrassment deterred me from ever doing those things again. We lived in a small neighborhood, so everyone knew what I had done. My parents moved to another community shortly after that.

In this new school, my problems with studies persisted. Though I was basically a terrible student and a discipline problem, I did cultivate some friends who were good students and athletes. I wanted to be an athlete, too, but I was afraid I would fail, and afraid I would succeed. I had no idea what to do with success. I lived a kind of double life that eighth grade year. In school I hung around with the president of the student council and dressed well. My after school friends barely made the fringe of acceptability.

During eighth grade, I spent many long periods sitting in classrooms without the vaguest idea of what was going on. Most times, this confusion concerned me. I remember being fearful because I was failing, but did not know what I could do about it. I didn't think I was dumb, but I began to believe that I just did not want to succeed. I spent so much time worrying about why I didn't want to succeed that I became a nervous wreck and very depressed. One marking period, my sister forced me to work and I wound up getting very good grades. Of course, this said to all the teachers and my parents, "You can do it if you want to." But without my sister's help, I slipped back into my old ways and left to my own devices, I just did not get the work done. I had to go to summer school that year.

Around this time, I began lying to my parents a lot. I think that in the beginning I lied because it seemed easy to do and my parents never challenged me much. My lies were really exaggerations of how I did in school. As I got older my exaggerations became more elaborate. For example, whenever we moved, I told the new kids what life was like in the previous city. I would tell them I had been a star athlete or that I got into a fight with another kid and inflicted serious damage. That kept the new kids at a distance. And I wanted things that way because I knew that I had lied about how successful I was and knew damn well that if someone hung around me long enough he would find out that my story was not true.

While my classmates didn't like me much, adults and older kids did. I think maybe they saw me as bright and appealing which are things kids don't necessarily see. I had a job as a bat boy for a minor league baseball club in the town where we lived. The players let me tag along when they went out socially. I loved that. Being a bat boy was ironic because I got cut from little league my first time out.

When I entered ninth grade, even though I had done so poorly in school, people still thought I was college material. In those days, you were either in college prep or dummy classes. So at that point I had mainly college prep courses, but I also had a few dummy courses because I couldn't pass subjects like basic algebra. I hated Monday mornings. They meant school. I only got by because of some benevolent teachers.

After ninth grade, my parents decided to put me in private school. As a requirement for acceptance, I had to start again as a freshman. I bombed out of that second rate prep school, and then went back to public high school. That public school had a lot of tough actors, and I had my usual problems, but I was happier there than I had ever been anywhere else. I made some friends. My football playing improved to the point that I showed real promise. The teachers did not ask much from me, or any of the students for that matter. Though I didn't do much academically, they passed me. I actually got a few C's and a B or two.

While at this school, I did not set the world on fire, but I was acceptable. Once again, I was living almost a dual life. My girl friend went to a prestigious private school, so when she was home, I turned my belt from the side to the front, buttoned my shirt, and went to see her. With my friends I dressed punk. With my coach, I was a different way. I just was not the same with anybody.

Meanwhile, my father was worried about how I would ever get into college. Somebody suggested to him that I needed to go to this school where they used a lot of discipline, straightened out kids with problems and got them into college. So I changed school for the millionth time and went to this place that was just short of being a military school. I had a terrible year there and did not go back.

From there, I went to another second rate prep school. That

environment was not too demanding. I played football and actually made all-state that year. I didn't do any studying, but two months shy of turning twenty, I actually graduated from this place. Still, I had a lot of sleepless nights because I certainly shouldn't have passed. I even went into a couple of final exams and didn't bother to look at the questions. But they passed me, probably because I had been accepted to a college for my football ability. Not too many kids from that school got accepted to college. Needless to say, I was not at all prepared for college and had serious academic problems. I left as soon as football season ended.

I felt very depressed, empty and afraid, like the jig was up. I had no idea what would happen to me or where I would end up in life. I tried some different things and nothing panned out and I felt more and more frustrated. I considered enlisting in the service, but I knew I didn't really want to do that, so I joined the reserves. For active duty, I played football. I didn't have to go to boot camp so I just slept, drank and chipped a little paint for the rest of my time. Back then I thought I had pulled a great coup, but now I wish I had gone through the regular program, because I didn't learn anything that the other guys did.

After active duty, I got a job selling advertising. My boss thought I seemed like a nice, bright guy but so unsure of myself and always uptight. Still, he liked my work and advanced me. My father, however, got a lot of good feedback and I got panicky. I felt so afraid that somebody would ask me to do something I couldn't and that I would fall flat on my face. Even though I had a job, a car, I had no confidence and didn't feel good about myself. So I decided to quit and move to the West Coast.

I had a similar experience there. My life was a farce. When I decided to leave my new job and move back east, my boss told me the same thing I'd heard before. "It's too bad you're leaving because it seems like you're at the point where you understand what we want and you're doing a good job." But I never felt a sense of permanence. Instead, I always felt like this good stuff is gonna pass and then what. I always worried about tomorrow.

Then I reached a point where I tired of dodging bullets. All the time I felt my life had no purpose, that it would always be painful, and that I would never be able to keep fooling everybody. I was at the point of totally bagging it when somehow, around the age of thirty, I got into counseling. Some of that helped, though I never felt like I really had a good sense of why I was such a mess.

But I did start to realize that I was succeeding somewhat in life. I think slowing down and maturing helped me to see that I had actually been doing better than I thought. I built on that realization a bit. I have always had a competitive nature and a high energy level. Where at times those traits had been destructive, they turned into positive factors for me. I had some more success, and like anything else, success leads to success. Even before I had a real sense of myself and knew that I had problems which were not of my own making that caused many things to be difficult for me, I started to get better.

Between the ages of thirty and forty, I made real strides in life. Though I changed jobs a lot, each move meant more responsibility and improved salary. The year I turned thirty-three, I got married, and in addition to my son from my first marriage, I had two more boys. Finally, I felt part of a family.

When my son David started to have his difficulties, I had a hard time believing he had a problem. Maybe one of the manifestations of this condition is not believing it exists or denying it. For as long as I could remember, there was always a lot of noise in my head. But I thought this was normal. I always thought of ten things at a time instead of one and could never focus. But I didn't know that made me different than anyone else. Whenever I got something right, it was always a great relief. You know, "Boy, I got through that," or "I hope I don't have to do that again."

I knew that my son and I had a bond of similarity and that many of the problems he had were like the ones I'd had. But when I had to learn about ADHD and go to professionals with David, I began to realize that maybe this life of fear and inability to get with the program and do what everybody else was doing might have been caused by some reason other than the fact that I'm a no good person.

I consider myself fortunate. I have had some success and been able to build on it. I think a lot of people with ADHD or similar conditions maybe pass the point where they are going to have success and then go down hill. Though I believe I have to work harder than many other people, I also know now that I have an edge. I know my strengths and how to play them. I'm driven less by what others expect of me and more by what I feel is right for me. I'm able to accept the fact that I have plusses and minuses and don't feel defensive about the minuses the way I did most of my life. I am able to bounce back from setbacks a lot faster and without going into a tailspin. Things are pretty good for me today. I feel optimistic.

I realize now that I am a capable person. I have talent. I'm not afraid to take chances or try new things. I think I've become a very reliable person and I've been able to establish relationships. I feel good about myself as a person and as a parent. So I'm not so sure ADHD is a handicap for me today. The people I know who have this condition have superior traits. They tend to be bright, energetic people.

What I want to impart to other people and what I try to get across to my son David is that you can channel your energies in a positive way. If you want to be successful and happy, you may have to try harder and delve deeper, but I think ultimately this struggle is a plus because you learn more about yourself. I think most people go through life without really knowing themselves. Learning about my weak points and my blind sides has been positive. Life can be structured around them.

Though I had always been taught that such things could be overcome, I now know that I can't overcome all my weak points, so I'm a lot better off recognizing them and taking steps to minimize their effects. Many people with ADHD have been very successful in life, despite their problems. What I try to tell my son is that there is no reason to be discouraged about this condition.

Whenever I told people that my son had Attention-deficit Hyperactivity Disorder, invariably they asked, "Is this ADD-thing something new?" Well, as my husband's story illustrates, generations of children with ADHD have passed through the stages of life never quite knowing why they had so much trouble or why they underachieved. Thanks to more public awareness and more recognition by the medical and mental health communities, ADHD children are being diagnosed and offered treatment. As a result, their ADHD parents are also learning for the first time that they were not problem children, but rather children with a problem.

ADHD is generally believed to be a genetically transmitted condition. Though it is not always passed directly from parent to child, the incidence of an ADHD child having an ADHD parent is common. Sometimes, the similarity between them is uncanny. Joe Curran, one father I spoke with, has never been diagnosed with ADHD. But he told me, "When I read the neurologist's and psychologist's reports about my son, all I had to do was change the name of the patient, and they described me as a kid exactly. Then, when a note on a report card came home from my son's teacher that matched word for word one of my report cards at the same age and the same grade level, I knew my school problems had been related to ADHD."

At one time ADHD had been considered to be a self-limited disorder which meant, like an ill-wind, it would blow away with puberty. Today researchers know for an estimated one to two thirds of the children with this disorder, ADHD symptoms are carried into adolescence and adulthood. As explained by Dr. C. Keith Conners, Professor of Medical Psychology and Director of the ADHD Clinic at Duke University Medical School, "kids go through phases of this disorder in which the intensity of it may be more apparent. For example, they often have a terrible time in the early years when they first go to school. They might settle down a little, but then suddenly as they go to junior high school, the rules of the game change and they become disoriented again."

Furthermore, Dr. Conners notes that as physiologic developmental changes occur, where before these children had little sense of self, they now begin to experience internal states. "The ADHD adolescents I talk to are full of fear and anxiety which I believe have been accumulated over time. They find they're in a heck of a mess because in school they have not been able to learn."

ADHD adolescents have good reason to feel so anxious. According to Dr. Sam Goldstein, a certified school psychologist, "The American education system is designed with the best interests of the ADHD adolescent at the bottom of the line." He explains that in junior high school, ADHD adolescents are expected to have more internal responsibility which they don't have. They experience even more trouble operating within the system because now they have seven teachers and must get from class to class with the appropriate materials. Because they are in a larger system where their teachers are responsible for one hundred plus children in the course of a day, the undiagnosed ADHD adolescent has to be "a real screw up" in order to be identified. By the high school years, Dr. Goldstein reports that research data suggests that eighty percent of kids with histories of ADHD are behind at least one year in one basic academic subject.

As a result of her difficulties negotiating within the junior high school setting, as an eighth grader, Christine McLean's ADHD did get diagnosed. Chris is adopted. Her mother Sally explained to me that she and her husband did not have any information about their daughter's biological background. Chris's biological mother also had been adopted.

Interestingly, Dr. Zakreski reports that research studies indicate the rate of ADHD in adopted children is four times higher than among non-adopted children. The McLeans had no idea why Chris, as a younger child, was such an emotional and impulsive little girl. However, Sally McLean reported that Chris's serious school problems did not begin until she got into junior high school. When Chris was faced with the task of getting from class to class and keeping track of her belongings, she fell apart. She also started to "pick the wrong kind of friends," her mother told me.

By the time undiagnosed and/or untreated ADHD children reach junior and senior high school, the cumulative effects of the disorder take a heavy toll. In addition to feelings of depression, they may present with problems associated with Conduct Disorder. Dr. Conners says that secondary problems are hard to disassociate from the primary ADHD problem. He notes that ADHD teenagers are often aggressive because they have developed a lot of anger over their failure to adapt to the home, school and social environments. Consequently, the ADHD adolescents he observes are often "angry, defeated and demoralized to the point where they openly rebel or get in trouble."

Dr. Conners notes that superficially an ADHD adolescent will often appear to have Conduct Disorder or Behavior Disorder. But he says, "if you take the history carefully, you'll see the antecedents to their behavior patterns are the impulsive, restless, inattentive, poor learning style culminating in rejection and rebellion of the things around them."

Some ADHD adolescents develop a pattern of lying and stealing. Dr. Conners explains that all kids lie occasionally. However, he observes that some ADHD kids appear to continually lie because they always get themselves in situations where they feel the need to cover up for something they did without thinking. Sometimes, Dr. Conners says, ADHD adolescents will also steal something because they are immediately attracted to it, but afterwards, they realize they were wrong.

Dr. Conners strongly believes that these behaviors in ADHD adolescents are very different from an antisocial behavior disorder pattern in which deeds are more calculated and premeditated. He said, "ADHD kids are not sociopaths. They make a lot more mistakes and get into a lot more trouble, but this behavior comes more from an inability to restrain themselves than out of calculated wantonness. Parents need to understand that the ADHD kid is not a bad kid."

Parents also need to be aware of the risks associated with the disorder for adolescents. According to Dr. Russell Barkley, a noted ADHD researcher, the risk of car accidents is three to four times higher for ADHD teenagers, so parents might want to postpone the youngster's acquisition of a driver's license or supervise the use of the car much more than they would do otherwise. Children with ADHD are more likely to begin smoking and using alcohol at earlier ages than peers, so parents need to monitor their comings and goings carefully. The risk of suicide, though very low among ADHD teenagers, is nonetheless higher than that of non-ADHD children.

Jean Bramble, a case worker at Primary Children's Medical Center in Salt Lake City, is also concerned that "raging adolescent hormones combined with the drives to be social and accepted by peers, the use of alcohol and the characteristic impulsivity are a set up for unplanned pregnancy in ADHD teenagers." She believes parents need to be vigilant and involved with their ADHD teenager's sex education.

The reason why ADHD adolescents face these risks is understandable. Dr. Goldstein notes that by the teenage years, "If you have ADHD, you are at greater risk because you've gotten a lot more quit it, stop it, cut it out, don't do it, just a lot more negative feedback than everybody else."

According to Dr. Paul Wender, Director of Psychiatric Research at the University of Utah Medical School, "Nobody knows for sure whether early treatment prevents subsequent psychopathology." However, Dr. Wender believes that parents and practitioners alike have to operate on the assumption that early treatment will prevent subsequent behavior problems and psychological scarring. He says it seems logical that if a child gets treatment, he performs better in school and gets along better with parents, siblings and peers. Thus, Dr. Wender says, "you would expect a good psychological experience rather than the bad one the child is likely to have without treatment."

The treatment for ADHD adolescents is much the same as it is for children. They require a modified school program, behavior management, psychotherapy, and in the cases indicated, medication.

A common misconception about stimulant medications is that they are ineffective for adolescents. However, Dr. Wender reports that stimulant medication is effective for the treatment of ADHD in adolescents, and adults for that matter. Furthermore, in a research paper, "Prognosis of Attention Deficit Disorder and Its Management in Adolescence," which appeared in *Pediatrics in Review* (January 7, 1987), Dr. Rachel Gittleman-Klein, a Professor of Clinical Psychology (Psychiatry) at Columbia University College of Physicians and Surgeons, wrote:

"The only small study in which the effect of methylphenidate (Ritalin) in adolescents has been examined confirms the now common clinical observation that these medications continue to be effective through this age range. The stimulants enable better self-control, do not induce euphoria, and are not known to lead to addictive behavior. To the contrary, the major management problem in adolescents with ADD-H is their reluctance to take the medication and to stay on it; as a result, they are difficult to engage in treatment. Psychiatrists are often resisted because their specialty is often interpreted by the adolescents as indicating that they are 'crazy.' "

Just as with ADHD children, the use of stimulant medication with adolescents needs to be carefully monitored. Dr. Bennett Shaywitz, Professor of Pediatrics and Neurology and Director of Pediatric Neurology at Yale University School of Medicine, finds that monitoring the clinical effects of medication with college students poses problems. He notes that because of the college student's erratic schedules, it is hard to pinpoint the student's target symptoms and when the student should take medication.

Furthermore, in the absence of a teacher or parent to report about the medication's effects, the clinical response proves hard to measure. In the case of one college student Dr. Shaywitz has treated with medication, to effectively manage this case, he and the patient made a tailored rating scale. They selected six areas in which the patient needed help and made a scale so the patient could rate the effectiveness of medical treatment in those areas.

Only in recent years has ADHD been acknowledged to exist in adults. Dr. Paul Wender, from the University of Utah, has pioneered much of the research about the manifestations of the disorder in adults and the appropriate treatment. Based on his research, Dr. Wender has imparted the following information presently known about ADHD and the adult:

1.   Identifying ADHD in the adult is fairly easy. However, the practioner must first know that the disorder can exist in adults, and second that an adult can have more than one disorder. "We certainly see people with combined major biological depression and ADHD." Thus, a differential diagnosis must be made and the patient treated in ways that discriminate between the various conditions.

2.   The average adult with ADHD is easier to distinguish from non-ADHD adults than a hyperactive kid is among non-ADHD peers on a playground. "The ADHD adult will tell you he can't sit at his desk very long. ADHD adults are always fiddling, tapping or drumming their fingers on the desk top. They are happier as oil field roustabouts than public accountants."

3.   The patient is evaluated on the basis of both inclusionary and exclusionary criteria. "The diagnosis of ADD residual type should be considered in patients with prominent complaints of impulsivity, restlessness, emotional lability, and hot temper with a history of ADHD in childhood, and who do not suffer from schizophrenia, major mood disorder, and do not have symptoms of schizotypal or borderline personality disorders." Thus, adults, like ADHD children must be diagnosed by a competent clinician.

4.   "In all instances ADHD has to be discriminated from manic depressive illness. The experienced adult psychiatrist should have little difficulty making the distinction. However, these disorders are common and some unlucky soul might have both." Manic depressive illness can be discriminated from ADHD

by assessing the frequency of the patient's mood changes. ADHD adults are labile and their moods go up and down quickly and several times a day, whereas in mild manic depressive illness, moods last for weeks or months.

The highs which the ADHD adult experiences can be described basically as an out of control excitement. In older ADHD adults the highs tend to go away. The lows which could be characterized by a sense of boredom, ennui, depression, on the other hand, tend to persist, particularly in those adults who "dig themselves into the ground because they are impulsive and do not think ahead."

5. In treating ADHD adults, an approach which employs both psychological and pharmacological intervention appears to work best. A practioner can use rationale psychotherapy to help extricate the ADHD adult from the hole he or she might be in. The patient will respond and get less depressed. However, "unless we work with the impulsivity both pharmacologically and rationally, the ADHD adult is likely to go back into the hole again." Most of the counseling presently given to ADHD adults is "by the seat of the pants." Nonetheless, just as with people who have biological depression, practitioners do try to educate ADHD adults to monitor themselves to learn under what circumstances their symptoms are aggravated and what they do incorrectly at those times.

Currently, Dr. Wender and his assistants are conducting a four-year research project with a sizeable budget to study treatment effects of medication in ADHD adults. From the results of the study, Dr. Wender hopes to scientifically validate and confirm in public a hypothesis about the effects of pharmacological intervention with ADHD adults which most practioners are satisfied is a correct hypothesis. As he reported, project results should confirm "that adults respond well to medication and if they continue to respond well they get their lives turned around. Their relationships last. They get into less social and financial difficulty partly because of decreased impulsivity. They also become better parents, spouses, students and workers."

In an earlier study which he and his colleagues conducted, adult patients who responded to stimulant medication reported relief from a number of symptoms. These adults noted an increase in the ability to concentrate and to stick to tasks and a decrease in motor activity, and talkativeness. Their minds also wandered less, their thinking slowed and many found themselves listening to their spouses for the first time.

Just as with children, physicians often note that adults on medication frequently cannot give an accurate appraisal of their clinical response. To demonstrate this point, Dr. Wender relates the following anecdote:

"One day a nursed stopped me in the hall to thank me. When I asked what I had done to deserve her thanks, she explained that she and her husband were in the process of splitting up their marriage when he entered our research project. In the interim, she had gone out of town for a period of time to take care of her ailing mother. When she returned, she found most of her husband's problems had diminished or gone away. When earlier marital counseling had not helped, now that he had pharmacologic treatment, they were able to work on their marriage. I was so impressed with this story that I went back to look at her husband's chart. He had rated his clinical response as slightly improved."

Dr. Wender explains the reason for the disparity between this husband's and wife's reports has to do with the fact that most ADHD adults "have been color blind since birth. They do not see that the rest of the world perceives things differently. So when they improve, they fail to notice any changes." This point was vividly made to me by Gene Conlin, a father I interviewed who has ADHD. He said, "When you start out at birth with a problem and you go through life not knowing you have that problem, you really just accept that this is how things are and think everybody else goes through life the same way. Now I see that is not true."

With regard to the use of stimulant medications in adults, Dr. Wender explains that a common criticism is that these drugs have recreational value and are therefore abusable. He acknowledges that no one knows whether these drugs affect the bodies of ADHD and non-ADHD adults differently. However, he adds, "We do know they affect the psyche of ADHD adults differently. For instance, many people enjoy speed, but most of our patients do not. They find if they take too much dexadrine it makes them irritable. From a practical point of view, ADHD adults like ADHD kids do not get tolerant of the medication and do not get euphoric in the doses we employ."

Judy Woodruff learned she had ADHD after her daughter had

been diagnosed. She was given a trial on medication and found that for the first time in her life she had self-control and even managed to get her house in order. Medication was not the only relief for Judy. As she explained, "From the time I was very young I knew I had something wrong with me, but I always blamed all my problems on my home life. When I saw the same symptoms in my daughter, I realized I was not neurotic and that something else caused my problems. When I learned about ADHD and that it was a genetic disorder, I felt so relieved to have a label and to know that this problem can be surmounted."

Summary

- One- to two-thirds of ADHD children carry symptoms into adolescence or adulthood.
- Intensity of symptoms fluctuates with changes in environmental demands.
- ADHD adolescents often feel anxious and depressed.
- Many ADHD adolescents experience great difficulty functioning within the structure of junior and senior high school. Problems with learning persist.
- Parents need to be aware of risks associated with ADHD.
- Early ADHD treatment more than likely prevents subsequent psychopathology.
- ADHD adolescents are treated with the multimodal approach.
- Stimulant medication has been proven effective in treatment of adolescents and adults.
- ADHD adults may have more than one disorder.
- Adults require a differential diagnosis.
- ADHD diagnosis in adults is made using inclusionary and exclusionary criteria.
- ADHD adults are treated with psychological and pharmacological interventions.
- Current research hopes to validate positive clinical response of use of medication in ADHD adults.
- Children, adolescents and adults with ADHD can lead successful, happy lives.

CHAPTER ELEVEN

In Appreciation of Children and Adults with ADHD

Over the last two decades, research has generated a great deal of knowledge to add to the understanding of Attention-deficit Hyperactivity Disorder. Yet, at this point in time, though much is known about the way the disorder manifests and its probable basis, any explanation about the actual neurological basis of the disorder remains theoretical. Through the course of writing this book, I learned that ADHD is as multifaceted as a prism. Though general patterns exist, each child is imprinted with environmental circumstances and varying degrees and symptoms of the disorder so that no two ADHD children are exactly alike. Still, in speaking with the authorities on the subject, I found some of the analogies they made to describe the "generic" ADHD child helpful in conceptualizing the struggle these children face daily.

Dr. Melvin Levine, Professor of Pediatrics at the University of North Carolina School of Medicine, explains the child's deficits in terms of an unskilled pilot who must manage the multitude of controls in an airplane's cockpit with such precision that the plane flies effectively and evenly. He developed a chart called the Concentration Cockpit which has a series of meters and dials depicting the various thought processes and/or behaviors the ADHD child needs to regulate in order to fly straight. Among the wide array of meters the ADHD child has to operate efficiently are the selective focus control, the consistency control, the tempo control, the motivational input control, the arousal control, the mood control, the memory control, the social control and the motor/verbal control. Understandably, a child innately deficient in the skills needed to operate these controls will experience difficulty adapting to the myriad demands placed upon him or her by the environment.

Dr. Russell Barkley, Director of Psychology and Professor of Psychiatry and Neurology at the University of Massachusetts Medical School, views the disorder as an inability to motivate and regulate behavior. He describes the ADHD child as a company highly motivated to maximize profits for immediate gain and not so motivated to plan for future development. According to Dr. Barkley, our society has a hard time accepting the notion that an individual's biology rather than one's will power is in control of one's motivation. Perhaps that is why ADHD children are often blamed for their characteristic inability to "get with the program."

Dr. C. Keith Conners, Professor of Medical Psychology and Director of the ADHD clinic at Duke University Medical School, says the ADHD child is like a company with too many workers but an ineffective boss or no boss at all to order them. Because the ADHD child suffers from a lack of appropriate energizing ability, he or she can not arouse himself or herself to the level necessary to effectively order the mind's workers who need a lot of executive input.

Though each of these analogies is different, a common thread runs throughout them. ADHD children are the children who *can't*, not the children who *won't*. So maybe we do not need to know any more about ADHD than that. Instead, maybe we need to know how to adjust our attitudes about the disorder, because like everyone else, ADHD children thrive on love and acceptance. By love, I mean an unconditional love given freely with no demands attached. Unfortunately, for children and adults with ADHD, approval, acceptance and love often come with a price tag.

Psychologist Sam Goldstein believes, "as a society we need to recognize that the demands of the culture actually play favorites with our kids' lives." He pointed out that one hundred years ago, those children who could not fit into the school system were probably sent out to work the land or roam the frontier. While this alternative may not have been the best, at least a place existed where people with ADHD could tap their potential.

"But, unlike a hundred years ago," said Dr. Goldstein, "we have no place to send these people. Today, we have no wilderness where they can go and be fur trappers, no farms they can work. We are between frontiers. Yet the demands of the culture are such that these people have a real hard time fitting in. When we do finally open up space, the last frontier, maybe we'll send these people out to be explorers, trappers and miners on the moon. And some of them will probably want to go. But why? Maybe the kid who wants to be an astronaut is saying, 'Gee, get me the hell out of here. I need a new frontier. I want to go some place where I won't bump into somebody all the time.'"

I think we need to ask ourselves if we view the children who do not "fit the mold," the children who cannot "get with the program," as square pegs. Rather than search for their intrinsic value, do we try to force these people into round holes? Maybe ADHD is not necessarily something gone amuck which needs to be fixed. Many of the traits associated with this condition can be either assets or liabilities.

Consider perseveration. Dr. Goldstein says, "being perseverative when you're a kid means you're a pain in the neck. Mom tells the child that she will take him or her to the park in half an hour and the child asks every thirty seconds if it is time to go. But being perseverative, which is rooted in the word persevere, is a valuable trait when you find something that interests you and you are willing to stick with it. Maybe a child with ADHD might someday find a cure for cancer because he or she has extraordinary energy and curiosity and is willing to stay up all night and test a million different hypotheses until the cure is found."

Admittedly, when my child was first diagnosed with ADHD, I had no concept that this disorder might have a plus side. Then, a parent sent me an article from Pediatric Clinics of North America-Vol. 29, No. 1, February 1982, titled "The Unhappy Wanderers: Children with Attention Deficits," by Melvin Levine, M.D., and Raun Melmed M.B., Ch.B. The authors discussed the potential dividends of ADHD. They suggested that the highly distractible child with the wandering mind might see things others lacking this trait might never perceive. The wandering mind may represent creativity. The child who is insatiable may become the adult with ambition. The trait of egocentricity may form the foundation of leadership. They also cautioned that "Environmental circumstances, patterns of nurturance, critical life events, and educational experiences can minimize or aggravate the effects of attention deficits. It is likely that the responses of adults have a significant impact on prognosis."

When I interviewed Dr. Levine for this book, he expressed his dissatisfaction with the ADHD label given these children. He explained why. "One of the remarkable things about kids with attention deficits is that they have extraordinary strengths and affinities. For that reason, I do not like to take a fully pathological view of them. We need to at least consider the possibility that the word deficit is wrong. Maybe ADHD is just an alternative way to be wired. I am worried that with the current label of the disorder we may be creating a self-fulfilling prophecy in which these kids feel they have brain damage which is sort of implicit in the name."

Dr. Levine acknowledges that applying some type of label to describe these children and adults leads to recognition and help. But he observes that "so many kids we see with attentional problems are highly entrepreneurial, and creative people who have certain foci of interest that are very sophisticated and exciting. Perhaps we need to direct our energies to help the child recognize the existence of these traits. It would be so much better for them to think they just see the world differently from a lot of other people and there are good advantages to that and there are problems created by it. The child needs to see his or her potential value." And so does the adult.

Though ADHD is a handicapping condition, it need not levy such a heavy toll on a person's life. As a society, we need to develop an appreciation of the struggles and play to the strengths of people with ADHD. I once read somewhere that in nature there is no right or wrong. There are only consequences. Maybe the label should be "handle with care."

Appendix A

Behavior Management Charts

Many variations of behavior management charts exist as do books to explain their use. The following charts are provided as samples. The home management chart depicts the type of chart we used with our son. The daily and weekly school charts have been used successfully by some of the parents I interviewed. For more information about the theory behind behavior management, see Chapters Three and Six.

Chart #1   Home Management Behavior Chart
Chart #2   Daily School Chart
Chart #3   Daily School Record Chart
Chart #4   Weekly School Chart

Sample Home Management Behavior Chart

CHILD'S NAME _____   WEEK OF: _____

	Sun.	Mon.	Tues.	Wed.	Thur.	Fri.	Sat.
NIGHT BEFORE BEDTIME ROUTINE: washes, takes bath, brushes teeth, changes into pajamas, gets into bed, turns lights out on time	3	2	3				
MORNING ROUTINE: gets up, washes, brushes teeth, gets dressed, eats breakfast, is ready on time	2	2	3				
BEDROOM: makes bed, puts books, toys, clothing neatly away by (time)	1	0	3				
HOMEWORK: brings home all necessary materials, completes all assignments by (time) without delays or arguments	3	2	2				
GENERAL COOPERATION AND RESPECT: listens to and follows house rules and directions, cooperates with requests, speaks to and treats other family members nicely	2	2	3				
TOTAL	11*	8*	14**				

RATINGS

Excellent = 3
Good = 2
Needs Improvement = 1
Poor = 0

DAILY TOTALS AND CONSEQUENCES

Excellent Day (12-15 points) Bed 9:30, unrestricted TV/Nintendo time, 50 cents, 2 stars
Good Day (8-11 points) Bed 9:00, 1 hour of TV/Nintendo time, 25 cents, 1 star
Poor Day (0-7 points) Bed 8:30, no TV/Nintendo, no money, no stars

WEEKEND PRIVILEGES = STARS

Excellent week (10-14 stars) = Super Special (e.g. sleep over)
Good week (6-9 stars) = One Special (e.g. rent video tape)
Poor week (0-5 stars) = No Specials

This chart is for an elementary age child whose normal bedtime is 9:00. For younger children—preschool through kindergarten age—it is often best to use a "sticker" or "star" chart. A younger child's chart would have only three behaviors listed. Similarly, rewards would be age-appropriate, e.g., ice cream cone.

Sample Daily School Chart

		DATE:	DAY: MONDAY '89
SUBJECT	DO YOU HAVE BOOKS/MATERIALS YOU NEED?	HOMEWORK ASSIGNMENTS	
PERIOD 1 READING:	YES/NO HOMEWORK? ☐	ASSIGNMENT: PAGES:	
PERIOD 2 SPELLING:	YES/NO HOMEWORK? ☐	ASSIGNMENT: PAGES:	
PERIOD 3 PENMANSHIP:	YES/NO HOMEWORK? ☐	ASSIGNMENT: PAGES:	
PERIOD 4 MATH:	YES/NO HOMEWORK? ☐	ASSIGNMENT: PAGES:	
PERIOD 5 COMPUTER:	YES/NO HOMEWORK? ☐	ASSIGNMENT: PAGES:	
PERIOD 6 SCIENCE:	YES/NO HOMEWORK? ☐	ASSIGNMENT: PAGES:	
PERIOD 7 SOCIAL STUDIES:	YES/NO HOMEWORK? ☐	ASSIGNMENT: PAGES:	
RESOURCE ROOM:			ARE THERE ANY NOTICES TO GO HOME? YES/NO
COMMENTS:			
POINTS TODAY:	POINTS TOTAL:	TEACHER(S):	PARENTS:
			89P1DEMO

Sample Daily School Record Chart

NAME: _____ DAY/DATE: _____

SUBJECT	WORK COMPLETION				CLASS BEHAVIOR			
Language Arts	3	2	1	0	3	2	1	0
Math	3	2	1	0	3	2	1	0
Science	3	2	1	0	3	2	1	0
Reading	3	2	1	0	3	2	1	0
Social Studies	3	2	1	0	3	2	1	0

RATINGS - Please Circle

3 = Excellent

Total = _____ 2 = Satisfactory

1 = Needs Improvement

0 = Poor

Language Assignment:

_____

Teacher initials: _____

Test/Quiz Grades: _____

_____

Reading Assignment:

_____

Teacher initials: _____

Test/Quiz Grades: _____

_____

Social Studies Assignment:

_____

Teacher initials: _____

Test/Quiz Grades: _____

_____

Previous Assignments overdue:

Math Assignment:

_____

Teacher initials: _____

Test/Quiz Grades: _____

_____

Science Assignment:

_____

Teacher initials: _____

Test/Quiz Grades: _____

_____

_____

Richard S. Zakreski, Ph.D.

_____
_____
_____

Sample Weekly School Chart

Name: _____ Date: _____

Ratings
3 = Excellent 2 = Satisfactory 1 = Needs Improvement 0 = Poor

Subject	Work Completion				Class Behavior				Teacher Initials
Language Arts	3	2	1	0	3	2	1	0	
Math	3	2	1	0	3	2	1	0	
Science	3	2	1	0	3	2	1	0	
Reading	3	2	1	0	3	2	1	0	
Social Studies	3	2	1	0	3	2	1	0	
Subtotal	_____				_____				
Total			_____						

Missing Assignments
English/L.A.
Social Studies
Math
Science
Specials

Test/Quiz Grades or Upcoming Tests
English/L.A.
Social Studies
Math
Science
Specials

Appendix B

National Support Organizations

ADDA—Attention-deficit Disorder Association
      Ms. Linda Phillips—ADDA Contact Person for
      National Referral to ADHD support services
      University of California, Irvine
      Child Development Center
      19262 Jamboree Boulevard
      Irvine, California 92715
      (714) 856-8700

CHADD—Children with Attention-deficit Disorders
(national information center for children with ADD)
Suite 185
499 NW 70th Avenue   Suite 308
Plantation, Florida 33317
(305) 587-3700

Learning Disabilities Association
(formerly ACLD-Association for Children and Adults with
  Learning Disabilities)
4156 Library Road
Pittsburgh, Pennsylvania 15234
(412) 341-1515

National Center for Children with Learning Disabilities
(formerly Foundation for Children with Learning Disabilities)
99 Park Avenue
New York, New York 10016
(212) 687-7211

NICHCY—National Information Center for Handicapped
Children and Youth
Post Office Box 1492
Washington, DC 20013
1-800-999-5599

Self-Help Clearinghouses in the United States
(for help in finding and forming Mutual Aid Self-Help Groups)

California* 1-800-222-LINK (CA only)
Connecticut (203) 789-7645
Illinois* 1-800-322-MASH (IL only)
Kansas (316) 689-3170
Massachusetts (413) 545-2313
Michigan* 1-800-752-5858 (MI only)
Minnesota (612) 642-4060
Missouri—Kansas City (816) 561-HELP
Nebraska (402) 476-9668
New Jersey 1-800-FOR-MASH (NJ only)
New York State* (518) 474-6293
NY—New York City (718) 596-6000
NY—Long Island (516) 348-3030
NY—Westchester (914) 347-3620
Oregon—Portland (503) 222-5555
PA—Pittsburgh (412) 247-5400
PA—Scranton (717) 961-1234
South Carolina (803) 791-2426
Tennessee—Knoxville (614) 584-6736
Texas* (512) 454-3706
Vermont 1-800-442-5356
Greater Washington, DC (703) 536-4100

For National U.S. Listings and Directories:

Self-Help Clearinghouse, NJ (201) 625-7101
Self-Help Center, Illinois (312) 328-0470
National Self-Help Clearinghouse, N.Y. City (212) 840-1259

Other Helpful Organizations:

O.D.P.H.P. National Health Information Clearinghouse
(U.S.) 1-800-336-4797

---

*Maintains listings of additional local clearinghouses operating within that state.

Appendix C

Special Education and
the Civil Rights of Handicapped Individuals

As mentioned in Chapter Eight, children whose handicapping condition is ADHD often fall through the cracks in the current educational system in both regular education and special education. However, Fran Rice, a child education advocate with Advocacy Association of Northern New England, advocates for a free and appropriate education for ADHD children under Public Law 94-142, 1975, and Section 504 of the Rehabilitation Act of 1973. Following is a brief discussion of how both these laws may protect the rights of the ADHD child in school.

Under the Education for All Handicapped Children Act (EHA) 1973, Congress mandated that all children regardless of their handicap were entitled to a free and appropriate public education. Furthermore, that education had to be meaningful to the child. Therefore, Congress insured that children with special needs would not only receive access to the public school system, but once in school, special needs children could not be placed in programs merely to pass the time of day. Congress then passed Public Law 94-142, 1975, the implementing rules and regulations for EHA. This statute reflects the minimum requirements expected of every state in serving handicapped children. Each state, thereafter, had to develop its own rules and regulations to govern special education in accordance with the public law.

Fran Rice explained that special education was intended to provide very specialized instruction for handicapped children whose impairments were of such a nature and severity that the child warranted this highly specialized instruction. Under PL94-142, students are eligible to have special programs designed to meet their unique and individual educational needs if they are mentally retarded, hard of hearing, deaf, speech impaired, visually handicapped, other health impaired, deaf-blind, multi-handicapped, or have specific learning disabilities, and determined in need of special education.

PL94-142 defines specific learning disabilities as "a disorder in one or more of the basic psychological processes involved in understanding or in using language, spoken or written, which disorder may manifest itself in imperfect ability to listen, think, speak, write, spell or do mathematical calculation. Such disorders include such conditions as perceptual handicaps, brain injury, minimal brain dysfunction, dyslexia, and developmental asphasia . . ." Because ADHD is not specifically stated, often school systems try to exclude these children from special education.

Under PL94-142, all children recognized are to have one or more of the physical or mental impairments previously listed. "A child with a disability means a child with one or more of the impairments listed in the definition of handicapped children if the child needs special education. In essence, there is a continuum of impairments. Where an impairment is of such a nature that the child needs special education, it is referred to as a disability in PL94-142 and the child is a handicapped child," Fran Rice said. In instances, however, where a clinical determination is absent, then the school follows a supplemental evaluation process when it suspects that a child may have a specific learning disability.

The child is considered to have a specific learning disability if no other primary handicapping condition is present and the child has been provided with learning experiences appropriate to the age and ability of the child but has not achieved commensurate with his or her age and ability levels in one or more of these areas: oral expression, listening comprehension, written expression, basic reading skills, reading comprehension, mathematics calculation, or mathematics reasoning.

This criteria has been interpreted by schools, however, as requiring that a severe discrepancy between the child's measured ability and his (her) success in a basic academic subject must exist in order to be considered handicapped and eligible. Fran

Rice said, "in practically every state now, the eligibility for special education seems to be based upon a need for the child to fail first or be so discrepant in achievement that he or she cannot be overlooked." This ability/achievement ratio is often an area for dispute in due process hearings. Discrepancy driven decisions which are used solely to rule children in or out of special education fail the federal test and Congressional intent.

The Education for All Handicapped Children Act followed closely on the heels of Section 504 of the Rehabilitation Act of 1973. The Rehabilitation Act is basically a Civil Rights Law that protects individuals with disabilities. It mandates that any agency in receipt of any federal funds cannot discriminate against a qualified handicapped person on the basis of his (her) handicap. Persons who have questions or who feel their rights under 504 are being denied can contact the Office for Civil Rights. Addresses for these agencies to follow.

Under Section 504 a handicapped individual is defined as "any person who has a physical or mental impairment which substantially limits one or more major life activities, has record of such impairment, and is regarded as having such an impairment." A child diagnosed with ADHD, 314.01 or Undifferentiated ADD 314.00 as codified in the *Diagnostic and Statistical Manual of the American Psychiatric Association Revised Third Edition* has record of such impairment. Physical or mental impairment is defined as any physiologic condition, . . . affecting one or more or the following body systems: neurological . . . Major life activity means functions such as performing manual tasks, . . . learning and working." Since ADHD is a neurologically based handicap which interferes with the child's ability to learn, Fran Rice advocates for educational services for ADHD children under the auspices of Section 504.

Furthermore, Section 504 states, "handicapped persons, regardless of the nature or severity of their handicap are entitled to a free and appropriate public education; handicapped students are to be educated with non-handicapped students to the maximum extent appropriate to their needs; educational agencies must undertake to identify and locate all unserved handicapped children . . ." Recently, as a result of investigations conducted by the Office for Civil Rights in response to complaints by parents of ADHD children that the rights of their children under Section 504 were being violated, the OCR ruled in favor of the parents. Thus, the school districts had to provide the appropriate education program. In one of these cases the OCR also found that school personnel were unknowledgeable about Section 504, and since the RHA stipulates that any agency in receipt of any federal monies be knowledgeable about the law, the court ordered the school to conduct a workshop to inform personnel about the law.

In addition to specifying the quality of education for handicapped individuals, Section 504 also called for evaluation procedures to be improved to avoid inappropriate education resulting from misclassification, and procedural safeguards to enable parents and guardians to influence decisions regarding the evaluation and placement of their children. Fran Rice points out that these basic requirements are common to PL94-142 as well as 504.

Under Section 504, in order for the services delivered to handicapped individuals to be appropriate, they must follow this criteria. First, the educational program must be designed to meet the handicapped individual's educational needs to the same extent as non-handicapped children. Second, an appropriate education could consist of education in regular classes, education in regular classes with the use of supplementary services or special education and related services. Special education may include specifically designed instruction in classrooms, at home, in private schools or institutions . . ."

Furthermore, and I quote from 504 "the quality of educational services provided to handicapped students must equal that of services provided to non-handicapped students: thus, handicapped students' teachers must be trained in the instruction of persons with the handicap in question and appropriate materials and equipment must be available." As explained by Fran Rice, 504 actually offers stronger protection for ADHD children, especially for those who do not qualify for special education as the regulations are currently interpreted by their individual school districts, and who can function in the regular classroom quite well providing modifications are made in their programs.

Included in the requirements common to both Section 504 and PL94-142 and its state equivalents, are evaluation procedures and safeguards to protect the rights of both parents and their children as well as schools. When a school district considers evaluating a child, parents or guardians must be given a copy of their parental rights and an explanation of the state's safeguards governing special education. As explained by Fran Rice, written notice which meets very specific requirements must be given to a parent a reasonable time before a school proposes or refuses to identify, evaluate, or place a child, or for the provision of a free appropriate public education. The notice must include a full explanation of all procedural safeguards available under PL94-142 and a description of each procedure, test, record, or report the school used as a basis for its actions written in language understandable to the parent. Notice is also required by Section 504. In cases where parents refuse consent, the school has the right to request an impartial hearing to determine whether the evaluation is warranted.

Fran Rice says that Notice in actuality represents the parental Miranda Rights. Notice not only enables parents or guardians to make intelligent decisions on behalf of their child, but it also insures the parents that the tests being administered are considered valid for the purpose for which they are intended. Furthermore, if the parent has had the child tested privately, the school must respond to the evaluation report(s) under the same exacting standards especially if the school rejects any or all findings or recommendations of independent evaluators.

In order to determine if a child is eligible for special education services, PL94-142 specified the following process: First, child study teams were created to annually identify, locate, and evaluate children with handicaps to determine the nature and extent of special education and related services that were needed by the child. The teams were to consist of the child's regular teacher, or in the absence of a regular teacher, a teacher qualified to teach similar age children; for preschool age children, an individual qualified by the state to teach a child of his or her age; and at least one person qualified to conduct individual diagnostic educational examinations of children, such as a school psychologist, speech-language pathologist, or remedial reading teacher. For a child evaluated for the first time, a person knowledgeable in the area of the disability must be included. The actual medical diagnosis of ADHD must be made by persons in the medical community or by a clinical psychologist. School psychologists would not usually offer such a clinical status. Each state has its own team configurations, however, these configurations must comply minimally with those specified in the federal law. Parents are also afforded the opportunity to initiate a child study team evaluation if they have evidence to suggest that their child has a specific learning disability or other handicapping condition.

Upon completion of an evaluation, the child study team must prepare a written report of their findings for the parents. The report must include the team's determination of whether the child has a specific learning disability, the basis of making the determination, the relevant behavior noted during the observation of the child, the relationship of the child's behavior to academic functioning, and the educationally relevant medical findings. The team must also determine whether there is a severe discrepancy between ability and achievement not correctable without special education and related services, and consider the effects of the child's environmental, cultural or economic disadvantage. This information must be documented. Each team member must certify in writing that the report accurately reflects his or her own conclusions or submit a separate statement presenting his or her conclusions.

Once a child is determined to be eligible for special education and related services, a representative of the agency qualified to provide or supervise special education, the child's teacher, parents, the child (when appropriate) and other individuals at the discretion of the parent or agency must meet to develop, review or revise an individualized educational plan (IEP) designed to meet that child's specific needs. Once the IEP is developed, parents are often asked to sign this document. However, Fran Rice says under federal law this is not a requirement. Parents are only required to give written consent twice: for the initial evaluation and thereafter permission for their child to receive special education services. The permission is not construed as "approval" of the IEP. Parents can also revoke their consent at any time. However, the school district can request an impartial hearing if it believes the child is in need of the special education and related services.

In discussing the IEP provisions, Fran Rice said, "The IEP is a very important legal document which parents should not enter into lightly." Your child's IEP must be centered around the effects of your child's diagnosed impairments on any area of education affected. It must state where the child is now (present level of performance), what progress the child can be expected to achieve in the next twelve consecutive months (annual goals), and what the measurable intermediate steps are (short term instructional objectives) between the child's present level of achievement and the specific goal. These objectives are to constitute a series of steps which are to lead to the accomplishment of the annual goal. They must be measured by objective evaluation criteria and evaluation procedures and conform to a schedule for determining progress. Each service provider must be listed for each area addressed in the IEP. The amount of time committed to the various services must be clearly stated and appropriate for that service. If modifications to the regular or vocational areas of education are found necessary through the evaluation, then every modification or accommodation must be included for each service. It is not complete until all parties at the IEP meeting agree on its contents. Once in place, the IEP cannot be significantly amended without written parental consent.

Fran Rice advises that parents learn all they can about their child's impairment(s) before entering into the IEP development. She adds that the U.S. Department of Education issued a very helpful clarification on IEP's January 19, 1981 in the Federal Register titled "Interpretation of the Individualized Education Program." It is obtainable from any State Department of Education, through the offices of your Congressional delegation or your state library. The paper presents answers for fifty questions about IEP's.

With regard to preparing for an IEP meeting, I have included a copy of The Surefire Four-step Record Decoder, source unknown, which was provided to me by Fran Rice. This decoder offers a step-by-step guide to help parents understand all their child's evaluations and recommendations so they can participate effectively in the IEP process.

If the school and parents decide the child is not in need of special education, the school still has an obligation to assist a handicapped child under Section 504 free appropriate public education requirements. These requirements are similar to those found in PL94-142. Section 504, subsection 104.33 states, "implementation of an individualized educational program developed in accordance with the Education of the Handicapped Children Act is one means of meeting this standard established in paragraph (b)(1)(i) which is the entitlement to a free appropriate public education.

Both PL94-142, its state equivalents, and 504 contain procedural safeguards should disagreements arise between parents (guardians) and schools regarding appropriate educational placements and interventions for a child. Thus, both schools and parents are afforded the right to due process, which means that their cases are presented before an impartial hearing officer, and that officer makes a determination based on the evidence presented. Under PL94-142 and its state equivalents, due process hearings are not formal court cases, but they are heard by an administrative law judge, and their rulings are enforceable under the law. Parents, even if they are not instituting due process procedures, are entitled to receive a copy of all pertinent school records pertaining to their child upon written request. Furthermore, at a hearing, parents are entitled to counsel and/or representation by an individual qualified to speak on behalf of their child's handicapping condition.

Prior to due process, or while waiting for a due process hearing, parents and the agency involved may choose to use mediation when disputes arise. However, mediation is not regulated by law. If mediation is used and the results are not agreeable to both parties, the parties involved in the dispute are still entitled to due process. Mediation proceedings must be conducted by a mediator who is trained in mediation techniques and special education laws and procedures and who is not affiliated with either party.

I strongly suggest parents make themselves knowledgeable about their state's equivalent rules and regulations for PL94-142. Furthermore, parents should seek the advice of people knowledgeable about education law when disputes arise between parents and the school. The following supplemental material will assist you in your efforts to advocate for your child's education needs. Included are: guidelines for establishing a record, sample telephone log for the purpose of record keeping, information about IEPs, The Surefire Four-step Record Decoder, addresses of the Regional Offices for Civil Rights, and addresses of national organizations which can assist you or direct you to local agencies for assistance with your advocacy efforts.

Establishing a Record

When dealing with any agency, including the public schools, your chances are better if you have a written record of all communications with that agency. The following suggestions should increase your chances in getting action and will strengthen your positions when confrontations arise.

WHAT SHOULD BE IN A RECORD
1. *All* letters *from* you to the school district and other agencies about your concern.
2. *All* letters to you from the school district and other agencies about your concern.
3. *All* reports from the school, doctors, other agencies, and others including: report cards, parent-teacher conference reports, diagnostic reports, minutes or reports of meetings with persons involved with your concerns, IEP recommendations, etc.
4. *A log of telephone calls* giving the dates and time and length of the call, who initiated the call, who participated in the call (i.e., sometimes calls are transferred to more than one person or are conference calls), a summary of the conversations (i.e., who said what, what conclusions were reached or what action was promised, etc.).

HOW TO DEVELOP AND KEEP A RECORD
The following are suggestions for establishing and maintaining a record of contacts with the schools or other agencies.
1. Purchase a three-ring notebook, pocket folder or small

205

file. This will be the one location where you will keep all information related to the record.

2. Organize the record in whatever way helps you to locate the information quickly. (It is suggested you use reverse chronological order with latest information on top.)

3. Place all written reports, minutes of meetings, letters, etc., in the record. (See 3 above.)

4. Write down all phone calls (see 4 above). You may want to have the telephone log as a separate section in your record.

5. For meetings and phone calls for which there is no record, ask the school or other agency people to supply a summary of the meeting or call. If you agree with the summary, file it.

6. If you do not agree with the record or summary of a meeting or phone call, put your own interpretation in writing, and send it to the persons who chaired the meeting and wrote the minutes or summary. Ask that person to respond if they disagree with your interpretation.

7. Make your own notes at every meeting. If you have trouble writing notes during the meeting, *use a tape recorder* and transcribe your notes later.

8. Write out a summary of your interpretation of each meeting or phone call. Send your summary to the chairperson and minute taker and ask that person to react to your interpretation if he disagrees with it.

9. Make enough copies of all your correspondence so that you can send copies to all persons related to your concern. Always keep a copy for yourself.

10. Always send copies of your complaint letter to the following people:
    a. Local Superintendent
    b. Local Director of Special Education
    c. School Principal
    d. Local School Board President

11. Notifications of formal action such as requests for a hearing or filing of a complaint should have copies sent by certified mail to all those listed in 10 above.

12. If your initial letter is not answered or responded to, you may wish to follow up by doing any of the following:

   a. Make a telephone call to any of the above listed persons

   b. Make a direct phone call or in person visit to your local Superintendent of Schools.

13. *Never* let anyone have the master copy of your record except your legal counsel. You may want to have photo copies made and sent to others to help make your point.

By Harold W. Spicknall
Provided to the author from:
Fran Rice
Advocacy Associates of Northern
New England, Montpelier, Vermont

Telephone Log

PERSON I TALKED TO   TELEPHONE   DATE

QUESTION/INFORMATION

FOLLOW-UP:
- I PROMISED TO —

- HE/SHE PROMISED TO —

- ADDITIONAL ACTION NEEDED —
  (i.e. letter documenting phone call,
  others to contact, etc.)

PERSON I TALKED TO   TELEPHONE   DATE

QUESTION/INFORMATION

FOLLOW-UP:
- I PROMISED TO —

- HE/SHE PROMISED TO —

- ADDITIONAL ACTION NEEDED —
  (i.e. letter documenting phone call,
  others to contact, etc.)

Provided to the author by Statewide Parent Advocacy Network SPAN
516 North Avenue East, Westfield, New Jersey 07090

Guidelines for Being an Effective Partcipant in the IEP Process

How Should Parents Prepare for the IEP Conference?

Although parents may not be experts in the area of special education, they are experts on their child's strengths, weaknesses and learning patterns. Therefore, the full participation of parents is important in developing an appropriate IEP. Further, the parents' knowledge of their child will help them in deciding whether a proposed IEP is "appropriate." Parents should not be afraid to ask questions at the IEP conference or to speak up if they disagree with the educators.

If the parents have an IEP for their child from the current or previous school year, they should review each section of that IEP prior to the conference. Do they agree that their child requires special education in each goal area listed? Are the "objectives" or tasks appropriate, or has the child already learned these skills? Should other areas be included? Are all necessary related services being provided and are the type and amount listed sufficient? Do the parents believe the child could spend more time in class with non-handicapped students? If no IEP yet exists, the parents should think about these IEP areas prior to the conference. The checklist below provides other areas for all parents to consider before, during and at the end of the IEP Conference.

IEP Checklist

Before Attending an IEP Conference:

- review all school records, including school district evaluations;
- review the results of any outside evaluation done on the child;

- talk with people who have worked with or evaluated the child;
- identify those areas in which the child needs special attention, including, if appropriate, vocational areas;
- identify and/or review the goals (both long- and short-term) for the child and the type of educational setting the child needs.

During the IEP Conference:

- get an explanation of all evaluation results, terms and recommendations;
- find out how much progress the child made in achieving the goals and objectives in the previous IEP (if one exists), which teaching methods and materials worked and which did not;
- review each aspect of the district's proposals, including current levels and goals, and compare these to the parents' own observation of their child;
- discuss parents' academic and vocational goals for the child and the types of skills they want their child to learn;
- make known any agreement or disagreement with the district's recommendations and ask that any modifications or additions be included in the IEP;
- discuss the type and amount of any related services the child requires;
- discuss the amount of special education and regular education the child requires;
- discuss any modifications to the child's regular education classes that may be necessary.

At the End of the IEP Conference:

- make sure that the type and amount of all related services appear on the IEP;
- make sure that the amount of time the child will participate in regular education appears on the IEP.

Excerpted from *The Right to Special Education in Pennsylvania: A Guide for Parents,* published by The Education Law Center, 225 South 15th Street, Philadelphia, Pennsylvania 19102.

The Surefire Four-Step Record Decoder

STEP I: ORGANIZE

1. After obtaining the *complete set of records* from the school system, separate reports about your child (teacher reports, psychological evaluations, social history, etc.) from the correspondence.
2. Make an extra copy of the records in order to have an original and a working copy you can mark, cut, paste and use in any way that will help you.
3. Arrange each set, reports and extra documents, in chronological order.
4. Secure the pages in a folder with a clip or in a loose leaf notebook.
5. Number each report and make a chronological list that can be added onto as new records are generated.

STEP II.   READ

1. Read through the entire record to get overall impressions, tones of the school's view of your child.
2. In the margins of your working copy, mark with a "?" the statements or areas of the reports with which you disagree or do not understand.

STEP III: ANALYZE

1. While re-reading the reports, underline the phrases or sentences, you feel best describe *both* your child's strengths and your child's problems. Put an "S" in the margin opposite a description of your child's learning strengths, a "P" opposite problems.
2. Using a worksheet, place the phrases or sentences about your child's strengths and problems within the categories of Oral Expression, Listening Comprehension, Basic Reading Skills, Reading Comprehension, Mathematical Calculation and Mathematical Reasoning, and Social Perception.
3. After each piece of data put the *source* and *date*. Often you

will find trends beginning to emerge. The same observation, said in similar language, may occur in several reports over a period of time. You can indicate this by simply recording additional sources and dates to the original data.

4. List *recommendations* in the last section of the analysis sheet that are made by each evaluator; for example, services needed, classroom environment, class size, type of school setting, recommendation for further testing, specific teaching materials or methods.

STEP IV: EVALUATE

Using the question mark quotations you have made in the margins and your overall sense of the records from your analytical work with them, evaluate their accuracy against the following criteria:

ACCURATE—

do these reports and portions of the records correspond with your own feelings, perceptions, observations and assessments of your child?

COMPLETE—

are all the documents required by the school system for the Eligibility, Individualized Education Plan (IEP) and Placement decision available in the file? For example, medical report, psychological examination, educational report and others as required.

JARGON-FREE—

do the reports describe your child in non-technical terms and/or language you can understand and use? In a good report diagnoses and technical language will be used and defined within the report.

CURRENT—   are the dates on the records recent enough to give a report of your child's present behavior and functioning?

CONSISTENT—   are the reports contradictory? Is there consistency between the descriptions of your child by each evaluator?

UNDERSTANDABLE—   is the language used meaningful, clear and understandable to you? Example of an unclear statement: "She appears to have a psychological learning disability, calling for treatment involving a moderation of the special focus on interpersonal sensitivity she has received so far." "WHAT DOES THAT MEAN?"

OVERALL INTEGRITY— considering the records as a whole, do they make sense and lead to the given recommendations?

Provided to the author from Fran Rice, Advocacy Associates of Northern New England, Montepelier, VT 05602

Department of Education Office for Civil Rights Regional Civil Rights Offices

Region I
Connecticut, Maine, Massachusetts, New Hampshire, Rhode Island, Vermont

Regional Civil Rights Director
Office for Civil Rights, Region I
U.S. Department of Education
John W. McCormack Post Office and
 Court House-Room 222
Post Office Square
Boston, Massachusetts 02109
(617) 223-1154   TTY   (617) 223-1111

Region II
New Jersey, New York, Puerto Rico, Virgin Islands

Regional Civil Rights Director
Office for Civil Rights, Region II
U.S. Department of Education
26 Federal Plaza, R33-130
New York, New York 10278
(212) 264-5180   TTY   (212) 264-9464

Region III
Delaware, District of Columbia, Maryland, Pennsylvania, Virginia, West Virginia

Regional Civil Rights Director
Office for Civil Rights, Region III
U.S. Department of Education
Gateway Building, 3535 Market Street
Post Office Box 13716
Philadelphia, Pennsylvania 19101
(215) 596-6772   TTY   (215) 596-6794

Region IV
Alabama, Florida, Georgia, Kentucky, Mississippi, North Carolina,
South Carolina, Tennessee

Regional Civil Rights Director
Office for Civil Rights, Region IV
U.S. Department of Education
101 Marietta Tower, Room 2702
Atlanta, Georgia 30323
(404) 221-2954   TTY   (404) 221-2010

Region V
Illinois, Indiana, Minnesota, Michigan, Ohio, Wisconsin

Regional Civil Rights Director
Office for Civil Rights, Region V
U.S. Department of Education
300 South Wacker Drive, 8th Floor
Chicago, Illinois 60606
(312) 353-2520   TTY   (312) 353-2540

Region VI
Arkansas, Louisiana, New Mexico, Oklahoma, Texas

Regional Civil Rights Director
Office for Civil Rights, Region VI
U.S. Department of Education
1200 Main Tower Building, Room 1935
Dallas, Texas 75202
(214) 676-3951   TTY   (214) 767-6599

Region VII
Iowa, Kansas, Missouri, Nebraska

Regional Civil Rights Director
Office for Civil Rights, Region VII
U.S. Department of Education
324 E. 11th Street, 24th Floor
Kansas City, Missouri 64106
(816) 374-2223   TTY   (816) 374-7264

Region VIII

Colorado, Montana, North Dakota, South Dakota, Utah, Wyoming

Regional Civil Rights Director
Office for Civil Rights, Region VIII
U.S. Department of Education
Federal Office Building
1961 Stout Street, Room 1185
Denver, Colorado 80294
(303) 884-5695   TTY   (303) 844-3417

Region IX

Arizona, California, Hawaii, Nevada, Guam, Trust Territory
of the Pacific Islands, American Samoa

Regional Civil Rights Director
Office for Civil Rights, Region IX
U.S. Department of Education
1275 Market Street, 14th Floor
San Francisco, California 94103
(415) 556-9894   TTY   (415) 556-1933

Region X

Alaska, Idaho, Oregon, Washington

Regional Civil Rights Director
Office for Civil Rights, Region X
U.S. Department of Education
2901 3rd Avenue, Mail Stop 106
Seattle, Washington 98121
(206) 442-1636   TTY   (206) 442-4542

Parents may obtain copies of PL94-142 and Section 504 of the
RHA by writing their Congressperson or by ordering them from
the U.S. Department of Education, Office of Special Education,
Washington, D.C. 20202

National Organizations for Advocacy Resources

The following list of resources may be helpful to you for purposes of obtaining information about how to receive the appropriate education program for your child.

NPND - National Parent Network on Disabilities
1600 Prince Street
Suite 115
Alexandria, Virginia 22314
(703) 684-6763 V/TDD
(Contact for the listing of the federally funded parent training and information center in your state. NPND also has listing of parent to parent groups and other nationwide support services, such as information regarding Social Security Insurance.)

Advocates of Children of New York, Inc.
24-16 Bridge Plaza South
Long Island City, New York 11101

Center for Law and Education, Inc.
955 Massachusetts Avenue
Cambridge, Massachusetts 02139

Disability Rights Education and Defense Fund, Inc.
1616 P Street, NW
Suite 100
Washington, D.C. 20036

Education Law Center
155 Washington Street
Room 209
Newark, New Jersey 07102

Education Law Center
2100 Lewis Tower Building
225 South 15th Street
Philadelphia, Pennsylvania 19102

TAPP (Technical Assistance for Parent Programs) Network
Federation for Children with Special Needs
95 Berkeley Street   Suite 104
Boston, Massachusetts 02116

HEATH Resource Center
(National Clearinghouse for Post-secondary Education for People
with Disabilites)
1 Dupont Circle NW
Washington, DC 20036

Learning Disabilities Association
   formerly the Association for Children
   and Adults with Learning Disabilities
4156 Library Road
Pittsburgh, Pennsylvania 15234

Mental Health Law Project
1101 15th Street NW
Suite 1212
Washington, DC 20005

National Center for Children with Learning Disabilities
   formerly Foundation for Children with Learning Disabilities
99 Park Avenue
New York, New York 10016

National Coalition of Advocates for Students
100 Boylston Street   Suite 727
Boston, Massachusetts 02116

Public Interest Law Center
125 South 9th Street
Suite 700
Philadelphia, Pennsylvania 19107

Youth Law Center
1663 Mission Street, 5th Floor
San Francisco, California 94103

Index

ABOUT THE AUTHOR

Mary C. Fowler, a former teacher and founder of an ADHD parent support group in New Jersey, is on the National Board of Directors of Children with Attention Deficit Disorders, CH.A.D.D. She currently serves as CH.A.D.D.'s Director of Government Affairs and is one of the country's leading education advocates for children with Attention Deficit/Hyperactivity Disorders. Ms. Fowler offers workshops and lectures exstensively to teachers and parents on the subject. She lives in Fair Haven, New Jersey.